The Buffalo Soldier Tragedy of 1877

The Buffalo Soldier Tragedy of 1877

Paul H. Carlson

TEXAS A&M UNIVERSITY PRESS COLLEGE STATION

First edition

The paper used in this book meets the minimum requirements
of the American National Standard for Permanence
of Paper for Printed Library Materials, z39.48-1984.
Binding materials have been chosen for durability.

Library of Congress Cataloging-in-Publicaton Data

Carlson, Paul Howard
The buffalo soldier tragedy of 1877 / Paul H. Carlson.— 1st ed.
p. cm.
Includes bibliographical references and index.
ISBN 1-58544-253-4 (alk. paper)
1. Comanche Indians—Wars. 2. United States. Army.
Cavalry, 10th. 3. Nolan, Nicholas, d. 1883. 4. Frontier and
pioneer life—Llano Estacado 5. Texas—History—1846–1950.
I. Title
E99.C85C36 2003
355'.0089'960730764—dc21 2002015456

For

Eric Strong

and again with appreciation

for Ellen

Contents

Illustrations

Maps

Preface

In a general way many of us are acquainted with Captain Nicholas M. Nolan's "lost troop expedition," even if we are not familiar with its painful details. The raw brutality of the 1877 tragedy will not allow us to forget its basic outline, for here were nearly forty African American troopers—buffalo soldiers—who with their twenty-two bison-hunting companions survived by drinking their urine and the urine of their horses, by sucking on the moist internal organs of their dead mounts, and by their own grim, voiceless determination to struggle forward through the heat and dust of the desert-like Texas High Plains. "The Staked Plains Horror" people called it at the time. Four men died, many deserted, one went mad, leadership failed, and the whole company broke up.

So, if we are acquainted with the failed expedition, why a book? There are several reasons: the oft-cited articles on the black troop tragedy in the *Southwestern Historical Quarterly* are more than sixty years old. The articles, moreover, represent little more than edited versions of the white officers' official reports. The best of the popular articles dates to thirty years ago. One of the most thoughtful books on the black regulars, also published more than thirty years ago, treats the expedition in just six pages, and a more recent one covers it in even less detail. Another book, one that contains a brief chapter on the expedition, dates to nearly a half century ago, and some of its interpretations are not sensitive to modern scholarship. As no book exists aimed solely on the black troop tragedy, the time has come for a new appraisal, one that will cover in some depth the context and multidimensional experiences of those who participated.

My purposes, then, were to reexamine the lost troop expedition and to place it in a broad perspective. I also wanted to assess it from more than the white officer and bison hunter viewpoints that dominate most discussions of the dramatic military operation. Testimony from the black soldiers of Troop A, Tenth Cavalry, at the court-martial afterward, for example, provides different opinions than what have been available, and several recent Comanche studies, influenced by newer approaches to American Indian history, form the basis for a fresh Kawhada view of the tragic affair. In the end, droughty weather, poor choices, bad luck, wrong decisions, and ultimately failed leadership combined with Comanche tracking skills and superb knowledge of the Llano Estacado doomed the July scouting campaign.

Relatedly, my goals have been to present the failed expedition from several viewpoints. That is, I have tried to see the July disaster from white, black, and Indian vantage points and to show how veteran military officers, seasoned bison hunters, and younger enlisted men experienced the events differently. For background, moreover, I have tried to assess the black military presence in West Texas to 1877, to examine the bison hunter activity to 1877, and to cover Kwahada Comanche experiences that led to the events of July 1877. One result is this caveat: in chapters two, three, and four there is a bit of repetition. In the three chapters I survey, although briefly, such preliminary developments as the Adobe Walls fight, the Red River campaign, the Yellow House Canyon fight, and the attack on Rath City from, respectively, bison hunter, Indian, and buffalo soldier perspectives.

The lost troop expedition captured national attention. Newspapers in cities all across the country in early August covered the story and pressed the army's division headquarters in Chicago and department headquarters in San Antonio for more information. In such a sense, although its "news life" was brief, it was a national tragedy. It was also a great American story of fortitude and will and determination, one in which perhaps we can all find admirable men.

I received an enormous amount of unstinting help, courteous assistance, and thoughtful advice on this project. Eric Strong got me started. When I told him during a conversation in my office that I was thinking of tackling from a Native American perspective an article-length manuscript on Nolan's lost troop expedition, he advised against it. Instead, Eric, who nearly twenty-five years ago with some friends on foot and horseback retraced the expedition's route, suggested a book, one that looks much like the offering presented here. I am indebted to him.

Without the efficient work of the staff at Texas Tech University's fine Southwest Collection, I could not have completed the project. As always, staff members there were gracious and professional. Among them, Jennifer Spurrier helped me work through the records management system; Freedonia Paschall retrieved materials from the National Archives and elsewhere; Janet Neugebauer located the photographs; Tai Kriedler offered suggestions; and Monte Monroe, the Collection's archivist, questioned everything as he supported the work and helped in numerous ways to push the project forward. They offered encouragement and good cheer, sometimes including cake and coffee. Their many assistants—especially Shane Sledge, Randy Vance, and Kyla Osborne—helped me through the reference files, catalogue collections, newspaper records, microfilm files, interview ledgers, and other materials that are part of the Southwest Collection's enormous holdings on the black military experience in the West. I am thankful.

People from additional archives also contributed to the study. At the Fort Concho National Historic Landmark in San Angelo, Evelyn Lemens was a great help. At the Rath City museum in Hamlin, Cheryl Lewis shared information and insight. At the Panhandle-Plains Historical Museum and Archives in Canyon, Betty Bustos and Dulcinea R. Almager answered my requests for information and photographs. At the West Texas Collection on the campus of Angelo State University, Suzanne Campbell, Tanya L. Norris, and their assistant Katie Marie Plum supplied photos. At the Fort Davis National Historic Site, Mary Williams gave information and assistance. At the Ronald Reagan Presidential Library, John Langellier provided guidance.

Lesle Nash Loughridge of Albuquerque, New Mexico, and Jerry Hall of Austin, Texas, provided a large collection of materials related to Nicholas Nolan. Lesle's father, the late Robert "Bob" Nash of Lubbock, had spent half a lifetime collecting Nolan records for a book he had hoped to write. Nash, before his death, loaned the materials to his friend Jerry Hall, who with Ms. Loughridge's concurrence gave them to me. I am most grateful.

Others helped. Ty Cashion read the manuscript and provided many good suggestions for improvement. Robert Wooster offered advice and guided me to additional sources. David J. Murrah, who read portions of the manuscript in its early stages, furnished information and made suggestions; he also made old maps available and identified physical and geographical features, place names, and site locations. Michael Harter produced the maps. Bryan Edwards assisted, encouraged, and prodded. He read portions of the manuscript and asked important questions. In an air-conditioned automobile in November 2001, he and I followed as closely as possible the route we thought Nicholas Nolan, Jim Harvey, and their men took on foot and horseback that hot, dry July in 1877.

Several colleagues in the History Department at Texas Tech assisted in one way or another. They include especially Alwyn Barr, Bruce Daniels, Jorge Iber, Joseph King, Randy McBee, Mark Stoll, Briggs Twyman, and Don Walker. I wish to thank a number of other people as well, including Peggy

Ariaz, Debbie Shelfer, Darrell Kitten, Bryson Vedder, Dino Bryant, Damon Kennedy, Dana Magill, Ron Power, Scott Sosebee, Todd Walker, and especially Robert L. Carr and Clint Chambers. In preparing the final manuscript, I leaned on Kevin A. Carlson and Tim McLaurin for computer assistance. I appreciate everyone's help, but also I accept full responsibility for any errors or misinterpretations that might remain.

Finally, and, yet again, I am happy to say, my wife Ellen, even as she recovered and rehabilitated from a crushing automobile accident, provided support and encouragement of the highest order. She remains a remarkable companion.

The Buffalo Soldier Tragedy of 1877

Chapter 1

Land of Sunshine and Space

It can be a brutal country, the Llano Estacado. A huge level, treeless plain that stretches across West Texas and eastern New Mexico, the region is a high tableland whose relentless winds, semi-arid climate, monotonous terrain, and mercurial temperatures mystified early visitors. Indeed, its unending distances coupled with its sometimes inhospitable weather—summer or winter—often intimidate even modern-day travelers.

Early-day sojourners saw the Llano Estacado as a high, shimmering, wind-swept grassland. An ocean of grass, they called it, and like the ocean it offered to travelers an almost hypnotic view, for it contained few places where one could reach any kind of eminence, thus compounding the maddening sense of being on an infinite plain with no great vista. In 1877, wrote C. U. Connellee, a surveyor who visited the area, "the plains was covered with a thick coat of grass and extended as far as the eye could see, and [it] was the broadest country I have ever seen." In the nineteenth century, the flat, empty, awesome vastness of the place caused problems for humans. July 1877 was no exception.[1]

Events this time began just after lunch on July 26. A party of twenty-two bison hunters and some forty men of Troop A, Tenth U.S. Cavalry—buffalo soldiers, people have come to call the black regulars—with their white officers and a guide left Double Lakes, twenty-five miles south of modern Lubbock, in pursuit of a band of Comanche warriors. Heading in a northwest direction, the hunters and soldiers soon ran out of water, lost their way, argued over the route to follow, and suffered terrible hardships before a few of the soldiers returned to the lakes some eighty-six hours later.

As a result of the debacle, four soldiers died and several left the command. The expedition itself fell apart. One soldier was missing and others

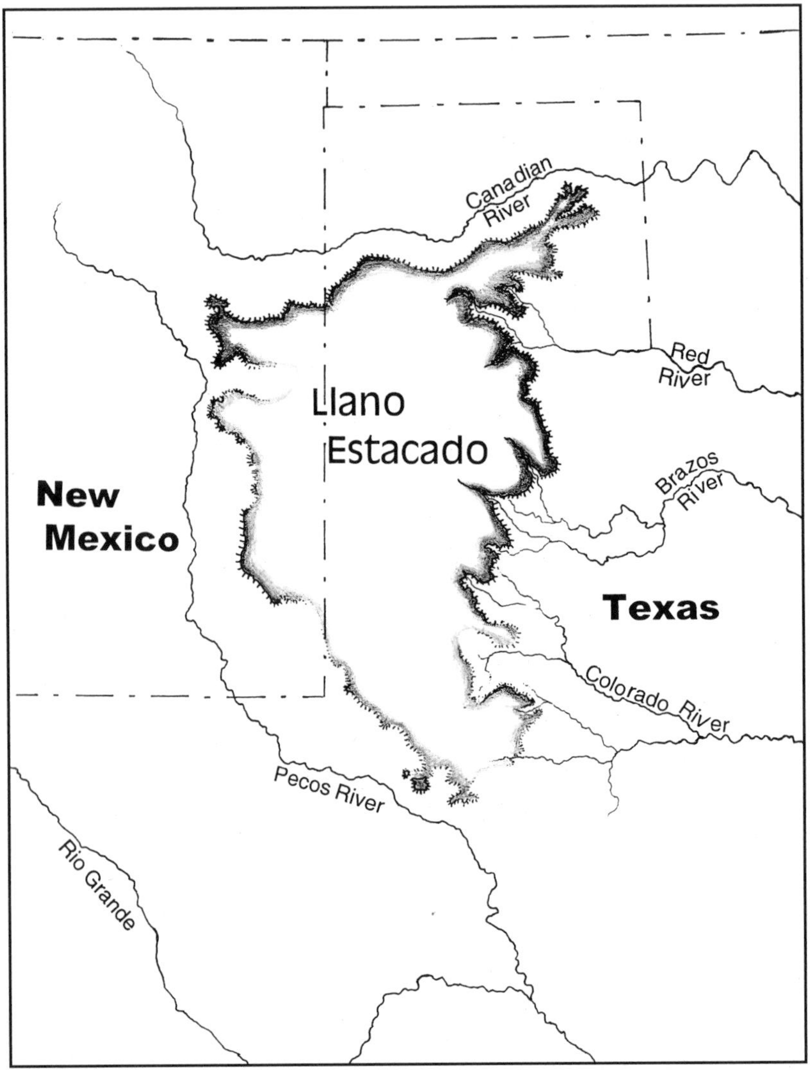

Map 1. The Llano Estacado sits astride the Texas-New Mexico border. Courtesy Michael Harter.

were scattered, some of them back up the trail unable to continue. The hunters separated from the soldiers and went their own way. Most of the horses and mules were dead, and the troopers, unable to carry them, abandoned the military supplies, including the rations. A routine army scout turned to disaster of the worst kind.

What happened? What went wrong? Why, when the region had been thoroughly mapped just two years earlier, could the men not find water, strike the Comanches in their favorite camps, or abandon the high tableland—the Yarner, as the bison hunters called the Llano Estacado, the land of sunshine and space—without suffering the shocking conditions that occurred.

The answers and the story are complicated. First, beginning on August 3, when three black soldiers rode into Fort Concho at modern San Angelo and reported that most men of Troop A and their officers were missing and presumed dead, the "Staked Plains Horror," as the *Galveston Daily News* called it, captured national attention. Word of the failed expedition flashed across the country's telegraph wires, and soon afterward reports of the "lost expedition" appeared in America's newspapers. Quickly, rescue parties started for Double Lakes, but for several days others waited to learn more about the black troop tragedy.[2]

Second, the story is complicated because of the ways in which over a four-day period it brought together the black soldiers, the bison hunters, and the Indian warriors. The Comanches were off their reservation in Indian Territory (Oklahoma), some of them without permission. And, in fact, others under the leadership of Quanah, one of the last great Comanche headmen, showed up at the soldiers' field camp. They carried with them an official letter, countersigned by a military officer, giving them permission to

An early wolf-hunting party; chaperones are in the buggy at far right. Courtesy Southwest Collection, Texas Tech University.

convince the missing warriors and their families to return to the reservation at Fort Sill.

The soldiers were there to find the Comanches and, like Quanah, to get them back to the reservation. They resented Quanah's presence and believed he helped the warriors escape. Some of the black troopers, along with their white officer, Captain Nicholas M. Nolan, two years earlier, in 1875, had been on the Llano Estacado seeking out Apache and Comanche bands at one water hole after another. In 1877, however, they found neither water nor Indians.

The bison hunters, operating in the last couple of seasons of the spectacular Southern Plains bison hunt, were searching a wider area and finding fewer animals, and they were frustrated. They also were angry at the Comanches, who, the hunters claimed, had killed popular hideman Marshall Sewall, and had stolen horses from the hunters' supply depot near the Brazos River in southern Stonewall County—a place called Rath City. The hunters wanted to find the Comanches, punish them severely, and secure the return of their mounts.

Finally, the story is complicated because of the mysteries of fate—if there is such a thing. What brought these varied groups together in that hot, dry summer of 1877? The Indian warriors, having been defeated in the decisive Red River campaign of 1874, should not have been on the Llano Estacado that July. But it was a region they knew well, one they had crossed over, hunted on, and for many generations in the past used often. The frustrated and bitter bison hunters, if they had paid better attention to their corralled horses at Rath City, would not have been chasing the elusive Comanches. In 1877, because of the Red River campaign, federal troops such as the buffalo soldiers had few Indians to pursue anywhere in Texas, except perhaps along the Rio Grande and in the Big Bend country. The federal military was already beginning to close many of its Texas forts, and cattlemen and settlers were pushing to the very edge of the Llano Estacado's eastern escarpment. Bad luck, missed opportunities, unusually hot weather, and ill-fated decisions all played a hand in the 1877 tragedy.

Elsewhere, there was much to write about in 1877. Thomas Edison, who invented the phonograph that year, had just recently moved his research laboratory to Menlo Park, New Jersey, and was now determined to concentrate on developing a workable electric light. On January 2, carpetbag government ended in Florida with the inauguration of George F. Drew as the state's Democratic governor. As part of the important Compromise of 1877, an Electoral Count Commission on March 2 selected by one electoral vote Republican Rutherford B. Hayes over Democrat Samuel Tilden for President of the United States. On June 14, the country observed its first Flag Day. A strike began on July 14 in Martinsburg, West Virginia, against the Baltimore & Ohio Railroad—a strike that spread to much of the country, including Galveston, and caused President Hayes to send federal troops to protect the line's property.

In the West other developments transpired. Anti-Chinese riots broke out in San Francisco. The Sioux War of 1876–77 wound down as federal troops forced one Indian band after another back to its reservation and Sitting Bull took his people to Canada. On March 3, Congress created the U.S. Entomological Commission to examine ways to ameliorate the damage grasshoppers caused farmers on the Great Plains, and it passed the Desert Land Act, a law designed to encourage irrigation and cultivation of semi-arid lands. In June, federal troops in Idaho and western Montana began a four-month-long campaign to capture Chief Joseph and his fellow Nez Perce and return them to their reservation. On September 7, Crazy Horse died in a botched attempt to remove him from Fort Robinson, Nebraska.

In Texas in 1877 events mirrored the national scene. Carpetbag government was on its way out, for example, and Democrat Richard H. Hubbard, a Georgia-born ex-Confederate officer, was governor of the state, having just recently succeeded Richard Coke who had resigned in favor of a senate seat. The state's farmers that year created the Southern Farmers' Alliance, a political and economic body designed to aid its members; the Alliance would grow into a powerful political organization with national membership. Cattle raisers drove most of their livestock northward along the western cattle trail. The route took them through Wilbarger County, over the Red River at a place that two years later became known as Doan's Store, and across Indian Territory to Dodge City.

San Antonio in 1877 was the largest city in Texas, and Galveston the busiest port. Most of the state's 1.6 million citizens lived east of a line that ran from Laredo northward through Austin and Temple to Fort Worth and beyond to the Red River—or, in other words, east of the long curve of the Balcones Escarpment. Only during the previous few years had settlers in any kind of appreciable numbers begun to broach the line. The Galveston, Harrisburg & San Antonio Railroad reached San Antonio in 1877, and other lines, which had stopped construction as a result of the national economic depression in the early 1870s, stood waiting to build farther west.

Silver Falls, Crosbyton. Courtesy Southwest Collection, Texas Tech University.

And far out in West Texas, high on the Llano Estacado, weather conditions soured. On the Llano, the summer of 1877 turned dry, with temperatures in July significantly higher than normal. Cloudless skies, a burning sun, and heat that day after day reached over 100 degrees discouraged activity on the Staked Plains, and even bison had begun to abandon the drier sections above Cedar Lake. Two years earlier, in the summer of 1875, when they had pursued Indian warriors across the same High Plains, Nicholas Nolan and other military officers had reported two or three bison herds of an estimated one hundred thousand animals each. Now, there were none—or very few.[3]

There were not many deer either. Deer preferred to hide and browse in woodland areas interspersed with meadows. As they also preferred an uneven landscape, they could be found in the canyons and deeper draws of the region, but even the larger mule deer seldom ventured onto the high Llano, a level land devoid of timber but rich in grass and sunshine. Still, most early travelers reported seeing and killing deer on the Staked Plains.[4]

Pronghorns, or antelope (as they are popularly called), had also declined in number, perhaps because in the summer heat of 1877 they had left for a drought refugium. Small, graceful, beautifully colored animals with distinctive horns, the curious pronghorns were once nearly as common as bison, and they would last on the Llano Estacado until deep into the twentieth century—probably because their hides held little commercial value.

Wild horses, often called mustangs, grazed on the Llano Estacado, sometimes in very large numbers. Below Cedar Lake, Johnny Cook and Sam Carr, bison hunters, while scouting for Indian campsites in July 1877, rode up on a herd. The men, probably in northern Martin County west of Sulphur Springs Creek and northwest of modern Big Spring, "had ascended a rise in the plain," remembered Cook, when west and southwest of them they saw "scattered over many thousands of acres of land . . . bands of wild horses." The animals, wrote Cook, "were ranging in unmolested freedom and in perfect quiet." The bison hunters, awed by the incredible scene, watched the horses for hours. "As evening came on," Cook concluded, "young colts came running and frisking around in reckless abandon in their wild unfettered freedom."[5]

Rabbits, both cottontails and jackrabbits, were also present in large numbers. Indeed, their populations continued to increase after settlers arrived, for their most dangerous enemies, wolves and coyotes, declined with the arrival of cowboys, farmers, and townspeople.

The wolves—plains lobo (or buffalo wolf) and gray wolf—and coyotes ate mainly small game. They sought quail, prairie dogs, skunks, and, of course, rabbits. Working in packs, the wolves also attacked young, old, or crippled bison and other large animals, such as young mustangs and pronghorns. Once settlers had introduced European animals to the region, the wolves and coyotes attacked younger cattle and sheep—or so ranchers claimed. In response, wolf and coyote hunting became favorite pastimes in West Texas as well as the special occupation of several men, such as Gus Hartman, Bill Benson, J. B. Sledge, and Rufe LeFors, who hired themselves out for the purpose of ridding the country of the predator lobos.[6]

After 1877 wolves may have departed on their own accord. In 1880, for example, some early settlers in the area viewed thousands of gray wolves, maybe "twenty abreast, and the pack must have been two or three miles in length," loping over the plains and up Yellow House Canyon. If true, it must have been a fantastic scene. John Lovelady, who maintained a ranch below the Caprock about twenty miles south of the mouth of Yellow House Canyon, noted that he saw the gray wolves "heading in a northwestern course across the plains." And, on "the same day some parties [perhaps including Willis S. Glenn, a former bison hunter] saw what was undoubtedly this same pack crossing Yellow House Canyon, still traveling in a lope and headed northwest." Lovelady concluded that "whether these wolves were following the buffalo or were governed by some mysterious instinct will always remain a mystery to me."[7]

In 1877, because of the absence of trees, few arboreal birds were present. Ravens, blackbirds, curlews, and some others, such as owls, could be found, and eagles flew out from their nests along the canyon rims to search for rabbits, prairie dogs, and other small prey, including on occasion young pronghorns. Bobwhite and blue quail nested on the Llano, and to a lesser extent one might find prairie chickens and wild turkeys near the ubiquitous sand hills where scrub oak grew. Ducks, cranes, and other migratory birds stopped in season at the wet-weather (or playa) lakes.[8]

Prairie dogs, or ground squirrels, were abundant in 1877. They may have been latecomers to the Llano, for, according to William Curry Holden, the early Spanish explorers, except for Francisco Vásquez de Coronado's chroniclers, made little mention of them when they crossed the Southern Plains. Albert Pike, who from New Mexico followed Blackwater Draw in 1832, killed and ate prairie dogs, and members of the Texan–Santa Fe expedition ten years later saw them. While they were present in 1875, William R. Shafter, who crossed and re-crossed the Llano Estacado that year, made no mention of them in his lengthy report on plains flora and fauna. But a dozen years later, in 1887, writes Holden, a prairie dog colony, or "town", stretched "from Colorado City to Amarillo," placing modern Lubbock "in the heart of a dense prairie dog population."[9]

Mesquite was another intruder. Slowly, over the course of many decades, the tough, hardy plant with its thin, lime-green leaves and large seed pods had been making its way northward out of deep South Texas—probably in response to a warming climate. Perhaps, as some have suggested, cattle, which ate and then disgorged the undigested seeds, aided its migration. Indian warriors had for a century been moving cattle from South Texas to comanchero camps along the Llano Estacado's edge. In 1875, Shafter reported six- to twelve-foot mesquite trees along water courses off the Llano's eastern Caprock. He wrote about "large mesquite flats" at Rendlebrock's Springs (in southern Mitchell County) and "considerable mesquite timber of small growth" north from there to the upper branches of the Brazos River in modern Garza and Crosby Counties.[10]

Except in the sand dunes where scrub oak occurred, there were few trees on the Llano Estacado. A few mesquite shrubs were found here and there, and during their 1877 ordeal several men of Troop A hung saddle blankets over the tiny and scattered shrubs to secure some relief from the burning sun. Mesquite roots could be dug near most of the water holes, but fire, which came naturally on the Llano about every three to five years, beat back the growth of most trees, including mesquite and the hardy junipers. In the deeper canyons on the eastern side of the Staked Plains one could find hackberry and cottonwood trees.

In 1877, then, the Llano Estacado was level to a great extent, treeless, and arid (or nearly so) with only scattered water holes. It was windswept grassland interspersed with shallow depressions plus draws and arroyos that many eons ago must have formed part of some mighty river systems but through the long centuries had filled in with blowing sand.[11]

Here and there occurred stretches of sand dunes, usually consisting of a range of low hills of sand with only sparse vegetation. For Nolan and his buffalo soldiers, the most important of these were the large Lea-Yoakum Dunes, which in some places are eight miles wide and extend northwest and southeast about forty miles on the south side of Sulfur Draw from Terry and Yoakum Counties through Cockran County in Texas to Lea and Roosevelt Counties in New Mexico. Bison hunters in 1877 called the dunes in Roosevelt County the Blue Sand Hills. Other sand hills associated with these dunes crossed Sulfur Draw along the Texas–New Mexico line, and there were dunes farther west in New Mexico. Even larger sand dunes (the

Road between Post and Lubbock, showing the difficult climb up the Caprock. Courtesy Southwest Collection, Texas Tech University.

Muleshoe Dunes) existed some twenty miles north, and the huge White Sand Hills, as they were called in 1877, were located about fifty miles south, stretching north from present Monahans.

The sand hills were favorite camping places for Comanches and Apaches. Water could be found in most of them by digging in the small depressions at the bases of the hills. Scrub oak and shrubs of various kinds were available for fuel. The sand dunes were good hiding places. In fact, from the dunes in New Mexico Quanah, Red Young Man, and their Comanche allies watched through powerful binoculars while the soldiers and hunters suffered from want of water on the unfortunately named Nigger Hill, a knoll near the Texas state line in Roosevelt County, New Mexico.[12]

Away from the sand dunes, the Llano's mid-section—the country crossed by Troop A and the bison hunters—was hot and often dusty in summer, with high temperatures in July averaging ninety-two degrees. Average annual rainfall was just over eighteen inches. Winds blew across the region at rates that regularly reached twenty to thirty miles per hour; they blew, someone has suggested, as at the seashore, nearly constant with gusts that sometimes reached forty to fifty miles per hour.

In altitude, the Llano ranged between 4,500 feet above sea level in New Mexico and 3,100 feet in parts of Texas, sloping gently downward from west to east. Even more slightly it sloped from north to south, so that people crossing the plains either to or from New Mexico in the nineteenth century needed to be aware of what experienced plainsmen called "drift" that might send them off course toward the south. In 1877, drift turned some of the bison hunters away from the main trail.

On this high, level land an early-day traveler might find thousands of slight, circular depressions called playa lakes. They held water during the rainy seasons but were dry much of the year. Permanent water existed at some of the larger lakes, along the headwater streams of the Colorado and Brazos Rivers, and at springs that existed here and there in the draws and arroyos through much of the Staked Plains.

Between the draws and arroyos that drained the high tableland, the region was exceptionally flat. In 1876, William R. Shafter, who in the summer of 1875 had been there with Nicholas Nolan, described the level country south and west of modern Lubbock as "high hard . . . prairie . . . with scarcely any timber and but few mesquite roots." Shafter wrote about the many large, "circular depressions" (the playa lakes) that were "filled with water for part of the year" and indicated that "the whole country is covered with luxuriant grass, affording pasturage for immense herds of buffalo."

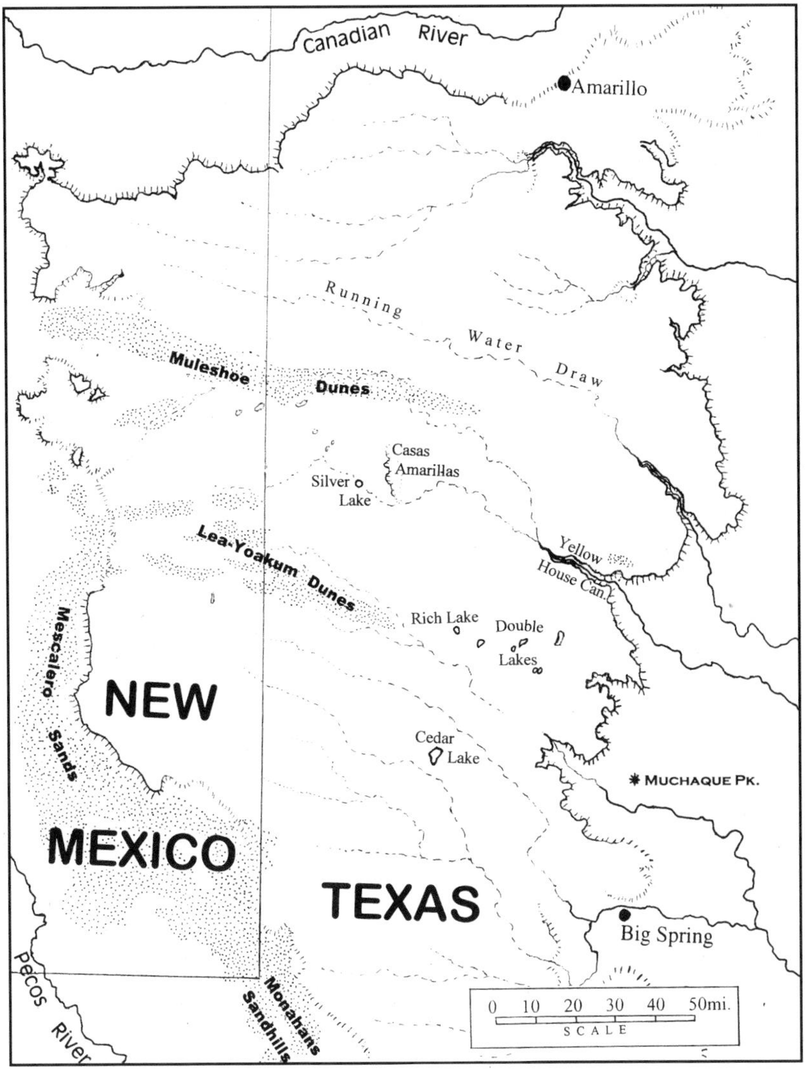

Map 2. This detail of the Llano Estacado shows sand dunes, sand hills, draws, and lakes of the region. Courtesy Michael Harter.

He also noted that cattle in huge numbers could be grazed on the rich grassland.[13]

"The great level expanses," wrote William Curry Holden, "were covered with buffalo grass intermixed with blue grama." Toward the west and north, short, thick, matted, curly mesquite grass was present, as were scores of other species, including weed varieties. In late summer the fine seed heads of many of the turf grasses, especially the blue grama, stood high, waving in the ceaseless wind and reaching the belly of a rider's horse. Shafter's 1876 report of the Llano Estacado mentioned, as indicated above, "luxuriant grass" and, again, "excellent grass" and "plenty of grass" and "good grass." In areas near streams and lakes where the ground was moist, Holden noted, one could find "tall switch grass, side oats grama, and bluestem."[14]

Several varieties of cactus grew on the High Plains, perhaps yucca the most prominent. With its light green stems and its tall, flowering stalk and white blossoms, the yucca, wrote Holden, "standing three to four feet above the ground, added a poetic touch to the vastness of the plains." But other species, such as cholla, were also present, and catsclaw acacia and bear and dagger grasses on the western Llano could make walking painful for horses and humans.[15]

Wild flowers of all kinds appeared in season. Some years, particularly after an early, wet spring, the flowers in May splashed the plains with many colors. Most common among the flowers were verbena, black daises, Indian paintbrush, buttercups, and Tahoka daisies, but dozens of others might add their colors of red, yellow, orange, or blue to spring. In May 1877, when they searched the plains, bison hunters marveled at the beauty and abundance of the wildflowers. By summer, however, when Nolan's buffalo soldiers crossed the plains during July's heat and drought, there were few Llano flowers in bloom. The short buffalo and mesquite grasses had, as was their custom in drought, browned and turned down, giving from a distance the appearance of a lifeless desert.

Wagon roads and Indian trails crossed the High Plains, and comancheros had been covering the region for a century or more. Bill Williams, an ornery and grizzled old mountain man, and Albert Pike, an adventure-loving Yankee who during the Civil War had become a Confederate diplomat, in 1832 led a party of forty-five fur trappers eastward from New Mexico down Blackwater Draw (sometimes called Thompson's Canyon) and Cañon del Rescate (now lower Yellow House Canyon) to the rolling plains beyond the Llano. They had little success in finding beaver dams, but they followed a well-worn trail, one that contained Indian camps and abundant signs of many previous ones.

Ranald S. Mackenzie, famed colonel of the Fourth Cavalry, in 1872 led troops of his command out of upper Blanco Canyon and westward through modern Petersburg. Once on the open plain, they discovered numerous Indian and Comanche trails. When they struck Blackwater Draw, the troopers followed one of the trails to New Mexico. The trail Mackenzie's men laid down was still visible in July 1877 when state surveyors and a large family traveling from Erath County to New Mexico encountered it. While the surveyors marked county lines and located section blocks in modern Crosby and Lubbock Counties, the family determined to follow the "McKenzie road," as a surveyor called it, to their destination. One hopes they made it.[16]

In 1875, after his exploration of the southern High Plains, William R. Shafter reported a number of well-traveled Indian and comanchero trails. In Seminole Draw, for example, a shallow arroyo that is one of the head streams of the Colorado River, one of Shafter's officers, Lieutenant C. R. Ward, discovered a series of wells. Afterward called Ward's Wells, but since having been filled with blowing sand, the place, in modern Gaines County, contained about fifty wells "in the space of one and one-half miles." The wells, Shafter said, were "from four feet deep at the western end to fifteen at the eastern, and having from two to four feet of water, of excellent quality and affording water for several thousand horses."[17]

Together with an arroyo about three miles distant, the region, Shafter guessed, "appears to have been a favorite resort for Indians." There were "deeply worn trails" and old, abandoned tipis in the vicinity. Because Shafter wrote that some skeletal heads of cattle were also present, the place may have been a location at which Indian families herded animals to butcher and to rest themselves and their mounts before moving to more permanent camps.[18]

Casas Amarillas (Yellow Houses), Shafter said, was another popular Indian camp. Comancheros also stopped there. Located in northern Hockley County, about forty miles almost due west of modern Lubbock, the place—a wide basin oriented north and south—got its name from the yellowish-colored bluffs, which, when seen from a distance, folklore suggests, resembled houses. A Tenth Cavalry officer, Captain Theodore A. Baldwin, wrote to his wife that "the appearance of the rocks [are] of a yellow color." Another early visitor, John R. Cook, referred to the site as a "bold rugged bluff with natural and excavated caverns dug" at the base and at the top "a stone half-circle breastwork," clearly the work of Plains Indians and comancheros. Cook's bison hunting and literary rival Frank Collinson remembered that "Yellow House proper was a large, yellow sandstone cave under the [Caprock], opening to the east, with sufficient room for twenty or more people to camp at a time."[19]

At Casas Amarillas, Shafter noted that "a large alkali and salt lake, of from one-half to three-quarters of a mile in width and about three in length . . . [drained] the country for several miles in all directions." He reported that "there are two dug springs at the base of the bluff on the southern side, and about a half mile further south, at the head of a ravine, a large tank of fresh water" was present. He believed that the springs, later called Yellow House Springs, fed the lake, for after camping there and watering his men and horses for two days, he "could not perceive any diminution in" the water supply.[20]

Shafter and his command also cut their own trails. One of the roads, he noted, "from about half way up" Blanco Canyon crossed the plains westward to "the head of [the] Double Mountain Fork of the Brazos" (modern Lubbock). Called Punta del Agua on Shafter's map, the head stream contained a small, spring-fed lake with a grassy marsh on the lower end. One of Shafter's officers complained about the place, writing to his wife that we "had a hard time for wood, could not get the buffalo chips to burn, and there was nothing else." The mosquitoes were "very bad," he noted, "10,000 to the inch."[21]

Two other roads cut through the heart of the territory traveled by Nolan and his troops. From the head of the North Concho River below modern Big Spring in Howard County, Shafter noted in 1876, "two large wagon roads into the plains have been made by my command." One took "the left hand valley and goes via Mustang springs," wrote Shafter, "to Five Wells, Laguna Sabinas [Cedar Lake], and Laguna Cuates," a series of four small lakes afterward called Double Lakes, the place where in 1877 the black troop tragedy began.[22]

The second road went up "the right hand valley to Big Spring," Shafter wrote, "thence via Sulphur Springs," to the head of the Colorado River. Shafter does not indicate that his route took him down off the Llano Estacado, but the trail here, he notes, is in the Muchaque (or "Moo-cho-ko-way," as Shafter spelled it) country located just off the Caprock on the high divide between the Colorado and Brazos Rivers in modern Borden County. From this important area—where Nolan set up his base camp in July 1877—the road ran north and a bit west to Double Lakes and thence north to the head of the Double Mountain Fork of the Brazos in modern Lubbock.[23]

Muchaque Peak, a major geophysical feature and ancient landmark, dominated the Muchaque region, which was situated in a rough, broken country between the upper Brazos and Colorado Rivers. Indian people had used the area for generations for hunting, camping, and trading. Grass existed in the river valleys, water could be found in Tobacco and Bull Creeks, and Muchaque (or Mushaway, as locals call it) Peak offered high ground from which to observe the movement of others approaching the vicinity. In 1877,

Even today the northwestern portions of the Llano Estacado still reflect the empty landscape soldiers and hunters faced in 1877. Author's photo.

a huge old pecan tree along Bull Creek provided shade for campers, including Nolan's buffalo soldiers.[24]

Shafter cut additional trails. From the north end of Cedar Lake, he established "two large wagon roads." The one on the right, he said, went "nearly due east to head of Tobacco Creek, distant thirty-five miles." He indicated that about "five miles of the road" ran through heavy sands, perhaps the far southeastern portions of the Lea-Yoakum Dunes in Dawson County. "The left hand road runs nearly northeast . . . to [Double Lakes]."[25]

North of there, Shafter carved out an even larger road. From Punta del Agua (at Lubbock) at the head of the Double Mountain Fork of the Brazos, with four companies of troops and his Black Seminole scouts, some 220 men in all, he cut a trail almost due west. It went about 40 miles to Casas Amarillas, the popular Indian and comanchero campground.

From Casas Amarillas, Shafter's command moved west about six miles to Silver Lake (Quemos or Lake Quemada, also known as Laguna Plata) in the northwest corner of Hockley County, a place the bison hunters and Nolan in 1877 sought to reach. From here the command moved southwestward, passing through heavy dunes of the Blue Sand Hills—the western portions of the Lea-Yoakum sands in Roosevelt and Lea Counties, New Mexico. Before leaving them, Shafter and his men made note of the scrub oak in the dunes. Then they crossed alkali flats of small brush and red sage with bear and dagger grass to the Pecos River, reaching it about twenty miles above the mouth of the Blue (Azul) River near modern Carlsbad. Shafter's men, including Tenth Cavalry troopers, suffered from lack of water on this portion of the scout, and they made the Pecos only after extreme hardships and partly because some of the officers with guns drawn forced the men to keep moving.

Because of recent rains, Shafter, when he began the scout, had expected to find water in the playas, or rainy-weather lakes. But on the march from Silver Lake to the Pecos, he found the playas dry and was unable to locate additional sources. His buffalo soldiers went two days without water. On the last night out many of them, because of swollen tongues, could not swallow and thus were unable to eat. Many could barely talk. Several men gave up on the idea of reaching the Pecos, and officers tied some of them in their saddles to keep them on the road.

Although they made the river safely, both the officers and men were fatigued—and they had barely started on their long march. After resting briefly at the Pecos, Shafter and his hardy black regulars headed downriver to the famous Horsehead Crossing. They then turned back up the river and marched through the White Sand Hills and then north to Silver Lake, where they struck their outward trail and returned to Punta del Agua and eventually to their supply camp near the mouth of Blanco Canyon. They had been on the march for some seven weeks and had covered over 860 miles.[26]

Nonetheless, once back at Fort Concho, Shafter was upbeat. His long report of the expedition was likewise positive. Despite the difficult conditions and severe problems caused from the shortage of water during his August crossing of the Llano Estacado, he was optimistic. Shafter noted, tragically as we shall see, that his "various scouts have shown how easily the plains can be traversed, in almost any direction, and to all the large watering places there are plain wagon roads that will show for years."[27]

It was an illusion—as it turned out—for, although many of the roads were visible to them two years later, Troop A soldiers in 1877 sometimes did not know which one to follow. There was a veritable maze of trails from which to choose.

Many of the trails came from comancheros. For a century or more the colorful traders, mainly Hispanics and Pueblo gardeners from villages along the upper Rio Grande in New Mexico, had crossed the High Plains at a number of points, but especially along Running Water, Yellow House, and Blackwater draws.

One of the favorite comanchero destinations was the Muchaque country. Located off the eastern side of the Llano and dominated by Muchaque Peak, as noted above, the well-watered region between the upper Brazos and Colorado Rivers was a long-popular landmark. Here, evidence suggests, comancheros traded their village wares and agricultural products to Indian groups, including Comanches, Kiowas, Lipans, Mescaleros, and others. They got in exchange bison robes and hides, dried meat, and other products, which sometimes included cattle taken from settlements toward the east and south or from large ranches in the central plateau of northern Mexico.

The Muchaque country was ideal for holding cattle. Shafter in 1875 called it "a magnificent grazing country." He said the "water is excellent and inexhaustible; considerable mesquite timber—sufficient for all necessary purposes of settlers, and stone convenient for building." For cattle raising, he thought the region was "unsurpassed by any portion of Western Texas," and Tobacco and Bull Creeks were fine sites for camping.[28]

On occasion human captives may have been part of the comenchero trade. One of the deep gulfs of the upper Brazos, Cañon del Rescate (Canyon of the Rescue), today known as Yellow House Canyon, was a popular trade site. Indian warriors, or so the argument goes, took prisoners from the settlements in Texas or from ranches in Chihuahua and Coahuila, hauled them to the Muchaque country, Rescate, or perhaps Casas Amarillas, and sold them to the comancheros. Back in New Mexico, the traders sought to sell the captives back to their families in Texas or Mexico.[29]

How often the trade in humans occurred is open to question. Many historians argue that it was a regular part of comanchero business in Yellow House Canyon (Rescate). They point to the Comanche practice of taking captives from ranches in Coahuila and Chihuahua and carrying them northward along the Great Comanche War Trail to Muchaque country or beyond to camps in the upper reaches of the Pease and Wichita Rivers. Other historians believe the trade in humans was rare and suggest that most Indian groups on the Southern Plains came to interpret the name Rescate as "trade fair," something far different from the dramatic exchange of human captives.[30]

There are mysteries associated with the Llano, and the trade in humans is but one of them. Although Indian people and early Spaniards in the Southwest used the Southern High Plains without trepidation, many of the first

Americans to encounter the Llano Estacado feared the awkward and incomprehensible land. They saw it as part of a larger desert, a waterless place void of landmarks and mysterious in its strange mirages and unpredictable nature.[31]

Two early West Texas cattlemen, Charles Goodnight and Oliver Loving, in 1866 drove their large herd south, around the Llano Estacado, rather than hazard a route shorter by some four hundred miles up Blanco Canyon and along Running Water Draw to New Mexico. Early stagecoach lines such as the Butterfield Overland Stage likewise veered around the southern edge. The idea was to avoid the dreaded "Sahara of North America."

And well they should—at least in droughty years. The experience of Nicholas Nolan and his buffalo soldiers as late as 1877 offers up a shocking lesson of what could happen during what should have been a minor, routine, and forgettable military patrol on the Llano Estacado—the expansive land of sunshine and space.

It began, of course, in 1877. Bison hunters from Rath City led the way.

Chapter 2

Bison Hunters and Rath City in 1877

Buffalo hunting," said J. Wright Mooar, "was a business and not a sport; it required capital, management and work, lots of hard work, more work than anything else." Speaking in 1928, a half-century after the great Southern Plains bison hunt had come to a close, the seventy-seven-year-old Mooar, one of the hunt's most successful participants, told his audience at a West Texas Historical Association meeting in Abilene that "the killing of the buffalo [was not] accomplished by vandals." It was an industrial enterprise, he was suggesting, one made possible by better rifles and new hide-tanning technology, and success went to the most daring and efficient of the hunter-businessmen. In 1877, many of the hunters based their operations at Rath City, a tiny, recently established trade center in West Texas—in the Brazos River country.[1]

By 1877 the destruction of bison had been going on for some time. The central herds—those in Kansas, Nebraska, and eastern Colorado—were gone or nearly so, and hunters had started on the northern herds. For some three years, in addition, hidemen had been working through the great southern herds in Texas, especially from bases in the Panhandle. Now, apparently, they had determined to cut below the herds and strike at the bison from southern camps scattered east of the Llano Estacado in the state's Rolling Plains section. Well-watered and ideal for grazing, the region included drainage areas of the upper Colorado and the Pease and Wichita Rivers, but mainly this was Brazos River country.

It was still Indian country, too. Although in 1874 and 1875 the Southern Plains Indians had agreed to settle on reservations in Indian Territory (Oklahoma), Comanches, Kiowas, and others continued to camp and hunt with passes in the Texas Panhandle and on the Rolling Plains. Too often, perhaps, younger warriors, who still needed success in hunting and raiding for

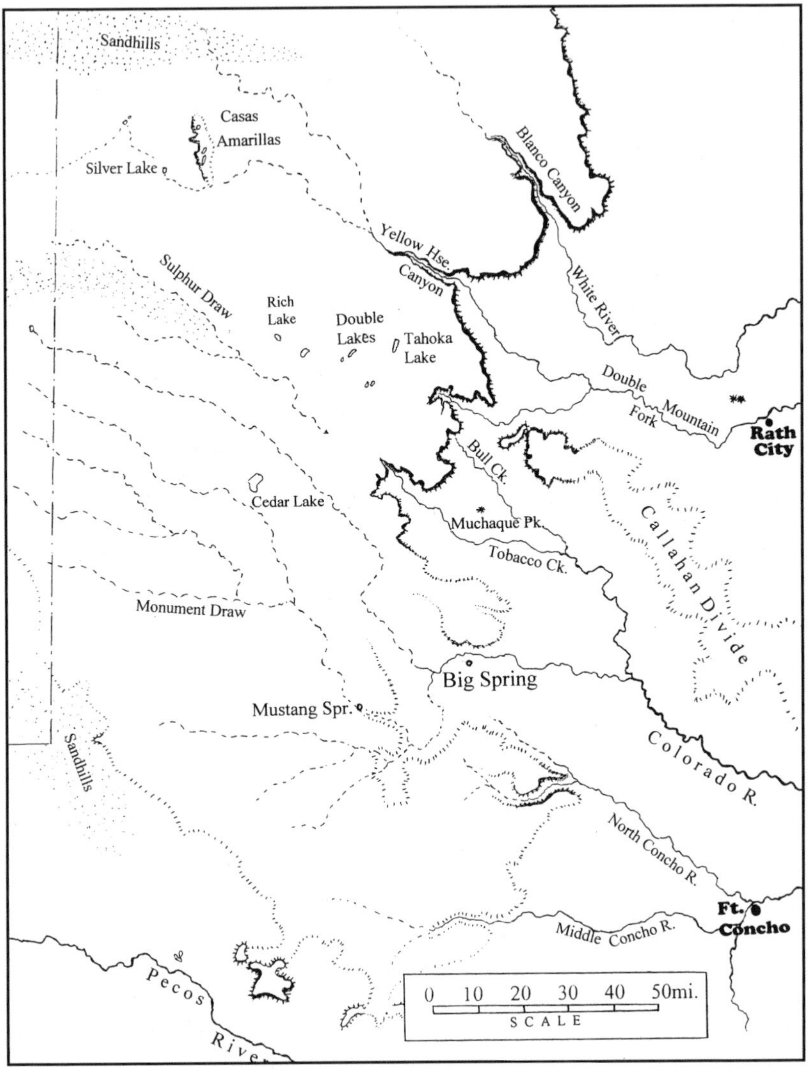

Map 3. Bison hunter sites on the Llano Estacado and the area to its east. Courtesy Michael Harter.

tribal prestige, splashed across the Red River without permission and searched the Texas plains for bison, horses, or other prizes—prizes that sometimes included settlers and hidemen.

Indian warriors and others found the hide hunters particularly distasteful. Richard Irving Dodge, a military officer who knew them, said the bison hunters were a rough and smelly bunch, as "unsavory as a skunk." Often heavy drinkers, the hunters were also fearless adventurers, sturdy fighters, and relentless foes. They may have been daring businessmen, as J. Wright Mooar remembered, but one of them, Jim McIntire, bragged—even if greatly exaggerating—that he had "killed Comanche and Kiowa Indians by the score, and once I killed and skinned [an Indian woman] and made a purse of her breast." Clearly, Plains Indians had reason to resent the hunters and their heavy assault on the bison herds.[2]

The bison slaughter began in earnest in the early 1870s. More specifically, it began in 1871, when William C. Lobenstine, a dealer in furs, pelts, and robes at Leavenworth, Kansas, got an order from an English firm for five hundred bison hides. The firm, using new technology, planned to experiment on the hides that up to that time had been used mainly for winter coats, robes, and rugs. Although the men involved offer slightly different versions of subsequent developments, their stories suggest that Lobenstine, in response to the order, contacted two men: Charles Rath, a profit-driven entrepreneur, Santa Fe freighter, and bison hunter. Born in Germany and just thirty-four years old, Rath supplied the Kansas railroad builders with meat and on occasion sent a few robes to Lobenstine. The second man Lobenstine contacted was A. C. (Charley) Myers, another of Lobenstine's suppliers and an occasional partner of Rath at Dodge City.[3]

Rath and Myers, in turn, contacted Josiah Wright Mooar and Jim White. Mooar, a Vermont-born New Yorker of Scot ancestry had come west as a nineteen-year-old in 1870. At Fort Hays, Kansas, he supplied the post with wood and sought a market for the discarded bison hides that Jim White, a hunter who provided bison meat to the post commissary, did not use. After the four men—Rath, Myers, Mooar, and White—gathered the five hundred hides, Mooar and White had fifty-seven additional robes. These, Mooar sent to his brother, John Wesley Mooar, a New York accounting clerk, asking his brother to dispose of them in New York City through a commission sales company to an American tanner. Eventually, a Philadelphia firm, which paid $3.50 each for them, received the hides, found an economical way to tan them, and asked for two thousand more. Quickly, other tanneries, including some in England and Germany, ordered bison hides.[4]

The big hunt was on. It consumed Kansas first and then spilled over into southern Nebraska and eastern Colorado. Within three years hunters had destroyed the central herds. As a result, many of them—led by Mooar, John Webb, Thomas L. (George) Causey, and the well-to-do English former seamen James H. and Robert Cator—in 1873 entered the Texas Panhandle. They concentrated in eastern portions of the territory and in the breaks of such streams as Wolf and Palo Duro Creeks and the Canadian River and its tributaries. The next summer, 1874, before a late-June attack by some two hundred Indian warriors on a short-lived hunting supply camp at Adobe Walls on the Canadian River, hunters swarmed over the Panhandle. There may have been fifty hunting outfits in the Panhandle at the time of the attack on Adobe Walls. And, after the federal army's 1874–75 Red River campaign, designed to punish the southern Plains Indians for the raid at Adobe Walls and return the Indian warriors to their reservations, hunters struck hard at the bison. Two years later many of the hunters determined to move south to get around the southern edge of the herds.[5]

Charlie Rath led the way. Born in Germany in 1836, he and most of his family had immigrated to Philadelphia when he was eleven, and shortly afterward his father had moved them all to Ohio. Young Rath, the second of eight children, left home in 1853 and headed west. He worked in Colorado for William Bent, the Indian trader on the upper Arkansas River, before setting himself up—along with some family members who joined him—in a succession of businesses in central Kansas. He married a Cheyenne woman, Roadmaker (Making Out Roads), but the marriage and two subsequent ones to white women ended in divorce. A tough, hard-nosed businessman, he spoke several Indian languages (among them, Cheyenne, Arapaho, and Kiowa) and knew the Plains sign language. He freighted along the Santa Fe trail, established trading houses and stage coaching stations along the trail, and hunted bison before the big break with Lobenstine's firm moved him into hide buying.

Rath was a dominant player in the southern hunt. From Dodge City, Kansas, where in 1872 he established Charles Rath & Co., a mercantile firm that advertised itself as "Dealers in All Kinds of Outfitting Goods, Ammunition, Groceries, Provisions, Etc.," his teamsters hauled supplies to isolated camps and brought back dried bison hides. When the hunt moved into the Texas Panhandle, he and his partner—Rath had a succession of them—Robert M. Wright, with Rath in the lead moved some $20,000 worth of equipment and supplies to Adobe Walls, arriving there on May 1, 1874, just eight weeks before the Indian attack. Rath and Wright lost a bundle at Adobe Walls, but after the Red River campaign and with a new partner, Frank E. Conrad, Rath set up another store. This one he located in 1875 at Fort Griffin along the Clear Fork of the Brazos in Shackelford County on the eastern edge of the herds. First established as a military post in 1867, the place soon attracted settlers, and a pioneer village, sometimes called the Flat, grew up below the fort. The Mooar brothers had already moved their operations to the community.[6]

The American bison or plains buffalo. Courtesy Southwest Collection, Texas Tech University.

About the same time, Rath and Wright reentered the Panhandle. With Henry Hamberg as their manager, they located a trading store on Sweetwater Creek near Fort Elliott, established in 1875, in modern Wheeler County. Called Hide Town—as many such outfitting camps were—the little tent, sod, and adobe community provided a marketing base and a "watering hole" for hunters. (It later became known as Sweetwater, then still later was renamed Mobeetie when it was relocated in 1878; Rath maintained various businesses there until the mid-1890s.) Rath and Wright sold groceries, tools, and other supplies—including whiskey, of course—to the bison hunters and bought and freighted their hides to Dodge City, some 180 miles away.

Near the end of the year, Rath moved again. In part because some hunters wanted to get south of the herds and in part because the Mooar brothers were enjoying great success in working bison herds west and southwest of Fort Griffin, Rath and others—both hide hunters and hide buyers—determined to move their operations out of the Panhandle. They hoped to intercept the Griffin trade, turn it north toward Mobeetie and Dodge City, and at the same time enter the very heart of the large Texas herds.[7]

Typically, Rath formed another partnership. This one he organized with William McDole (W. M. D.) Lee—an aggressive competitor and post sutler at Camp Supply (located south of Dodge City in modern Oklahoma) and Fort Elliott who became a highly successful rancher-businessman—and Albert E. Reynolds, a former Indian agent who was Lee's associate in a number of enterprises. Lee (who wanted to control the entire Texas hide trade even if he could do it only with a partner) and Reynolds provided mountains of trade goods, groceries, flour, equipment, tools, lead, powder, tobacco, and whiskey from their large stores at Camp Supply. Additional items came from Dodge City.[8]

Rath cut the trail. Late in 1876, at the head of a small group of men, he moved due south from Fort Elliott to build a new trade center. He "rode on his horse in the lead with a compass on his saddle horn," J. Wright Mooar recalled, and with him went "a wagon and team with about twelve men with picks, shovels and axes who fixed the crossings on ravines and creeks." A few days and some distance behind came John Russell, a Rath teamster and wagon master. Russell directed a train of fifty wagons, some drawn by six yoke of oxen and loaded with Lee and Reynolds trade goods plus supplies and equipment to build an outpost. The bison hunters used horses and mules to pull wagons loaded with tents, guns, ammunition, and other camp equipment. Hunters, skinners, freighters, hide buyers, and others, including a few women, followed Rath south. Among the hunters were John Cook, Willis Crawford, Joe Freed, Hank Campbell, Mortimer "Wild Bill" Kress, Limpy Jim Smith, Sol Rees, and Harry Burns, the group's Scot-English poet who the hunters claimed was related to Robert Burns (1759–96), sometimes called the national poet of Scotland.[9]

After nearly two weeks on the trail, Rath and the town builders reached their destination. Just before or after Christmas—accounts differ—they selected a site on a high mesa of some two hundred acres about seventeen miles southeast of Double Mountain in Stonewall County and a few miles below the Double Mountain Fork of the Brazos River. Here, two hundred miles south of Fort Elliott and sixty miles west of Fort Griffin, they laid out the town, known to most hunters as Reynolds City, but variously called Rath City, Camp Reynolds, and Rath's Store.

The main street, if it can be called that, ran north and south. On the east side facing west, the men laid out Rath's store. Thirty by one hundred feet, the place, which included a cookhouse and a sleeping area, consisted of adobe walls built over a limestone foundation, a roof of sod-covered boards supported by juniper and cottonwood poles, and a dirt floor. Carpenters framed the building's few windows with lumber, nails, and glass hauled from Dodge City, and Rath used hides to separate the cooking and sleeping areas from the rest of the store. The hides made the store smell of rotting tallow and drying leather—not, apparently, a pleasant odor. The sleeping room contained several narrow bunk beds in an open, barracks-style arrangement. In the business area, Rath and the store manager, W. H. (Harvey, not George) West, who was Lee and Reynold's agent, stocked the shelves with canned and dried groceries, ammunition, including a plentiful amount of powder, and other supplies. On the floor they placed the large sacks of flour, the heavy bars of lead for bullets, and the great kegs of whiskey.[10]

In a little shack adjoining to the store, Charlie Sing established a laundry. Of Chinese descent and a friend of Rath from Dodge City, Sing, who may once have worked on one of the big railroad construction crews, tended his cleaning supplies and old equipment. He had hauled the equipment in huge Murphy wagons (as nearly all building supplies and material were moved to Rath City) from the Fort Elliott area, where Sing had run a laundry before moving south.

On the west side of the street, facing east, George Aiken laid out a com-

Pictured here are dead bison from a "stand." Slaughter such as that represented in this photo angered the Comanches and contributed to their need to raid cattle herds for food. Courtesy Panhandle-Plains Historical Museum.

bination saloon and dance hall, and Jim Hopkins, apparently in the same building, had a restaurant and hotel. The hotel may have served as a brothel, with the "working girls" coming from Fort Griffin, at first in the "big blue hide wagons" and later in coaches of a short-lived stage line, but such a use is a matter of some debate. The crude, rough building, thirty by eighty feet in size, consisted mainly of hides stretched across juniper and cottonwood poles, but eventually adobe and sod walls went up. Its roof may have been sod-covered canvas stretched across poles, and its floor was dirt. Aiken's establishment was popular and did a large volume of business until Dick Flemming, on the same side of the street, opened a saloon with a plank floor, one much more comfortable for dancing and more attractive to the women from Fort Griffin.[11]

West of Aiken's saloon, the early arrivals in Rath City constructed sod corrals. In one corner they also erected a tiny bunkhouse for guards, including the teamsters, who were responsible for the oxen, horses, and mules. In the town's heyday the pens and adjacent wagon yard held hundreds of animals and dozens of wagons.

In the weeks following the original construction, the place grew. Little sod or adobe and hide shanties sprang up, the corrals expanded, and ricks made like cotton bales but of hard, bound hides (flint hides, they were called) awaiting shipment to Dodge City or Fort Griffin appeared in an area they called the hideyard. James Knight, a Rath employee who ran the hideyard, built a shack north of the store, and Dick Flemming, as indicated, opened a second saloon. Willis Crawford opened a barbershop, where he cut hair, shaved beards, and, if folklore is reliable, extracted teeth. Later, a blacksmith who had come down the trail from Camp Supply set up a small shop.

Smokey Thompson, an entrepreneur and former bison hunter who owned the wagon yard, found additional sources of income. Because the spring that provided drinking water for livestock and humans was two miles from town and, as the village's population grew, more and more inconvenient, he dug a cistern and lined it with rocks. He located the reservoir on the main street in front of Aiken's saloon, hauled water in barrels from the spring to fill it, and sold the water by the bucket. When he noted that the hunters often disliked the watered and rotgut whiskey available at the saloons, Thompson tried his hand at making beer, and he may have attempted brewing other alcoholic beverages as well.

More hunters rode into Rath City than the buildings could accommodate for sleeping. Soon the hides, stacked in ricks ten to twelve or more feet high, provided ample protection for bison hunters; the men simply spread their blankets between the ricks in the hideyard. Other hunters pitched camps with their low-slung tents along a nearby stream, and some folks scattered in shanties north along the road toward Fort Elliott.

Rath City boomed until the bison were gone—or, for about two years. At its height in the winter of 1877–78, claimed Pringle Moore who in 1878 guarded livestock there, the little community "consisted of some half a dozen adobe and cedar buildings . . . [that included] the main store, a magazine house, [Jim] Hopkins restaurant and hotel, George Aiken's saloon and dance hall, Smokey Thompson's wagon-yard, Charlie Sing's laundry, . . . a barber shop, and a blacksmith shop."[12]

It was a busy place. At the peak of the hunt, perhaps four thousand men (hunters, skinners, buyers, teamsters) sought hides across the wide West Texas country. Many of them traded at Rath City, coming to town on a regular basis to sell their hides, purchase supplies, and take in the few attractions that existed. Carl Coke Rister wrote that the "entertainment was . . . brutally raw." He indicated that bison hunters, area "cowboys, and transients played cards, patronized the bars, quarreled, and brawled." If, in fact, the hotel served as a brothel with prostitutes from Griffin, the men surely patronized it.[13]

How often the Griffin women came to Rath City is a matter of conjecture, for extant records do not indicate. Did they arrive weekly with the wagons? Or did they appear less often? In the spring of 1877, James W. Stell, a bison hunter and Rath City resident of sorts, began driving a mail and express stage between Griffin and Rath City. Did they ride along with Stell?

Without question women came for a big dance, or western "ball," as the term was used at the time. At least one, and maybe two or three, such balls occurred at Rath City. W. J. Bryan, who was there and who later owned a ranch in the area, recalled one in which cowboys off the open ranges, bison hunters, and women from Fort Griffin all danced through the night to the fiddle music of Cadmus Brown. Favorite songs included "Turkey in the Straw," "Sal, Spank the Baby," and "Sally Goodins." No doubt Brown fiddled a few waltzes, too, for they were among the most popular of all dances in the early West. The women were the big reason for the popularity of the event; "the men went calico minded as soon as they got a whiff of that Hoyt's cologne," Bryan remembered, "and they swung those gals so fast that they got dust in their pockets." The biggest event occurred in September 1877 to celebrate the successful return of bison hunters from the Llano Estacado and the return of the horses and ponies the hidemen brought with them.[14]

Business, however, was the purpose of the town. And when bison herds

The Mooar brothers, John W. and Wright, are pictured with the hide from a rare white buffalo they purchased from the man who killed the animal. Courtesy Southwest Collection, Texas Tech University.

were thick and large, as during the rut in July and August, business was good. One hunter, Jim McIntire, wrote that "next to owning a ranch buffalo hunting was the most profitable enterprise on the frontier." Hoping to dominate the market, Charles Rath and his partners W. M. D. Lee and Albert E. Reynolds kept prices for their goods low and paid about two dollars for a good bull hide and a bit less for a female one. In the two month period from December 1877 through January 1878, perhaps 200,000 hides sold at Rath City, and before the place shut down in 1879 some 1.1 million of them passed through the boomtown, most handled by Rath's Store.[15]

W. H. (Harvey) West, Lee's agent, managed the busy store for Rath and his partners. Instructed to treat the hunters fairly, West complied. He extended credit liberally, and on occasion he provided new outfits, including wagons and equipment, to men who had lost their supplies, most often by damage through accidents or on occasion by Indian raiders. West's efforts brought results, for the firm not only collected all the hunter debts but also enjoyed their support and good will.[16]

For buyers like West, the business was not always easy. Poorly skinned or damaged hides, including ones with bullet holes in them, held little value, but sometimes the hunters attempted to slip one past the buyers. To disguise nicked and cut hides, writes Jerry Eckhart, "hunters sometimes turned the flesh to the inside so the hair would obscure the holes." When they could, buyers inspected each hide.[17]

The business was always in flux. In 1878, for example, Rath's partner at Griffin, Frank E. Conrad, bought the Lee-Reynolds share of the enterprise, and the next year Rath bought out Conrad's interest. Rath then teamed with the Mooar brothers briefly. Hunters came and went, and as they destroyed herds in the Double Mountain region, the killing fields shifted to other areas. So-called hide towns appeared at Buffalo Gap south of Abilene, Deep Creek at modern Snyder, and elsewhere, and roads connected Rath City or Fort Griffin with most of them.[18]

The road north through Fort Elliott and Camp Supply to Dodge City became known as Rath's Trail. It was well marked, with stream banks cut and difficult spots graded; modern U.S. Highway 83 closely parallels it. The trail was for a brief two years or so heavily used, including for a time by stagecoaches from the line that ran from Fort Griffin to Rath City with an extension to Fort Elliott. Here and there, travelers piled bison skulls along the trail, sometimes writing notes on the skulls. On occasion hunters cut messages on soft limestone rocks and pointed the "way stones" in the direction of Rath City.

Rath, Lee, and Reynolds at first sent their bison hides north to Dodge City. But in the rapidly changing business, Rath and most other buyers, some representing William C. Lobenstine in Leavenworth, Kansas (the dealer who started it all), soon moved them eastward in the high-stacked, six-yoke, ox-drawn Murphy wagons. The hides went to Fort Griffin where, having formed another partnership, Rath and Frank Conrad maintained a large trading post and hideyard. From Griffin, depending on the buyer, the hides moved by wagon either through Denison, Texas, to Kansas or to Fort Worth. Railroads at Fort Worth carried the hides to tanneries in the East. The Griffin market, dominated by Rath and the Mooar brothers, quickly captured the bulk of the hide trade.

For Charles Rath, the change in delivery points to Fort Griffin marked a significant downward shift in the volume of his Dodge City hide trade. In response, at his Dodge City mercantile establishment Rath began to cater to Texas and other cattlemen. By this time, 1877, Dodge City had become the major shipping point for moving cattle to northern markets, and the place was already known more for its livestock trade than for its bison-hide business.

Nonetheless, even while he maintained a home and a business in Dodge City, where he lived well and expansively, Rath stayed active in the Texas hide trade. During the years of the big hunt in the state (1875–78), he spent most of his time in Kansas, but he traveled often to Texas. Sometimes his second wife, Caroline Markley, who was daughter of an old family friend in Ohio and whom he had married in 1870, rode along on the difficult journeys. Caroline went to Mobeetie a few times and may have visited Fort Griffin by way of Rath City, but she preferred her large home in Dodge, especially after the railroad arrived in the early 1870s.

Meanwhile, not long after Rath City appeared, Indian warriors attacked hunting camps. After leaving their reservations in early February 1877, the warriors, who had women and children with them, struck over a wide area in West Texas, destroying camp equipment, stealing horses and mules, and killing the hated bison hunters. Many of the Comanches established a small village in Yellow House Canyon just below its junction with Thompson's Canyon (Blackwater Draw) in modern Lubbock. They attacked Billy Devins's camp first, but he and his skinners escaped. A bit later the well-liked Marshall Sewell, whose camp was near the head of Salt Creek just off the Caprock, died in an assault while he was hunting on the Llano; the warriors also burned the wagons, supplies, and equipment of Harry Burns and Harold Bradstreet—the two Englishmen—who were camped not far away.[19]

As word of these and other attacks spread, the bison hunters headed for Rath City. They arrived—perhaps 175 men—from distant camps in all directions, seeking protection and planning to strike back. But, it turned out, not many wanted to fight Indians. In the end only 45 men agreed to go. Angry, wanting revenge and to get the horses back, and fortified by liberal amounts of whiskey, they determined to find and destroy the Comanches. Well-armed and with plenty of ammunition, horses, wagons, and, unfortunately for them, booze in a large keg, they headed in the general direction of the Comanche camp.

After establishing a temporary base at Buffalo Springs in Yellow House Canyon, the bison hunters located the Comanche camp several miles upstream and on March 18 attacked. The fight did not go well. Some of the men, as it turned out, were too frightened to fight effectively and some were too drunk. Leadership of the little hunter militia was short of sterling, and few of the men had military experience. When the Indians withdrew, the hunters, who suffered several hard injuries but no deaths—although two

Hide yards at Dodge City showing bison hides drying and being pressed into bales for shipment by rail. In the back, a mound of bison bones is stacked and awaiting shipment. From Harper's Weekly, *April 4, 1874; courtesy Panhandle-Plains Historical Museum.*

months later Joe Jackson died of wounds he had sustained in the fight–claimed victory and headed with as much dispatch as possible back to Rath City.[20]

Back at Rath City, the Indian fight caused trouble. The "buffalo militiaers," as several men called them, suffered heavy ribbing. Because few hunters dared to return to the camps, even to gather the hides they had left behind in early March, little hunting took place during March and early April, but in the saloons at both Rath and Griffin much mocking of the militia occurred.

Sometimes the joking was mean-spirited. Tom Lumpkin (not Lumpkins, as some have written), a twenty-six-year-old, quarrelsome, and hot-tempered Iowan had refused to go in search of the Indian raiders. "I have not lost any Indians," he had said, so he did not want to go find any. He voiced annoying contempt for the expedition's lack of success in cleaning out the Comanches, and he did not let up.[21]

Shortly, matters turned tragic. As hidemen began to return to the range in mid-April, Comanches once again swept through the camps. One party struck within five miles of Rath City. Three hunters died, and as usual the raiders stole livestock, damaged equipment, and destroyed supplies. Two

Hunters cleared the Llano Estacado of bison in 1877 and 1878, when hides were in high demand. The hides stacked here are at Charles Rath's firm in Dodge City. Courtesy Panhandle-Plains Historical Museum.

days later Lumpkin stood drinking in Dick Flemming's saloon where Limpy Jim Smith, one of the buffalo militiamen, tended the bar. Other hunters were there, and in a corner one of them, an enthusiastic but impulsive Swede named Oleson, was getting his hair cut. Lumpkin, drinking heavily, made disparaging remarks and snide comments about the men who back in March had chased after the Comanches. According to John R. (Johnny) Cook, who was present, the Swede, who had not been in the Indian fight, came to the defense of the hunters, and Lumpkin shot the unarmed man, breaking his arm. Willis Crawford, who *had* been at the fight and was cutting Oleson's hair, intervened, and Smith ran up to them, pulled Lumpkin aside, and shot him. Lumpkin backed out of the saloon firing away, and Smith emptied his weapon into the fatally injured Iowan. Lumpkin got a decent burial, and in the Fort Griffin law courts Smith got an acquittal.[22]

Meanwhile, the army had sent two expeditions in search of the Indian warriors, who were making life miserable for the bison hunters. In one, a detachment of Troop I, Tenth Cavalry, from Fort Richardson, covered over a thousand miles in an unsuccessful effort to find the Comanches.[23]

The other achieved mixed results. On April 9, muscular and square-shouldered Captain Phillip L. Lee, Troop G, Tenth Cavalry, left Fort Griffin with six Tonkawa scouts and seventy-two men of his command. He stopped briefly at Rath City before heading west to the High Plains. Nearly a month later, on May 4, 1877, he and his troopers found and charged the missing Comanches at Silver Lake (Laguna Plata, sometimes called Lake Quemado or simply Quemos), far out on the Llano Estacado. They killed four Indians in the attack and captured six women and sixty-nine horses. They suffered one death themselves: First Sergeant Charles Baker. The Indian families not killed or captured escaped to the southwest, probably heading toward the Blue Sand Hills. On their return to Griffin, Lee (perhaps a relative of the southern Civil War hero General Robert E. Lee) and his troops again stopped at Rath City, this time reporting the results of their engagement and dividing some of the stolen horses.[24]

John R. Cook and others insisted that Black Horse, a hot-tempered Kwahada war leader, was among those killed in Lee's Silver Lake fight. He was not. Nor was Black Horse the Comanche leader in the March 1877 battle of Yellow House (sometimes called Thompson's) Canyon. He was not there. Black Horse, rather, was in the Fort Marion Military Prison, Saint Augustine, Florida, in the spring of 1877, a place he had been since the summer of 1875, and he could not have led the warriors. After he had completed his sentence in 1878, Black Horse left the military prison and returned to the Comanche reservation. In the summer, he led a small group of his followers—this time with passes—from Indian Territory to the area about Big Spring, where Texas Rangers under Captain June Peak found them.[25]

Lee's favorable report on the fight at Silver Lake raised spirits. Thinking the region was safe, a few bison hunters once more turned to the range. They were wrong. Indian warriors hit outlying camps, and shortly after Captain Lee and his African American troops had passed through town on their way back to Fort Griffin, a group of perhaps seventy-five warriors struck Rath City in a pre-dawn raid. They shot up the place and took all the horses—more than one hundred of them—and mules. Everyone there, including the guards, was asleep. It was early May.

For most hidemen, the hunt was over; it was not safe on the prairie, or even in Rath City, for that matter. Many of them left, heading to Fort Griffin and other points toward the east to await a more healthful season. Some hung around the saloons, waiting for a chance to reenter the hunting ranges. Others determined to chase down the Comanche raiding party, secure their horses, and punish the thieves.

The latter group organized what became known as the Forlorn Hope expedition. They got horses and pack mules from area ranchers, received supplies from Harvey West at Rath's Store, and made plans: take wagons to a base camp and then pack the "supplies and roam the Staked Plains until [they] found" the Comanches. They hoped to get their horses back and planned to fight the Indians, if that was necessary. Altogether, just twenty-four men, including a guide, José Piedad Tafoya, a former comanchero who knew the Llano thoroughly, headed west.[26]

The expedition left Rath City in mid-May. With James Harvey, lately of the Fourth Cavalry, in command, the men followed a familiar route to their destination, the mouth of Blanco Canyon. They established a base camp at Silver Falls, where the river rushes from the canyon to form the head of the Freshwater Fork of the Brazos, not many miles east of modern Crosbyton. Near here, Ranald Mackenzie, William R. Shafter, and others in the past had located supply camps from which to scout the Llano Estacado, or "Yarner." Water, timber, and grass were plentiful at the site, which after the turn of the century would become a popular picnic ground.[27]

From their base camp, the hunters, with supplies on pack animals, headed up the canyon. At what Cook called "the head of White Canyon," they met *ciboleros* (bison hunters) from New Mexico. With an enormous sense of self-importance, the Texas hidemen told the New Mexicans to pull back off the Llano, to retreat to the Pecos River, and to tell any additional *ciboleros* or comancheros to do the same thing. Moving south, Harvey's group, mainly from curiosity, inspected the site of their March fight with the Comanches. They found no Indians.[28]

Now the bison hunters scoured the High Plains. They visited sand dunes that Cook called "the tunneled sand-hills" northwest of Lubbock, camped at the long water hole in modern Lubbock, rode up Thompson's Canyon, and visited Casas Amarillas and Silver Lake. They followed an Indian trail that took them in one direction after another, for obviously the Comanches knew the hunters were on their trail. They camped again at Casas Amarillas, rode south to Double Lakes, and from there marched all the way to Big Spring on the Colorado. Now off the Yarner, they moved north along the eastern edge of the Llano Estacado to the Bull Creek area, south of where Comanches had killed the popular Marshall Sewall in February.

Again the bison hunters climbed onto the Staked Plains and, as Cook wrote, visited "every place where water could be found that we knew of or could find." They marched and counter-marched "from place to place." They found one Indian trail after another, but each time the Comanches eluded them.[29]

Time passed. Days turned to weeks and then months. The rains stopped, the temperatures rose. Cook and other members of the Forlorn Hope, particularly the Scot-English poet Harry Burns, noticed how the flowers of May and June, so full of color and bloom, had shriveled before the heat of July. In May, Cook remembered, "we could smell the sweet perfume from them and admire their beauty; and for the next six weeks . . . the air was fragrant with their sweet odor." In July, however, the Llano turned brown and dusty; the men were tired; the playas were empty; and the waterholes, like the Comanches, had become elusive.

On July 4, 1877, the bison hunters again camped at Casas Amarillas. They celebrated Independence Day by making a flag from stripes of cloth from red and blue shirts, plus a white flour sack. The men used, wrote Cook, "the tin-foil from around our plug tobacco for stars. Our standard was a tepee-pole." They planted the flag at the top of a large stone pyramid they had built on the "bluff above the natural and excavated caves." After they hoisted it, the flag "floated about twenty-five feet above the ground."

The men ate. Then, to continue the celebration, they "delivered patriotic orations." According to Cook, they "declaimed some of Daniel Webster's and Henry Clay's speeches to Congress." They condemned all Englishmen (Burns and Bradstreet excepted, they said) and damned former King George. Finally, around their evening campfire they held a series of kangaroo courts, with Mortimer "Wild Bill" Kress as the judge.[30]

About two weeks later, on July 17, the hunters camped just off the Caprock in the Muchaque Peak country along Bull Creek, one of the head streams of the Colorado River. To the well-watered spot they had relocated their supply camp from Blanco Canyon. While the bulk of the tired party rested there, Harvey sent men in pairs with large field glasses onto the Llano Estacado to search for Comanches. The scouts saw neither Indians nor signs of them. They found little water at the familiar sites, and what little rain fell was localized and spotty. They were ready to call off their long, but failed, pursuit and in the heat and droughty conditions return to Rath City.

About noon, however, a large number of black soldiers, Troop A of the Tenth Cavalry, rode into camp. After a short parley, the buffalo soldiers and the bison hunters agreed to join forces. The hunters would serve as guides, and the soldiers, if necessary, would do the fighting. It was an informal agreement that produced disastrous results, but it had grown from the perceived need to protect not only hidemen but also ranchers, farmers, and townspeople from Comanche raids along the western edge of settlement in Texas.

Chapter 3

Comanches and Settlers in 1877

After the Civil War, two facts of life above all others slowed the settlement of West Texas: Indian raiding and insufficient rainfall. "Figuratively speaking," wrote William Curry Holden, "the settler had to hold his rifle in one hand and his plow in the other." Under such conditions, a pioneer farmer or rancher had trouble acquiring hired help, needed to watch his stock and buildings closely, and ran the danger of losing his home and family. Even without Indian raids, moreover, the region was not considered farming country. As early as 1851 General William G. Belknap had reported that "it is not probable that white settlement will be made [here] for a century to come, if ever." Two decades later a citizen in Shackelford County noted that "owing to the long and awful droughts, agriculture is not, and doubtless never will be, followed here." For settlers in the 1870s, then, farming, and to a lesser extent cattle raising, in West Texas was a tough proposition.[1]

For Comanche people, the decade of the 1870s was no less difficult. Once they had made a living hunting and trading below the Arkansas River in Kansas, Texas, and New Mexico, a region often called Comancheria. In the 1830s and 1840s, however, Texas Rangers and federal troops narrowed the hunting range of the Comanches—Penatekas mostly—in Texas, and in the 1850s they confined it to West Texas. During the Civil War years Indian warriors, now including Kiowas along with Kickapoos and Lipan Apaches from Mexico, sought with mixed success to ride across the state to hunt or to reclaim some of their former Texas lands. By stealing Texas cattle and driving them to Mexico, for example, the Kickapoos and Lipans made something of a living in the state, but the Lipans did not regain their lands, most of which Comanches had taken from them in the late eighteenth century.

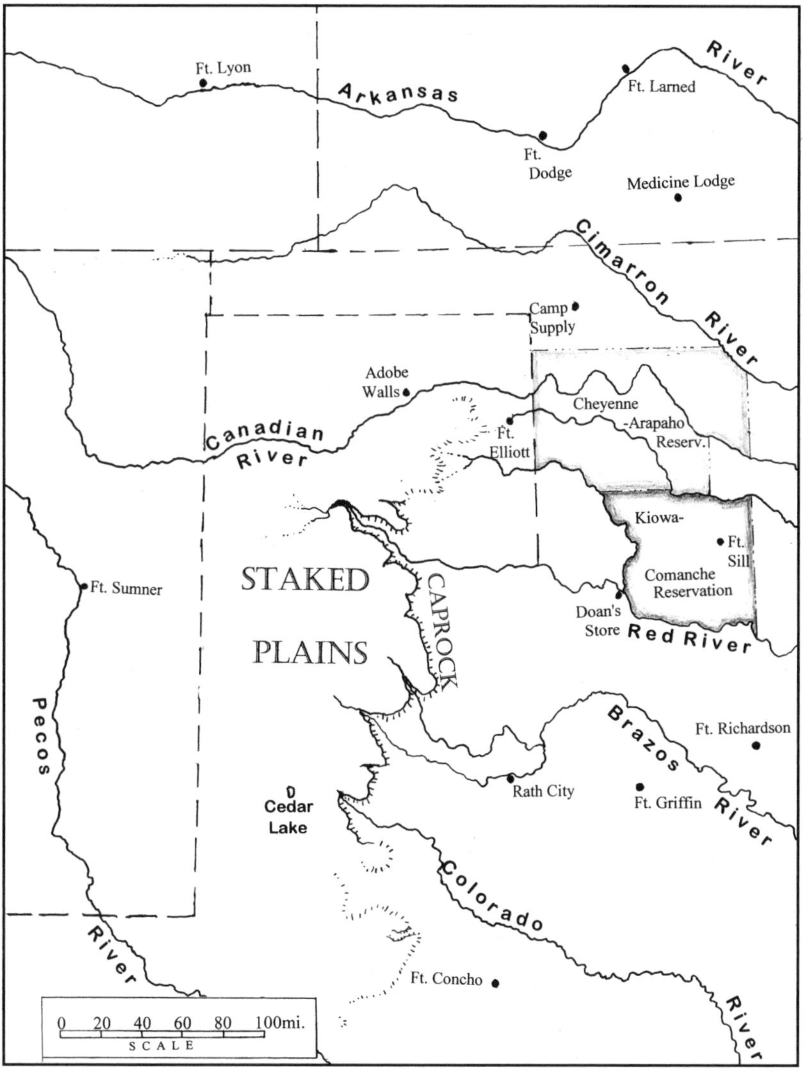

Map 4. Reservations and military posts of the Llano Estacado and in Oklahoma. Courtesy Michael Harter.

The Comanches with their Kiowa allies were more successful. In one of the treaties of the Little Arkansas in 1865 they accepted as their own a huge region in western Indian Territory (Oklahoma) and western Texas. It included the Llano Estacado, all of the Texas Panhandle, and most of Indian Territory west of the 98th meridian. Although legally it was not federal land to give away, the government, according to the treaty, set it "apart for the absolute and undisturbed use and occupation of the" Kiowas and Comanches and "no white person except officers, agents, and employees of the Government shall go upon or settle within the country. . . ." Kiowa and Comanche leaders who signed the treaty agreed that this region below the southern border of Kansas was "their permanent home." Of course, they also agreed not to raid in Texas or to leave the territory without written permission from federal authorities.[2]

Two years later in the treaty of Medicine Lodge (1867), the Comanches and Kiowas lost all their reservation outside of Indian Territory. At the urging of Paruasemena, a Yamparika Comanche leader, however, the treaty "reserved" for the tribes "the right to hunt on any lands south of the Arkansas River, so long as the buffalo may range thereon in such numbers as to justify the chase, and no white settlements shall be permitted on any part of the lands contained in the old reservation. . . ." The "old reservation," defined in this treaty as the region set aside for the Cheyennes and Arapahos in their 1865 Little Arkansas treaty, also included land in Kansas below the Arkansas River.[3]

Thus, in the late 1860s and in the 1870s, the Kiowas and Comanches found their hunting territory restricted. When the government did not provide adequate, proper, and treaty-specified amounts of flour and food, clothing and blankets, livestock, training in farming and animal husbandry, and tools and equipment for farming, they suffered desperately from material shortages basic to sustaining life. To some extent, raiding was necessary to live.

Moreover, young men, required by tradition and tribal codes of honor to achieve success in fighting and hunting to gain prestige, position, and influence, left the reservation to hunt and raid in Texas. With permits, they hunted bison in the Texas Panhandle and in West Texas below the Red River. Some men, including older warriors, raided ranches, supply wagons, settlements, and, later, bison hunter camps—doing it, probably, more for economic reasons than for honor.

Paruacoom, Quanah, and Black Horse were among several Kwahada Comanche leaders in the 1870s, a time when the Kwahada group was coming into its own from remnants of the Kotsoteka, Penateka, Yamparika, and other Comanche divisions. Paruacoom, described as the "mighty leader" of the Kwahadas, dominated the group in the 1860s. He did not attend the 1867 Medicine Lodge conference or sign the treaty, however, and in 1874 because of illness (pneumonia) he was not among the Comanche, Kiowa, and Cheyenne warriors who attacked bison hunters at Adobe Walls in the Texas Panhandle.[4]

Quanah was tall, dark, and commanding in appearance. He rose to prominence during the 1874 attack at Adobe Walls. On the reservation after 1875, he easily adjusted to white ways and became an influential and favored, but perhaps spoiled (by whites), young "chief" of the Kwahadas.

Black Horse is often incorrectly identified as the leader of the Kwahada holdouts during the 1877 black troop tragedy. An aggressive and boastful war leader, Black Horse spent two years in prison in Fort Marion, Florida; he was there in the summer of 1877. Once out of prison and back on the reservation, he led in 1878 what some call the last Comanche raid into Texas.[5]

In the late 1870s, the Kwahada leaders dominated Comanche hunting and trading in West Texas and on the Llano Estacado. Also in the late 1870s, the once-powerful Kotsotekas and the now-peaceful Nokonis—both of whom had once hunted and traded in the upper Red and Pease Rivers and in the lower Texas Panhandle—were living on the Comanche-Kiowa reservation. They received some of the so-called benefits of the Medicine Lodge treaty.

The Kwahadas, however, because they did not sign the Medicine Lodge treaty, had little access to the treaty's political and economic gifts. As a result, the Kwahadas needed to hunt bison, and stealing cattle for food and trade remained their principal economic resource. Accordingly, they engaged in the comanchero trade, as had other Comanche and Apache groups before them. They took horses and cattle from farmers and ranchers on the rim of settlement in Texas and trailed the animals to favorite campgrounds on the Llano Estacado or just off the eastern Caprock (Muchaque country for example). Here, they traded the horses and cattle plus dried bison meat and hides to comancheros who had come from villages in New Mexico with hard bread, blankets, equipment, tools, and other commodities unavailable to the Kwahadas.

The Indian attack in 1874 at Adobe Walls, then, should be seen as a way to protect an economic resource. Bison hunters in the Texas Panhandle had put the Kwahadas in jeopardy, and some of the Yamparika leaders, such as Tabenanaka, saw the hunters as damaging their own trade north across the Arkansas River. Other Yamparika leaders (Cheevers, for example), the Nokoni leader Terheryaquahip, and most of the Penateka people held different political-economic goals and did not push for the attack.

Less convincing is the argument that the attack was an effort to create some kind of Comanche "nationhood" or pan-Comanche movement. Isatai, a young Kwahada warrior and shaman, worked hard to produce such a movement, and his Sun Dance in May 1874 may have been part of the effort.

The Comanche camp pictured here in 1871 was located along Cache Creek near Fort Sill in southwestern Indian Territory (Oklahoma). Courtesy Southwest Collection, Texas Tech University, Ernest Wallace Papers, 442-E1.

If so, it failed, for many Comanche leaders refused to bring their people to the ceremony. Moreover, Kiowas, Cheyennes, and Arapahos were also present at the ceremony site near the junction of Sweetwater Creek and the North Fork of the Red River. And when militants on the course to follow gained control of the month-long gathering, many Yamparikas, Nokonis, and Penatekas headed back to Fort Sill, the reservation's principal agency town.[6]

In either case, at the end of June 1874 perhaps 200 to 250—accounts differ—Comanche, Kiowa, and Cheyenne warriors attacked Adobe Walls. Lone Wolf led the Kiowas; Stone Calf and White Shield, the Cheyennes; and Mowway (a Kotsoteka), Quanah, and Isatai of the Kwahadas led the Comanches. The attack did not go well, and after the death of some fourteen or fifteen warriors, Indian leaders called off the battle.[7]

But raiding continued. In the weeks that followed, Cheyennes, Kiowas, and Comanches continued to hit bison hunters, wagon trains, travelers, and others who ranged through their territory. Determined to keep whites from their favorite hunting grounds, they struck over a wide area of the southwestern plains. The Native Americans, especially the Kwahadas, raided out of economic necessity and because whites continued to press into territory the Indian people regarded as their own.

In response, the federal government ordered all the southern Plains Indians—the "offending" groups—to report immediately to their reservation agencies. It gave them until August 1. Many groups reported. Many others, especially the Cheyennes, refused, and the government saw the holdouts as hostile. In response, the Indian bureau in the Interior Department allowed the army in the War Department to pursue Indian people onto reservations.

The army acted with force. During the late summer and fall of 1874 it sent some three thousand troops into the Texas Panhandle, where most of the non-reservation Indians were living, hunting, and camping. Between August and November Indian warriors and soldiers fought fourteen engagements. Colonel Ranald S. Mackenzie, the hard-charging leader of the Fourth Cavalry, struck the most telling blow. At the end of September, he surprised Comanches, Cheyennes, and Kiowas who were camping in five villages along the Red River in Palo Duro Canyon. Mackenzie killed and captured few Indians in the canyon fight that followed, but he rounded up fourteen hundred horses and mules, moved the animals to nearby Tule Canyon, and shortly afterward shot them.[8]

Without horses and having lost their supplies, the southern Plains Indians who had been in the canyon had little chance. To escape the cold as winter approached, one small band after another reported back, surrendered to soldiers, or showed up at another reservation. A few Kiowas, under Satanta and Big Tree, for example, rode to the Cheyenne reservation before cold weather set in. In February 1875 Little Wolf led his Kiowa followers to their reservation, and in March about sixteen hundred Cheyennes reported back to their agency in Indian Territory. Finally, in June, Quanah, Isatai, Black Beard, Wild Horse, and some four hundred other Kwahadas with more than two thousand horses went to Fort Sill.[9]

Red Young Man, who had never been to the reservation, and his small band of Kwahadas stayed out. In 1875, they moved south and west deeper onto the Llano Estacado, hid in the sand hills, hunted bison when they could, and camped in such familiar places as Casas Amarillas, Silver Lake (Laguna Plata, sometimes Quemos or Lake Quemada), and the long water hole in Yellow House Canyon. From time to time others—including Batsena, Cotopah, Hishorty, and Esatema—joined them on the High Plains.

On the Comanche-Kiowa reservation in 1875 and afterward, life for many Indian people became a struggle for survival. The men balked at learning to farm, the government was slow to teach cattle-raising, and food shortages were common. Even when the men tried farming, difficulties arose, for the region was arid, with thin soils. Most of the reservation lands were unsuited to nineteenth-century farming techniques. Sometimes the work animals were so weak from lack of feed and forage that the horses could not pull a plow. Moreover, the Comanches needed to spend three days a week seeking government rations: one day traveling from their rural villages to the agency town, one day at the agency to collect the rations, and one day returning to their camps. The result was neglected crops and livestock. As noted, government annuities, clothes, food rations, and other supplies often arrived late, often arrived in pitiful condition, and often arrived in quantities insufficient to sustain good health. The cattle they received on ration days were sometimes scrawny animals that provided little beef. The Indians consumed salted pork, which they got as a supplement to the fresh beef, only with great difficulty.

After 1875, Comanches and Kiowas, mainly from economic necessity, continued to leave their reservation. Younger warriors, sometimes with their families, struck isolated bison hunter camps, cattle herds, pioneer homesteads on occasion, and stagecoach lines. Some of the spoils the Comanches took to comanchero trading camps on the Llano Estacado or along its eastern edge. Some they trailed back to the reservation, where the comancheros from New Mexico showed up for business, but it was a dwindling trade.

Available trade figures attest to the decline. Official traders on the Kiowa-Comanche reservation purchased from Indian people in 1876 robes and furs worth over $70,000. They bought $64,500 worth in 1877 and only $26,375 the following year. The comanchero trade took even sharper declines, in part because the journey from New Mexico across the Llano Estacado to the reservation was a two-month-long affair—and then of course another two months back.[10]

Settlers complicated the economic difficulties. They stole Comanche and Kiowa horses. Comanches loosely herded their stock, and white men who had taken such temporary positions as cutting and hauling hay or wood could and did leave their jobs, round up a dozen horses, and, as William T. Hagan writes, "ride home in style." Indians at Fort Sill in 1874 lost 2,000 horses and mules. The next year authorities arrested some twenty horse thieves, but courts, especially Texas courts, passed sentences light enough that the lucrative business continued. Indians sometimes pursued the thieves. In September 1877, they may have hanged two men who had run off with 133 Kiowa horses.[11]

In 1877, the Comanche population was approximately 1,550 people, a fifty percent decline since the 1867 Medicine Lodge Treaty. Older division lines had blurred, and tribal spokesmen, as Hagan has written, more and more spoke "as Comanches rather than" as Kwahadas or Yamparikas or Penatekas. Some older leaders had died and some, such as Mowway (a Kotsoteka), were about to step aside. In meetings with the agents, Hagan suggests, "Tabananaka, Horse Back, Quanah, and Cheevers talked most frequently."[12]

Meanwhile, in December 1876 a band of approximately 170 Comanches —Kwahadas for the most part—fled the reservation. They headed for the Llano Estacado, a place where they had hunted for decades and whose colorful breaks and deep canyons had often served as winter camping sites. Many of them joined Red Young Man's small band, and from their favorite Llano high country retreats, they struck with increasing frequency at bison hunters, supply trains, stage lines, and isolated horse and cattle herds.[13]

In early 1877, from their scattered winter camps along the Llano Estacado's eastern escarpment, the Comanches searched for bison hunters. Probably they were hungry; clearly they were angry. "We would often see great wagon loads of hides being hauled away," remembered Herman Lehmann, a white captive raised as a Comanche, "and would find the carcasses of thousands of slaughtered buffalo. It made us desperate to see this wanton slaughter of our food supply." In response, they destroyed Billy Devins's hunting camp near the mouth of Yellow House Canyon and took all the horses. The hunters, said Cook, "barely escaped with their lives." A few miles away they wrecked the camp of Harry Burns and Harold Bradstreet, the hidemen from Britain, burning the hides and wagons and taking the ammunition and horses.[14]

At the end of February about fifty Comanches rode up on Marshall Sewall, who was shooting bison and did not notice the Indians approaching. Sewall's outfit was near the head of the Salt Fork of the Brazos River, probably in modern Garza County and about five miles northeast of Devins's camp. The Indian warriors, noted Lehmann, "circuled [sic] around [the] lone hunter" and shot at him, and soon enough they killed and scalped him, and they took his long range .45 Creedmoor Sharp's bison gun. They also chased after two of Sewall's skinners, Wild Skillet and Moccasin Jim (if Cook is correct), who managed to escape by running down a brush-lined draw. At Sewall's camp the warriors destroyed everything they did not want to carry off.[15]

The Comanches then hurried away, riding onto the Llano Estacado and into camp in one of the shallow side draws of Yellow House Canyon. But, wrote Lehmann, "the buffalo hunters took our trail and followed us. . . ."

Part of the Comanche village of Chief Mowway along Cache Creek near Fort Sill on the Comanche-Kiowa Reservation, winter 1872–73. Courtesy Southwest Collection, Texas Tech University.

When a fight ensued, the Comanches divided, circled around to the rear of their pursuers, captured all but three of the enemy horses, and wounded four of the hunters.[16]

The "Indian who had [Sewall's] big gun," Lehmann recalled, "was killed. Another Indian got the gun and claimed it for his own. He, too, was killed." A third Comanche took possession of the weapon, "and he fell with it in his hands." Finally, "an Indian known as Five Feathers used it for a long time, when he, too, was killed." Seeing that the Creedmoor "had an evil spirit," the Comanche shaman later buried the gun and Sewall's scalp-locks in the tunneled sand hills northwest of modern Lubbock.[17]

Meanwhile, the Comanches could not overrun their pursuers. Using their long-range weapons, the bison hunters held off the warriors and eventually retreated. When the hunters pulled off, the Kwahadas moved away, most heading up Yellow House Canyon and going into winter camp just below the long water hole in present Lubbock. As weather conditions improved in March, some warriors, operating in small groups, struck at bison hunting camps, farms and ranches, and exposed cattle and horse herds. They ranged over a wide area in West Texas.

The bison hunters, however, were not finished with the Comanches. Seeking revenge for the popular Sewall's death and reinforced by additional men from Rath City, the hunters gathered at John Godey's camp, located about ten miles east of Sewall's destroyed hunting ground. About forty-five men, some in wagons and some on horseback—with plenty of bravado, plenty of determination, and plenty of ammunition, but, fortunately for the Comanches, with too little experience in military leadership and supplied with too much liquor—headed for Yellow House Canyon. After some difficulty, the hidemen located the large Indian camp and just after daylight on March 18 attacked.

The Comanches were caught unprepared. During winter months the Kwahadas were less watchful, less alert. Their military fervor slackened. They rarely posted camp guards, and they watched their horse herds with less vigilance. Despite their own recent attacks, they really did not expect to fight. The fight came, recalled Herman Lehmann, "at a time when we least expected to be attacked."[18]

When the attack came, remembered Lehmann, the women "mounted and got our horses out of the camp." The men "took refuge under a hillside and held the enemy, who were in the open, at bay for several hours, when they finally retreated." Well-protected, the Comanches, if Lehmann is correct, suffered only two men wounded and lost no lives. When the hunters withdrew, the Indian men "gathered up [the women] and children and horses and moved away from there."[19]

While the bison hunters trailed back to Rath City, the Comanches "traveled across the plains and met the Apaches." The meeting did not last long; presumably some trading took place, but it was not an altogether friendly meeting. The Apaches rode away before nightfall. Within a few days the Comanches were camping near Silver Lake on the modern Hockley-Cochran county line. It was a good place to rest. Just east of the lake stretched the large and game-rich Casas Amarillas basin, and northwest of the lake in modern Bailey County were wetlands that attracted game of all kinds.[20]

From Silver Lake, small groups of Comanche warriors rode off the Llano Estacado to sweep through bison hunting camps, ranches, and outlying settlements. In mid-April, one bold group struck within five miles of Rath City, killing three hunters, destroying supplies and equipment, and stealing livestock. Another "large party of us," remembered Lehmann, "went down on the San Saba and Llano Rivers and got a big lot of horses." The early settlers in that area, he wryly noted, "were very kind to raise horses for us, for it saved us a lot of trouble." The Comanches hurried back to the Llano Estacado with the captured animals, but when "we reached our camp," he recalled, "we found it had been attacked by a body of soldiers."[21]

In response to the renewed Comanche raids, both Texas Rangers and federal troops had gone in pursuit. The rangers at the end of April gave chase to Herman Lehmann and his Comanche horse thieves in the upper Llano and San Saba Rivers, but the Kwahadas got away, driving the stolen animals with them. Some black regulars of Troop I, Tenth Cavalry, from Fort Richardson rode for more than one thousand miles in the region north of the tunneled sand hills, but without success in finding Comanches.

Federal troops under Captain Philip L. Lee of the Tenth Cavalry proved more successful. They found the large Comanche camp at Silver Lake, and on May 4, 1877, with their Tonkawa guides they struck hard. The men of Lee's Troop G also found mainly women and children. "When the attack was made on the camp," wrote Lehmann, "most of the [women] ran away and hid, but five" people died in the fight. The Indians also lost six women who were captured and sixty-nine horses. One of the dead was Batsena, "a very brave warrior," whose body the Tonkawas scalped and multilated. Also among the dead was Batsena's "daughter, Nooki, a beautiful Indian maiden, who had been disemboweled and scalped."[22]

The Kwahada warriors who had been on the San Saba arrived at Silver Lake on May 5 to discover the carnage. They found bodies "horribly mangled," camp equipage wrecked, guns and ammunition gone or destroyed, and women and horses taken to Fort Griffin. We "soon found our scattered women and children and old men," remembered Hermann Lehmann, "and heard the sad details of the attack." Everyone was "badly demoralized," but before seeking revenge, the Comanches determined to reorganize—"to get our forces together and move to another part of the country."[23]

The Comanches moved deeper onto the High Plains. They also scattered into smaller groups, and some of them headed back toward their Indian Territory reservation. The younger warriors, however, were not finished with the hidemen. Cotopah, Hishorty, Esatema, and others struck again at bison hunter camps just off the Llano Estacado Caprock, and in early May a large party of them—perhaps seventy-five men—raided Rath City, this time riding right down Main Street, shooting up the place, and taking more than one hundred horses and mules. The Rolling Plains country of West Texas was not a safe place for white settlers.

Nonetheless, white settlers moved through the region as they edged toward the High Plains. Although some men in May 1877 (especially after the Comanche raid on Rath City) quit the range and settled temporarily into saloons at Fort Griffin, many bison hunters continued to search the broken country for bison stands. Here and there they established so-called hide towns, some of which (such as Snyder, Texas) grew into cities. Cattlemen pushed their longhorn herds into the Rolling Plains, and they drove their market animals north across the Red River and through Indian Territory to Dodge City, which had recently emerged as a major cattle-shipping town. Farmers and townspeople moved with increasing vigor into the West Texas lands they thought the Indians had surrendered some two or three years earlier. When railroad construction again moved toward western lands in the late 1870s and afterward, the westward push of white pioneers increased. Indeed, the "white settlements in Texas," write Ernest Wallace and E. Adamson Hoebel, "advanced more in the decade from 1874 to 1884 than in the fifty years preceding."[24]

On the Llano Estacado, the white assault began after the Red River War. Sheepherders from New Mexico—*pastores,* they were called—took the lead. Some of them were former comancheros who knew the Llano well and who knew that in the Canadian River Valley they could pasture huge flocks of sheep. Casimero Romero, for example, a successful comanchero, rancher, and businessman from Mora County, New Mexico, in November 1876 led his family, a dozen employees, and three friends each with their families down the Canadian River to where Tascosa later developed. They trailed some forty-five hunderd sheep, several horses, and enough cattle to provide beef and milk for the pioneers. They also placed household goods, lumber, and ranch equipment on a dozen or more large freight wagons, each pulled by a team of four oxen.[25]

Soon others followed. The Canadian River Valley filled with sheepherders who established small *plazas* along the river or its tributaries. From their *plaza* headquarters, the men grazed their flocks onto the high tableland on both sides of the wide valley. Some herders may have pushed sheep as far south as Tahoka Lake, and one Antonio Baca claims to have trailed sheep as far north as the modern Oklahoma Panhandle. For a half-dozen or more years, until about 1882, sheepherders dominated the Canadian River Valley and the High Plains region just south of the river. Cheyennes, Kiowas, and Comanches from their reservations may have come west to trade with the Canadian River *pastores,* but the Indians rarely raided the *plazas,* perhaps because many of the *pastores* were former comancheros.

The *pastores* did not stay in the Panhandle. Cattlemen soon forced them out. As early as 1876, in fact, the celebrated plainsman and cattle trailer Charles Goodnight, moving a herd of fifteen hundred cattle from Colorado, wintered near Casimero Romero's *plaza*. In the spring of 1877, about the time that the Comanches and bison hunters were fighting in Yellow House Canyon, the determined and enterprising Goodnight pushed into Palo Duro Canyon to establish the JA Ranch. Although Goodnight stayed away from the sheepherders, the *pastores* were not so lucky with other ranchers—cattlemen who followed close on Goodnight's heels. Before 1884, the *plazas* were deserted.[26]

Closer to the favorite Kwahada camps on the central Staked Plains, ranches appeared. Henry Clay "Hank" Smith, a forty-year-old Fort Griffin businessman and former overland freighter, built the first. In 1876 he searched Blanco Canyon for a favorable ranch setting and located a site northeast of modern Crosbyton. In the summer of 1877, while Comanches eluded bison hunters and buffalo soldiers on the Llano Estacado, workmen started building a large rock house on the Blanco Canyon property—a place at first called Tasker's Ranche [sic]. In the fall, Clay finished construction on the two-story home, and in 1878 with his wife and several employees from Fort Griffin he settled on the 2,560-acre ranch. The Smiths were the first permanent white settlers in the South Plains region of the Llano Estacado.

Even as stonemasons erected the rock house, land surveyors were at work in the region. In early May 1877 (about the time that Captain Lee and his soldiers of the Tenth Cavalry's Troop G attacked the Comanches at Silver Lake) a party of surveyors employed by the Dallas firm of Daugherty, Connellee and Ammerman headed for the Llano Estacado. They planned to "locate" lands from "the then unlocated public domain." Among the surveyors was O. W. Williams, a native of Kentucky with an Illinois law license who had come to the dry Southwest to recover from tuberculosis. When they reached Jacksboro in early June, the men heard, wrote Williams, that Comanches had left the reservation at Fort Sill some months earlier and were raiding bison camps "in the very country into which we were to do our work." Buffalo soldiers—a detachment of Troop I, Tenth Cavalry—from Fort Richardson, they heard, were in pursuit.[27]

As they moved west from Jacksboro, the surveyors made special note of the land and animals. In Archer County they ran "through a country marked by a great number of glistening skeletons of buffaloes, apparently slaughtered one or two years earlier." The bones covered two "spots of ten acres each," wrote Williams, with an estimated one hundred "skeletons closely lying, as the result of a hunter getting what was called a 'stand.'" Farther west, they encountered a big cattle trail, "which our boys from West Texas, called 'The Famous Colorado Cattle Trail.'" The road (the Western Cattle

Quanah, a Kwahada Comanche leader, took the name Quanah Parker after he entered the reservation. Courtesy Southwest Collection, Texas Tech University.

Trail) crossed the Red River at what in 1878 became Doan's Store in Wilbarger County and continued north from there to Dodge City.[28]

On July 4, while the bison hunters who were pursuing Comanches on the Llano celebrated Independence Day in Casas Amarillas, Williams and his surveyors worked their lines. But they stopped work early, located a source of fresh water, and camped that evening near two separate parties of bison hunters. One of the camps belonged to the Mooar brothers. Ten days later in Blanco Canyon the surveyors "went into camp some two miles below an unfinished house"—the rock house that stonemasons and Hank Smith would complete in the fall.[29]

A mile away, the surveyors found a family from Erath County, Texas, on its way to New Mexico. The family and the surveyors, as we have seen, camped together and the family followed the surveyors westward onto the High Plains. Ten days later, in what must be considered a bold, or even dangerous, move, the Erath County family (a husband and wife with "two good looking girls") left the surveyors to follow the Mackenzie Trail to their destination.[30]

Now, in mid-July 1877, Williams and his fellow surveyors were noticing the effects of the summer drought. In Blanco Canyon and on the High Plains west of the canyon, Williams noted first that the "country was dry and parched" and later that "the country appeared to be exceedingly dry." On the seventeenth, the surveyors camped on the plains at a small lake "that was the only water we had seen in the 22 miles of our day's run." On July 30—the same day that some forty miles to the southwest bison hunters and buffalo soldiers were killing horses to drink the blood—Williams, without water and "under a hot sun," shot a coyote so that he might drink its blood. But, because the coyote was infected with scabies, he let it be.[31]

On August 1, the surveyors were in Thompson's Canyon (or Black Water Draw) within the limits of modern Lubbock. At some springs just above the canyon's junction with Yellow House Creek, they discovered "many relics of Indian camps . . . rather recently abandoned." Bison and pronghorns were grazing near the springs. Below the junction of the two streams, in Yellow House Canyon, the surveyors found dry creek beds "choked with the skeletons of buffaloes."[32]

About noon two days later, pointing "up the mesquite clad valley," a surveyor shouted that Indians were approaching. The men quickly prepared to defend themselves. They "got out arms and cartridges, and under [the] wagon lined [their] guns on the spokes of the wheels." The people approaching were not Indians, however, but "some horsemen, clad in ragged clothes,

. . . and yelling 'friends.'" The "friends," led by "chief narrator" John R. Cook, related "a rather dramatic story of a chase after [Comanches], ending in the death, as it then appeared of a number of the United States soldiers and some hunters, due to lack of water in a desert."[33]

Some twenty-four bison hunters, the surveyors were told, had gone after the Comanches who back in May had stolen their horses at Rath City. For two months the hunters had stayed on the trail, crisscrossing the Llano Estacado as they followed the elusive Kwahadas from one water hole to another and back again. Then, on July 17, while they rested along Bull Creek in the Muchaque country just off the Caprock, the hidemen met some sixty black regulars of Troop A, Tenth Cavalry. The soldiers and hunters quickly agreed to join forces in pursuit of the Comanches.

In the meantime, on the Comanche-Kiowa reservation related developments occurred. At Fort Sill, Ranald S. Mackenzie, colonel of the Fourth Cavalry, and James M. Haworth, a forty-one-year-old Quaker, peace policy advocate, and Indian agent to the Comanches, asked Quanah, a Kwahada leader, to ride with four others to the Llano Estacado. They wanted him to convince the Comanches there to return to the reservation.

Quanah agreed and on July 12 left Fort Sill for the High Plains. Nine days later, about 4:00 P.M. on July 21, Quanah and his companions rode into the bison hunter–buffalo soldier camp at a large playa lake near modern Tahoka. In the discussions that followed, Quanah spoke about his mission, showed the hunters and soldiers his military and Indian-bureau instructions, and asked that he be given a chance to get the Comanches off the High Plains. No agreement was struck.

With that, Quanah and his companions left. Although knowing that the Comanches they sought were to the west in the Blue Sand Hills, they headed toward the southwest, planning to draw the soldiers away from the Kwahadas. They rode to Cedar Lake (Laguna Sabinas), the place where Quanah may have been born, and, after the soldiers arrived at the lake, the Comanches entered Captain Nolan's camp. This time they stayed six hours, eating, resting, talking, and perhaps measuring the soldiers' strength. Or, perhaps, Quanah just wanted to spend some time at his birth place.[34]

Upon leaving Nolan's Cedar Lake encampment, Quanah and his companions headed southwest. Then they turned west again before riding quickly northwest to join Red Young Man's band in the Blue Sand Hills. After reaching the small Indian village (located north of modern Milnesand in Roosevelt

County, New Mexico) about July 26, Quanah, Red Young Man, Hishorty, and others (including Herman Lehmann) debated in council over a three- or four-day period whether to return to the reservation. Quanah won them over.[35]

While the Indians counseled between July 26 and July 30, disaster of the worst kind struck buffalo soldiers in Troop A of the United States Army's Tenth Cavalry.

Chapter 4

Buffalo Soldiers and the Army in 1877

Some 180,000 African American soldiers fought in the Civil War, and from all accounts they fought well. Indeed, the United States Congress was impressed enough that in July 1866 it created six new and permanent black regiments: four of infantry plus what became the Ninth and Tenth Cavalries. Although in 1869 the War Department reduced the four infantry regiments to two (the Twenty-fourth and Twenty-fifth Infantries), the segregated units remained an important part of the American military until World War II.

The cavalry troops, particularly the Tenth Cavalry, became known as "buffalo soldiers," from most points of view an honorary sobriquet. They spent the post–Civil War period at stations mainly in the Southwest. Soldiers of the Tenth guarded mail routes and railroad builders, built and maintained military posts, chased outlaws and cattle thieves, protected Indian Territory (Oklahoma) from white incursion, and like most western army units engaged in a number of other civilian-related activities. The buffalo soldiers are remembered most, however, for the role they played in Texas and the Southwest during the soldier-Indian wars of the post–Civil War period.[1]

Organized at Fort Leavenworth, Kansas, in 1867, the Tenth Cavalry engaged in a number of activities in Kansas and Indian Territory before moving to Texas. With various white infantry regiments, it manned such stations as Forts Hays, Harker, Larned, and Wallace, all in Kansas. Its Troop H in September 1868 helped to rescue men of Major George A. Forsyth's command from the disastrous battle of Beecher's Island on the Arikaree Fork of the Republican River, a place in northeastern Colorado where Cheyenne and Lakota warriors had pinned down the white soldiers for several days. In November the Tenth, now scattered to such places as Forts Arbuckle,

Cobb, and Gibson in Indian Territory and Fort Lyon in Colorado Territory, participated in the Washita campaign. The operation, occurring in western Indian Territory and in eastern portions of the Texas Panhandle, marked another of the army's efforts to strike Indian villages during the winter months when Native Americans were hunkered down, less alert, and at a disadvantage. In the spring of 1869 the army ordered six companies (troops) to Camp Supply and six to Camp Wichita, both in western Indian Territory.[2]

Headquarters for the Tenth Cavalry also shifted. From Fort Leavenworth, it moved to Fort Riley, Kansas, for the winter of 1867–68 and to Fort Gibson, Indian Territory, for the following winter. In the spring of 1869 the army ordered the Tenth's headquarters shifted to Camp Wichita, located near Cache Creek in sight of the Wichita Mountains at modern Lawton, Oklahoma. In August the place became Fort Sill, and it remained the unit's headquarters until March of 1875, at which time the army moved the Tenth to Fort Concho at modern San Angelo in West Texas.

Benjamin H. Grierson, a scar-faced, shaggy-bearded Civil War hero from Illinois, was the African American unit's colonel. A former music teacher who did not particularly like horses, Grierson was white. In fact, until Captain Henry O. Flipper arrived from West Point in 1878, all the commissioned officers of the Tenth Cavalry were white. They included, among others, Captains Henry Alvord, George Armes, Theodore A. Baldwin, Edward Byrne, Louis H. Carpenter, G. W. Graham, William B. Kennedy, Alexander B. Keyes, Thomas C. Lebo, Phillip L. Lee, Thomas Little, Nicholas M. Nolan, George T. Robinson, Charles Viele, and J. W. Welsh.

John W. Davidson in December 1867 joined the Tenth as lieutenant colonel. A West Point graduate who had participated in the Mexican War, Davidson had seen extended service in the West before the Civil War. During the war, he rose in rank from captain in the First Cavalry to brigadier general of volunteers, and in 1864 he became Chief of Cavalry, Military Division of the West. By war's end he was brevet major general, and the army on several occasions had recognized him for gallant and meritorious service. Called an able but erratic officer who was a strict disciplinarian, he remained with the regiment until 1879. In 1877, Davidson was in command at Fort Richardson near modern Jacksboro.[3]

Like Grierson and Davidson, most officers of the Tenth Cavalry were Civil War veterans who after the conflict had sought and obtained a permanent place in the United States Army. Most were Yankees. At first many of them resented their assignment with black troops, and in fact some rank-

Eight cavalrymen of Troop A, Tenth Cavalry. Courtesy University of Texas Institute of Texan Cultures, San Antonio.

ing officers, such as George Armstrong Custer, refused service with black soldiers. Nearly all officers of black troops, however, soon came to respect the high level of competence, the enthusiasm, and the integrity among African American soldiers.

The Tenth Cavalry numbered twelve troops, designated A, B, C, D, E, F, G, H, I, K, L, and M. The army assigned some 90 soldiers to each troop but seldom in the early years did the Tenth enjoy a full complement of men and officers. In 1877, for example, the unit's authorized strength reached 1,202 men, but in uniform it numbered only about 900 soldiers. It possessed a small band, however, one that in 1877 contained 16 members. Colonel Grierson, perhaps because of his music background, had put together the little group, and it soon became a source of pride for the buffalo soldiers.[4]

The entire regiment was rarely together. Instead, it found itself scattered along troop lines among several federal army posts, and, of course, detachments of varying sizes often spent weeks at a time in the field. In the spring and summer of 1877, for example, Troop A was at Fort Concho, Troop G at Fort Griffin, and Troop I at Fort Richardson. Troops B, D, and L were at Fort Clark, and other troops camped at Fort Duncan and in the field along the Rio Grande below the Big Bend region. In other words, nearly all men and officers of the Tenth were in West Texas.

Although they may not have enjoyed it, most men of the Tenth welcomed and appreciated their service in the cavalry. Many were former slaves, illiterate when they entered, but hardworking and dedicated to the army. In the army, they got a rudimentary education—when they wanted it—and received a steady pay envelope, comfortable room and board (much of the time), and relatively good boots and clothes. Usually, there was considerable leisure time and plenty of opportunity for traders, sutlers, and off-post saloons, brothels, or other businesses to separate the troopers from their monthly income. Some men sent money home, of course, and others banked it, but in either case their monthly salary did not go far.

Buffalo soldiers received salaries of thirteen dollars a month. Meager pay it was, indeed, but as William H. Leckie has written, many African Americans "were eager to enlist because the army afforded an opportunity for social and economic betterment difficult to achieve in a society all but closed to them." The salary, as low as it was, may have been better than what most young black men "could expect to earn as civilians, and when food, clothing, and shelter were added, a better life seemed assured."[5] In addition, black society after the Civil War accorded relatively high status to army careers.

Not all the soldiers had been slaves, and not all of them were from the South. Although Memphis, Tennessee, and other cities and towns of the Upper South provided some of the first soldiers, the Tenth soon sent recruiters to Philadelphia, Boston, New York, and Pittsburgh, where Colonel Grierson believed he could "recruit men sufficiently educated to fill the positions of Non-Commissioned Officers, Clerks and Mechanics. . . ." He was right, and recruitment, which was slow at first, picked up in late 1867 and early 1868.[6]

A problem perhaps more difficult to solve was the quality of equipment and horses. Because of their assignment to remote stations, both the Ninth and Tenth Cavalries sometimes received secondhand weapons, camp equipage, and nonperishable supplies. Other times, however, as in the case of the army's adoption of Model 1873 Springfield rifle and carbine, they received new weapons before any of their white counterparts. Horses were always in short supply, and some of their first mounts may have been twelve years old. Later they received discarded horses from white regiments, including castoffs from George A. Custer's famed Seventh Cavalry. Such problems continued until at least the War with Spain in 1898.[7]

The African American soldiers also encountered racism. For the Tenth, problems of racial discrimination began at Fort Leavenworth in the first days of regimental organization, and they continued to plague the unit for years, decades even, afterward. In Texas, perhaps, considering the time (post–Civil War) and place (a former slave state), some racism may have been expected. Much of it was petty meanness that smacked of white resentment toward the successful black soldiers.[8]

In West Texas near Fort Concho in 1877, however, the racism turned uglier. According to Leckie, minor clashes had occurred at some of the saloons and "resorts" of Saint Angela (San Angelo) across the river from the post, but no major problem developed until the fall, when a detachment of Texas Rangers arrived. At one of the saloons, a place called Nasworthy's, writes Leckie, the rangers, resentful of finding the black troopers singing and dancing, "pulled their six-shooters and pistol-whipped the soldiers." Shortly afterward, the troopers, now armed, returned to Nasworthy's, shot up the place, and killed an innocent bystander.[9]

A similar incident occurred a few months later. At another Saint Angela saloon, a place called Morris', some bison hunters with area cowboys hazed a Tenth Cavalry sergeant by mutilating his uniform and, according to Leckie, having "a good laugh over" the man's situation. Not long afterward, the sergeant, having gone back to the post for help and weapons, returned to Morris' with some troopers. A gunfight followed. One trooper and one hunter died in the confrontation, two hunters and one trooper suffered wounds, and the saloon was badly shot up.[10]

In 1879 at Fort Giffin a white officer shot and killed a black infantryman. The officer, Captain S. H. Lincoln, who shot the man "in front of everybody in town," eventually received a "not guilty" verdict from the white jury.[11]

Although not usually ending in gunfights and death, confrontations continued, and as late as 1881, killing occurred. This time a tired Tenth Cavalry trooper, short of money but dancing for drinks at a local saloon near Fort Concho, decided to quit entertaining the bar's patrons and head for the post. One of the drink-buyers, taking offense at the trooper's decision, shot him to death. It was, it seems, a cold-blooded murder, but the incident subsequently resulted in a "not guilty" verdict for the accused, one Tom McCarthy, a white sheepherder in West Texas.[12]

Army posts in West Texas varied in size and comfort. Fort Davis in the upper Big Bend country, Fort Concho at modern San Angelo, Fort Duncan at Eagle Pass, Fort Griffin near modern Albany, and Fort Clark at modern Bracketville were all large, adobe or stone and mason strongholds that could accommodate hundreds of troops. The army listed many others, such as Camp Hudson on the Devil's River or Camp Charlotte west of Fort Concho, as sub-posts or temporary camps. Army fortifications in the West, including

Texas, however, were always in a state of flux. Soldiers occupied the buildings even as they constructed the forts; the army saw most of the forts as temporary, with many of the posts operated for twenty or so years; and the army often abandoned a garrison only to reopen it a few years later.

For the Tenth Cavalry life at a Texas army post was filled with routine assignments. Drilling and training, policing the grounds, hauling water and lumber, and constructing corrals and buildings represented usual and common duties. Occasionally, a detachment of troops might guard a stagecoach, help string or repair a telegraph line, or engage in some other civilian activity, but those were off-post assignments, activities that many soldiers welcomed to break the monotony of post life.[13]

Off-duty, or leisure-time, pursuits ranged across a wide spectrum of activities. In 1877, the men enjoyed holiday diversions, with July 4 and Christmas marking perhaps the favored celebrations. Sporting events, especially baseball, were popular, as were gambling at cards and other games of chance. Many of the men took advantage of the army's efforts to educate its troops and attended reading and writing sessions administered by the post chaplain. Off the post at the little towns that sprang up nearby, the men, as we have seen, found pleasures of all kinds. But mainly, life at a West Texas military post was pretty routine.

Some aspects of post life, however, were far from routine. Food was not always good or fresh. Coffee and other nonalcoholic beverages, except water, were often in short supply. Getting adequate laundry facilities and personnel were constant problems. Housing could be hot in summer and cold in winter, and the beds were too often uncomfortable. The buildings contained no bathrooms, no running water, no central heat, no plumbing. Candles or oil lamps provided the lighting. Some of the posts in West Texas could be hot, dry, and dusty places marked by a drably brown, dull environment that inspired little more than loneliness and a yearning for the green hills and clear streams of Virginia, Pennsylvania, North Carolina, or Massachusetts and home.

Despite the mostly dull routine of army life, the racial prejudice, second-rate equipment, poor mounts, and low pay, black regulars rarely deserted. Although the numbers for 1877 were not good (as we will see), at other times, such as 1880–81, the desertion rate for black troopers was the lowest in the army. For all black commands, infantry or cavalry, low desertion rates were common. By comparison, for example, while the Tenth suffered 18 and the Ninth Cavalry 6 desertions in 1876, the Third, Fifth, Seventh, and Eight Cavalries that year counted, respectively, 170, 224, 172, and 174 such departures.[14]

In the 1870s the United States Army contained three divisions: the Atlantic, Pacific, and Missouri. The latter was responsible for the Great Plains. Each division held several departments, and the departments might be divided into districts and sub-districts. The Department of Texas, reorganized and reestablished in 1870, became part of the Division of the Missouri, which included such other departments as Dakota, Platte, Missouri, and Arkansas. The army located headquarters for the Department of Texas in San Antonio at Fort Sam Houston. In 1877, Brigadier General Edward O. C. Ord commanded the department.

In the post–Civil War years, including the 1870s, federal military operations in Texas were complicated. First, the government in response to a perceived threat from French-backed troops under "the tinsel empire" of Archduke Maximilian, Napoleon III's puppet in Mexico, for more than a year stationed large numbers of troops along the lower Rio Grande. When the empire collapsed and Maximilian with his principal Mexican supporters died before a firing squad in 1867, the threat ended.[15]

At the same time—that is, the end of the Civil War—federal soldiers replaced Confederate and state ranger (or militia) forces. The new troops provided for the safety of the state's citizens, including former slaves, and the Washington government used the troopers to restore the authority of the United States in Texas. The problem was difficult, however, because civil government in the state had disappeared as the war drew to a close and afterward many old Confederates resented the presence of the blue-clad soldiers.

Moreover, when military commanders in Texas, especially Joseph J. Reynolds, tended to side in state politics with the Republicans (mainly Unionists), Democrats (mainly ex-Confederates) refused to support their government. Sometimes chaos and near-anarchy existed, at least in the short term, and, unfortunately, for a decade or more an unstable political climate prevailed.

A third complication related to American Indians, particularly Comanches, Kiowas, Lipan Apaches, and Kickapoos. Indian raiders struck at western farms, ranches, and settlements, threatening lives and property. As the state and Confederate organization for western defense collapsed in 1865, westerners received less and less protection. Some people abandoned the western country, pulling the line of heavy settlement back toward the east—in some places, a good distance. Between 1860 and 1870, for example, the combined populations of Wise and Young Counties declined by over fifty percent. In other places of northwest Texas the population continued to increase, and cattle ranching actually expanded. Still, in much of western Texas at the close of the Civil War, Native Americans had their way.[16]

For these reasons and others, therefore, the federal government in the aftermath of the war moved some forty thousand troops into Texas. It stationed most of the men along the lower Rio Grande to guard the border with Mexico, as we have seen, but others occupied strategic points elsewhere in the state, including such cities as Galveston, Corpus Christi, San Antonio, and Austin. Only a few soldiers guarded the western settlements.

Then, suddenly, with the threat from Mexico ended in 1867 and civil rule (for the most part) restored in Texas, the federal government quickly pulled most of its troops from the state. When Indian raiding again increased in northwest Texas, the army during the winter of 1868–69 conducted a major campaign against Comanches, Kiowas, and Cheyennes in western Indian Territory and in the Texas Panhandle. Successful, the operation cowed Kiowas and Comanches—at least for a time. A year later, in 1870, about forty-eight hundred soldiers remained in Texas, and the army used only a portion of them to establish, or reestablish, a line of military posts in the state along the western edge of settlement.

At the time, the military posts with their troops provided little protection. The federal government under President Ulysses S. Grant in 1869 had established what became known as the Peace Policy. Under it, western soldiers could not pursue Indian warriors onto reservations, and soon Kickapoos and Lipan Apaches raided western settlements from Mexico, and Comanches and Kiowas struck from their reservation in western Indian Territory. The Indian warriors stole horses and cattle, killed sheep, burned buildings and homesteads, and hurried back to Mexico or to the their reservations, places Texas pioneers unfairly saw as sanctuaries where Indian raiders remained free from retaliation. Western settlers complained often and loud, but to little avail—until 1871.

After a gruesome attack in May 1871 on Henry Warren's supply wagons en route from Fort Griffin to Jacksboro, William T. Sherman, General of the Army, reconsidered the army's policy of peace with American Indians. With a small escort, while Kiowa warriors watched, Sherman had passed the Salt Creek Prairie massacre site just hours before the Kiowas struck the wagon train; only a shaman's promise of a "bigger prize" had saved Sherman. The Indian raiders killed or wounded most of the twelve teamsters with the train and stole the mules, and Sherman, realizing now that cattlemen and settlers in western Texas had good reason for their loud complaints, ordered out the troops.[17]

There followed an aggressive series of military strikes on Indian positions in Texas. Colonel Ranald S. Mackenzie, considered by President Ulysses S. Grant as "the most promising young officer in the army," led the way. Mackenzie, who graduated first in his West Point class of 1862, was a tough and aggressive officer who got results. He quickly became a favorite of Texas pioneers who lived along the Rio Grande or in western portions of the state.[18]

With his Fourth Cavalry, Mackenzie in 1871 struck twice at suspected Comanche camps on the Llano Estacado. The second expedition, which ran from September to November, produced mixed results, but the Comanches now understood that soldiers would pursue them even onto the high plains of West Texas, where they had thought they were safe.[19]

Others, including Lieutenant Colonel William R. Shafter of the Twenty-fourth Infantry, led black troops of the Ninth and Tenth Cavalries in pursuit of Apaches in the upper Big Bend region. Additional detachments of the Ninth Cavalry and Twenty-fourth Infantry skirmished with Indian groups near Fort McKavett and on the Llano Estacado.[20]

Through the spring and summer of 1872 the army kept up its new offensive. The Twenty-fourth and Twenty-fifth Infantries and the Fourth and Ninth Cavalries dominated the military activities. Perhaps the major operation was Mackenzie's September expedition (his third in all) to the Llano Estacado. With his Fourth Cavalry supported by Shafter's Twenty-fourth Infantry and a party of Tonkawa scouts, Mackenzie crossed and re-crossed the upper Llano Estacado, attacking Indian camps, capturing Indian ponies, and taking some 130 Indian women and children prisoners. The operations of 1871 and 1872 brought a measure of relief to western farmers and ranchers.[21]

In 1873, as a result, the army turned to the Rio Grande border. That year Mackenzie, supported by Lieutenant John L. Bullis and twenty-four Black-Seminole scouts, led his Fourth Cavalry into Mexico. His troops struck four separate Lipan Apache and Kickapoo villages near Remolina. They captured horses and took women and children prisoners before returning to the United States. For a couple of years afterward border crossings from Mexico declined, and Kickapoo raiding in Texas all but disappeared.[22]

The next year, as bison hunters swarmed over the eastern Texas Panhandle, the Red River War dominated Indian-soldier clashes. In June 1874, Kiowa, Cheyenne, and Comanche warriors, in response to hidemen's entery onto lands that Indian leaders believed to have been reserved for Indian people, struck Adobe Walls, a trading and outfitting camp in the Canadian

Nicholas M. Nolan. Courtesy Lesle Nash Loughridge, Albuquerque, New Mexico.

River valley near modern Borger. The attack, which bison hunters and traders repulsed, precipated Comanche and Kiowa raids on isolated positions along the western edge of settlement. Bison hunters, ranchers, farmers, and townspeople all experienced attacks.[23]

In response, the federal government ordered the Southern Plains Indians to report before August 1 to their reservations in Indian Territory. Many Indian people refused. When the deadline for enrolling at the agency towns had passed, the army sent out its troops. About three thousand men marching in five commands each from a different direction converged on the Texas Panhandle, where most of the Native Americans were hunting and camping. The campaign, which became known as the Red River War, lasted from August to November. Colonel Ranald Mackenzie with his Fourth Cavalry delivered perhaps the crushing blow when he destroyed five Indian villages in Palo Duro Canyon.

Lieutenant Colonel John W. Davidson with nine troops of the Tenth Cavalry also participated. Davidson searched the region between his Fort Sill home base and the main fork of the Red River. He and his black troopers captured nearly four hundred Indian people and more than two thousand animals, and they destroyed scores of lodges and much camp equipment. Not long afterward, most of the Kiowas and Comanches agreed to come to their reservation, and in June 1875, when some of the last Comanche holdouts under Quanah came to Fort Sill, the war was over.[24]

But military operations continued. Buffalo soldiers scoured the Llano Estacado. Six troops of the Tenth Cavalry, plus two companies of the Twenty-fourth Infantry, one of the Twenty-fifth Infantry, and Black-Seminole scouts searched the region. Under the command of Lieutenant Colonel William R. Shafter, an overweight and over-aggressive martinet who in 1898 would lead American troops to Cuba during the War with Spain, they looked for Mescalero and Comanche groups on the high tableland.

From July to November, 1875, Shafter's large command, which numbered nearly 450 men, remained in the field. It captured few Indian people, but it scouted the entire area of the Staked Plains, for a time cleared the region of American Indians, mapped the high tableland, noted important water holes, connected by wagon road some of the permanent points of water, and dispelled some, but clearly not all—as we will see—of the mysteries associated with the Llano Estacado.[25]

The command left Fort Concho on July 14 and headed north to establish a supply camp in Blanco Canyon. On the way north at Rendlebrock Springs in modern Mitchell County, Shafter ordered Captain Nicholas Nolan with two troops of cavalry, including Troop A, to scout west before rejoining him at the supply camp. Nolan's force, about ninety men with very little military training, rode west, and about noon on the second day picked up an Indian trail. For a couple of hours, guides followed the trail to a large camp, but before the troops could get in position to strike, the Apaches fled to the southwest, leaving most of their equipment behind. Nolan's men burned seventy-four lodges and destroyed cooking utensils, bison robes, and a large supply of food. When a heavy rain prevented the buffalo soldiers from giving chase, Nolan gave up pursuit and ordered his men to head for Blanco Canyon. They reached Shafter's supply camp in early August.

Shafter, angry that Nolan had given up pursuit, relieved the captain of his duties and ordered him back to Fort Concho. Afterward, the two men were never again friends, and Nolan planned to use his 1877 command on the Staked Plains to gain redemption for what had happened to him there in 1875.

Troop A, meanwhile, continued with the expedition, and for the next several months it gained valuable experience in Indian pursuit. The men of Troop A, particularly Privates Isaac Thompson and Smith Johnson, also acquired geographical knowledge of the Llano Estacado, its trails, wagon roads, and water holes. The information saved lives in 1877.[26]

In 1876 the army again turned its attention to the Rio Grande border. As Mexican and American outlaws and desperados, Lipan Apaches, and others (including Kickapoos) struck from camps and villages in northern Mexico, raiding increased. The army countered. The most active officer was William R. Shafter who led black units of his Twenty-fourth Infantry and various troops of the Tenth Cavalry plus the Black-Seminole scouts of Lieutenant John L. Bullis. The men chased Apaches in the lower Pecos River country and in the summer of 1876 three times crossed into Mexico, striking a Lipan Apache village near Zaragoza, a Kickapoo camp in the Santa Rosa Mountains, and another Indian camp in the Sierra del Carmen. They destroyed two villages and captured four women and more than a hundred horses and mules.

Understandably, the cross-border operations stirred international tensions. Mexican authorities protested the violations of their border, complaints that taxed already strained relations between the United States and Mexico. In the United States a special committee of the U.S. House of Representatives, led by Edward S. Bragg of Wisconsin, criticized Shafter's raids. In a presidential election year, the border crossings had created a politically sensitive situation.[27]

Although politically sensitive, the problems remained. Texas citizens along the Rio Grande worried about lack of protection, and they got support from Governor Richard Coke, who complained to Washington authorities and to federal army officials in the state. Brigadier General Edward O. C. Ord, commanding the Department of Texas, and Shafter, who was in charge along the Rio Grande, received most of the criticism. Ord, whose position was more visible, needed to stop Indian and desperado raids from Mexico and to stop cattle rustling and horse stealing without angering Mexican authorities.[28]

To solve his dilemma, Ord in late 1876 created the District of the Nueces in the upper Rio Grande border country. He placed Shafter in charge of the new district and ordered large numbers of available troops, both infantry and cavalry, to concentrate at Forts Clark (at modern Bracketville), Duncan (at Eagle Pass), and San Felipe (near Del Rio).

By early 1877, Ord and Shafter had eighteen companies stationed at the three posts. During the year more arrived, and Ord, in addition, concentrated seven companies at Ringgold Barracks and seven more companies at Fort Brown, both along the lower Rio Grande. Of the thirty-three hundred troops in Texas in 1877, by far the great percentage of them camped along the Mexican border.[29]

Despite the large number of troops along the border, Indian and desperado attacks continued. Americans complained, and Secretary of State William Evarts instructed John Watson Foster, the American minister to Mexico, to convince the Mexican government that its soldiers ought to cooperate with the United States army. Porfirio Diaz, the new president of Mexico, thought it a good plan but, he claimed, his government could not spare the troops. Besides, not surprisingly, he wanted the United States to recognize his presidency before any military cooperation occurred. Thus, the spring and summer brought few changes, and raiding was common. The impatient Shafter grew testy, but he kept his troops north of the river—at least for a time.

Still, the border operations in 1877 drained Fort Concho of soldiers. The one Twenty-fifth Infantry company at the post left for the border early in the year. On July 8 Troop F, Tenth Cavalry, left the post, and on July 16 Troops D and L departed for Fort Clark, Shafter's headquarters for the District of the Nueces. With other units converging on the border, Lieutenant Robert G. Smither, referring to the movements there, wrote to an absent Colonel Benjamin Grierson, who had left for West Point, "I do not know what is up." But, after July 16, Concho was left with only fourteen soldiers—all privates; they were members of the Tenth's band. Lieutenant Smither, who in the absence of Grierson and Nolan commanded the post, had at his disposal only the small band, Chaplain George W. Dunbar, a couple of sick troopers, surgeon Joseph H. T. King, a few private citizens, and women and children.[30]

Among the departing units was Troop A, commanded by Captain Nicholas M. Nolan. It went in search of Mescaleros, who had been attacking stagecoaches along the San Antonio–El Paso road, and Comanches, who had been making life miserable for bison hunters and cattlemen in West Texas. A Comanche raiding party from the Llano Estacado stole more than one hundred horses from hidemen and others at Rath City before fleeing back to their camps on the Staked Plains. Having been ordered to search for Indian raiders along the Llano's eastern Caprock, Nolan and his men left on July 10. They headed northwest for the Big Spring, in modern Howard County, and from there followed the Caprock to Bull Creek, one of the head streams of the Colorado River in the Muchaque Peak country of present

Borden County. Here about noon on July 17, 1877, the soldiers rode into the camp of Jim Harvey and his party of twenty-four bison hunters—the Forlorn Hope. The hunters for more than two months had been in pursuit of the same Comanches—the Indian warriors who had stolen their horses from Rath City in May.

The *mise en scène* was set. The Comanches of Red Young Man camped on the High Plains, and those with Quanah were about to arrive. The weary hunters and young buffalo soldiers prepared anew to go once again in pursuit, but this time as they climbed onto the high Yarner their lives took shockingly different directions.

Chapter 5

Onto the High Yarner

Instead "of having . . . the forty rational men who left camp with us," wrote Lieutenant Charles L. Cooper to his father, "our party now consisted of eighteen madmen." Cooper, one of two white officers with Troop A, Tenth Cavalry, was describing the condition of his few remaining black soldiers. The day was July 28, 1877, and Cooper's command was breaking up. The men had no water. Although very hungry, none of them could eat; some could not speak or hear; and many were walking around in "blind staggers." Some of the men were falling behind or deserting. A few were dying.[1]

Little hope for success remained. The officer responsible for guarding the supply camp later testified that one of the deserters had told him: "Sergeant, they are all dead—perished to death for water on the Staked Plains." They did not all perish, of course, but all the survivors experienced terrible physical hardship and incalculable mental anguish.[2]

The disastrous military expedition had started in a routine fashion. In December 1876, a band of perhaps 170 Comanches had slipped away from Fort Sill in Indian Territory and headed for the Llano Estacado, where they joined other Kwahadas under Red Young Man. Through the winter of 1876–77 they struck bison hunting camps along the Caprock and in the Double Mountain country, sometimes hitting sites in the region northeast of Fort Concho. The killing led to the March 18 Yellow House Canyon fight with bison hunters. When other warriors, some of whom were off the reservation with agency passes to hunt or trade, attacked settlers in the Fort Griffin area, federal and state officials took action.[3]

The army moved first. Because it wanted to maintain its larger role in Indian-white relations, it determined to get troops onto the Llano Estacado before the state sent its Texas Rangers after the Comanches. In Texas, however, most of the army's attention in 1877 centered on military activities along the Rio Grande, especially from Eagle Pass up river and through the Big Bend to Presidio. From the region, the army was considering some strikes into Coahuila, raids against Lipan and Kickapoo villages that, of course, would violate Mexican sovereignty.

Nonetheless, when reports of Indian depredations in the Double Mountain country continued to reach military headquarters in San Antonio, Brigadier General Edward O. C. Ord, commanding the Department of Texas, took action. He telegraphed Colonel Benjamin Grierson of the Tenth Cavalry at Fort Concho, instructing him to take appropriate action. Grierson in turn on July 4 ordered Captain Nicolas M. Nolan with his Troop A into the field. The order came on the same day, a Wednesday, that bison hunters were celebrating Independence Day at Casas Amarillas.[4]

Fort Concho in July was as hot and dusty as the Llano Estacado. January had been cold, with sleet and icy wind. The spring weather, as on the Llano, had produced "a riot of color and alluringly sweet" prairies, "but dust storms in April warned of the drouth to come." On July 7 temperatures at noon reached ninety-seven degrees, and they climbed over the century mark in the heat of the afternoon.[5]

Established in December 1867, Fort Concho in 1875 became the headquarters post for the Tenth Cavalry. Located at the junction of the Main and North Concho Rivers at modern San Angelo, the post was part of a line of forts stretching along the western edge of settlement from the Red River to the Rio Grande. Colonel Grierson, who had come to West Texas with the Tenth in 1875, was post commander. The army abandoned Concho in 1889.[6]

In 1877, Fort Concho became one of several Texas centers for the Southern Plains bison hunt. Almost daily, tall-sided Murphy wagons with their seven-foot-high wheels and loaded with "flint" hides passed the post on the way to markets at Fort Griffin or elsewhere. As the slaughter neared its peak, the tiny community of Saint Angela, just across the North Concho River, on the north bank, attracted bison hunters and off-duty soldiers who haunted "the miserable hovels which made up" the village. Former Confederate soldiers among the hunters, some of whom were native Texans, did not always get along with the black troops, but most of the racially inspired difficulties developed in 1878 and afterward. Benficklin, the county seat, stood three miles from the post.[7]

In mid-July 1877, few soldiers remained at Fort Concho. Most of the men from the Twenty-fifth Infantry and several troops of the Tenth Cavalry had left for posts closer to the Rio Grande, especially Forts Clark and Duncan.

Concho Avenue, San Angelo, in 1887. Courtesy West Texas Collection, Angelo State University.

The army still stationed a couple of the Tenth's companies at Forts Richardson and Griffin. A week after Nolan's Troop A departed, Lieutenant Robert G. Smither, acting post commander, counted only fourteen soldiers—all privates—at Concho and worried about Indian depredations at the post; he considered calling Nolan home. Unfortunately, he did not.[8]

Captain Nicholas Merritt Nolan (1835–83), a "bull-headed" Irish immigrant who in 1852 had enlisted in the United States Army at Fort Hamilton, New York, was a Civil War veteran. He had served in the Union cavalry during the war, and afterward the army had transferred him to the Tenth Cavalry, one of its newly created but segregated black units. After the Red River War of 1874–75, he went to Texas and Fort Concho with his Troop A. Always a favorite of Colonel Grierson, Nolan, described as "very fine and soldier-like" with a large "overhanging moustache," experienced personal as well as professional problems. Grierson saved him from a court-martial in 1875 as a result of what others considered his lack of vigorous pursuit of Indian warriors. His wife died suddenly in February 1877—on the eve of Saint Valentine's Day, and "bewildered and forlorn," he "bore his cross . . .

awkwardly." At the time, his daughter Katie attended Ursuline Academy in San Antonio and his seven-year-old son Ned remained in the care of a servant.[9]

Meanwhile, on July 6, Nolan took command of Fort Concho. Colonel Grierson left that day for West Point, New York, and the U.S. military academy, where his twenty-one-year-old son Charles had suffered a "breakdown." Grierson took official leave to get his son and to help the young man recover from his emotional instability. The two returned together to Concho in the fall.

Four days after Grierson had left the post, Captain Nolan began his painful odyssey. With Lieutenant Charles L. Cooper, sixty men of Troop A, and four six-mule wagons to carry supplies for a two-month scout, Nolan on July 10 splashed across the North Concho River and headed up the river valley. His troops represented a mix of experienced soldiers, including some who had been on the Llano Estacado during the 1875 scout, and new recruits. Also along, although neither Nolan nor Cooper mentioned him in their reports, was a young man from Boston—a runaway who had left home for Texas in search of adventure. Nolan carried orders to locate a camp at Big Spring or another suitable spot and scout from there for the missing Comanches.[10]

The command, sixty-three in number, was, with the exception of Nolan, Cooper, and the Boston youth, African American. It headed up the North Concho River toward Big Spring following the Mackenzie Trail, a route named for Colonel Ranald S. Mackenzie, Fourth Cavalry, who had used it in 1872 and 1874. The weather, whose temperatures had been high earlier in the week, continued very hot and dry, and few clouds blocked the burning sun. The command covered about forty-five miles the first two days, but as a result of the oppressive heat one soldier "was sun struck." The man recovered soon enough and the march continued, but two days later Nolan, unable to find a place called White Springs, left the North Concho River and headed north for Big Spring on one of the upper forks of the Colorado River, arriving there late on July 13.[11]

During the march, Nolan and his troops passed Spotted Jack, a part-Anglo, part-Indian, part-Mexican bison hunter and former scout, and three other former hunters, including a Mr. Perkins. The men guarded a herd of longhorns. They were, they claimed, in the employ of a rancher who was moving his cattle beyond the western line of settlement to the edge of the High Plains. Near the head of the North Concho, the men indicated, they had lost some horses to Comanche raiders.[12]

From Big Spring, Nolan, intending "to find a suitable point to establish a supply camp," led his men "north easterly" along the eastern Caprock. During the next few days Nolan and the buffalo soldiers crossed the main fork of the Colorado, searched some of the river's head streams, and looked for a place at which they might set up camp. On July 17, the day Lieutenant Smither considered recalling Nolan's command, they found it.[13]

Nolan and Troop A selected a site on Bull Creek, a northern head stream of the Colorado. Located 140 miles north of Fort Concho and 7 miles northeast of Muchaque Peak in modern Borden County, the spot served as Nolan's supply camp throughout the ordeal that followed. The region around Muchaque Peak was well watered, with plentiful good grass and, even in this dry year, plenty of forage for the horses. Some timber for fuel existed in the form of mesquite, cottonwood, and hackberry trees, plus one could dig roots of the mesquite trees.

Also at the place was a huge, old pecan tree. About two hundred years old, sixty-five feet tall, nearly thirteen feet in circumference with branches that spread over eighty feet from the trunk, the tree provided an abundance of shade to the hunters and soldiers. As pecan trees are not native to the Muchaque country, one must guess that Native Americans had carried nuts back to the place from the Concho River area or from regions farther to the southeast.[14]

The site also stood across Bull Creek from the camp of Jim Harvey's bison hunters. The hidemen had been on the Llano for ten weeks but had stopped at the creek to rest briefly before continuing their search for the Comanches who had attacked Rath City and run off their horses and mules back in early May. Captain Nolan recognized some of the bison hunters. Jim Foley, a former Union soldier, was the hunter who, when the men first saw the troopers in the distance, rode out to confer with Nolan. Indeed, it was probably Foley's invitation that brought the black troopers to their Bull Creek campsite. Nolan also recognized Jim Harvey, a former member of the Fourth Cavalry and a person with whom he had campaigned in 1868. If John R. Cook's memory is correct (and often it is not, at least on details), Nolan gave the bison hunter expedition its nickname when, upon seeing his old comrade, he said, "Well, the saints deliver us! Jim Harvey! And are you with this Forlorn Hope?"[15]

Despite the familiarity, the meeting was a bit tense. Several of the hunters were Southerners who had fought for the Confederacy in the Civil War. Led by Charles "Squirrel-eye" Emory, a native Texan, they viewed Nolan and his African American troops with suspicion. Some of the Yanks did as

Surgeon Joseph Henry Thomas King. Courtesy Susan Miles Papers, West Texas Collection, Angelo State University

well. On their part, Nolan and his experienced troops probably "looked the hunters over with a tinge of the soldiers's contempt for civilian Indian fighters." The hunters, at least in their own minds, must have been recalling and comparing—and surely with some embarrassed discomfort—their own difficult struggle with Comanches in the Yellow House Canyon fight back in March and Captain Phillip L. Lee's easy success in May with black troops against the same Indians.[16]

Nonetheless, after the hunters gathered around him, Nolan explained his orders. Then, the hidemen and Nolan agreed to join forces. The hunters would serve as guides in finding the Comanches, in traversing the high Yarner, and in securing water every twenty-four hours. The soldiers would provide supplies, equipment, and medicine and would undertake any fighting with the Comanches that might be necessary. The hunters wanted their livestock; Nolan wanted to vindicate himself for the troubles associated with his 1875 scout of the Llano and to reestablish his good reputation.[17]

Nolan was particularly satisfied with the agreement, for among the hunters was José Piedad Tafoya, a former comanchero who may have been with Mackenzie in the 1874 Red River campaign. Tafoya understood only a little English and spoke none of it, but among the hunters were several men, including Johnny Cook, who spoke Spanish and could serve as interpreters. Tafoya, who had spent many years on the High Plains, knew the Llano Estacado thoroughly—he "knew every 'waterhole' and possible camping-place." As an experienced and successful Staked Plains trader, he may have known key Comanche words—perhaps he knew the language well—and probably could handle the Plains Indians sign language. Like the bison hunters, Tafoya had lost horses in the Comanche raid on Rath City, and he was anxious to retrieve his mounts.[18]

During the meeting, Nolan indicated that Phillip Lee had received orders similar to his own. Captain Lee, marching west out of Fort Griffin with Troop G, Tenth Cavalry, was to scour the Brazos River, including its Clear, Fresh Water, and Double Mountain Forks. Lee, perhaps Nolan reasoned, might find the Kwahadas first, and by doing so, wreck his own chances for redemption. Such may not have been the case. But, although Jim Harvey explained to him that the hunters believed the Comanches were in what the hunters called the Blue Sand Hills about fifty miles west of Double Lakes, Nolan reported that Tafoya said the Indian warriors were at Cedar Lake (Laguna Sabinas), near the site of Nolan's 1875 troubles. A few days later, granted, Tafoya would in fact point to the large lake as place where a small party of Comanches might be camping, but at the initial meeting Tafoya and all the bison hunters insisted—correctly as it turned out—that the Comanches were in the sand hills. From this first meeting to the end of the ordeal the information and messages the two groups left for historians to sort through were divergent.[19]

Johnny Cook, a six-foot two-inch tall, rail-thin bison hunter, and Nicholas Nolan, a cautious, twenty-four-year veteran trying to secure his reputation, remembered the "lost expedition" differently. Cook, writing nearly thirty years later, was more detailed but less precise and occasionally confusing. Nolan, writing shortly after his return to Fort Concho, was more accurate and more circumspect but more defensive. He left out a lot—unfortunately. Some of Nolan's version is supported by Lieutenant Cooper's letter to his father, Cook's view by testimony at the courts-martial afterward.[20]

The next day Captain Nolan and his troops rested a bit and began preparations for a scout of twenty days. Planning to use mules for pack animals, they unhitched the lead animals from each of the four wagons. Nolan then left orders to send the empty wagons, each now with a four-mule hitch, back to Fort Concho with instructions to the teamsters to get additional rations. His men set about establishing a permanent base camp and getting their equipment and supplies together for the long scout. He designated Private Steven Floyd as the scout's farrier (although Private James Jackson was also a blacksmith) and named Privates Isaac Thompson and John A. Gaddie its chief packers.[21]

The bison hunters made similar preparations. Harvey, the veteran with the strong military bearing, was in command. Dick Wilkinson became the chief packer; Solomon "Sol" Rees, who had attended the 1876 Philadelphia Centennial Celebration, took charge of medical supplies; Cook and Louis Keyes, the latter a mixed-blood Cherokee, served as interpreters for and assistants to José Tafoya, the honest, loyal, and gallant company guide. Seasoned and confident plainsmen, the hunters carried an abundance of ammunition and packed plenty of supplies. Also, each of them carried a half-gallon canteen of water or a six-pound powder can filled with water, covered with blanketing, and attached to a strap that could be placed over the shoulder. A few carried both.

On July 19, preparations complete, the combined force left the Bull Creek supply camp. It consisted of Captain Nolan, Lieutenant Cooper, the runaway boy from Boston, forty enlisted men of Troop A, and twenty-two bison hunters under Jim Harvey's separate direction. Nolan left Sergeant Thomas Allsup with nineteen men to guard the supply camp and get the wagons to Fort Concho for additional supplies. Two hunters, Hiram "Hi" Bickerdyke and Billy Devins—who was still recovering from a wound to his arm received during the March 18 Yellow House Canyon fight—stayed in camp to look after the equipment and wagons of the hidemen.[22]

The command, not having left Bull Creek until 5:00 P.M., made only fifteen miles before going into camp along Tobacco Creek, a head stream of the Colorado River. Such a westward course might suggest that the command was headed for Cedar Lake rather than Double Lakes and the sand hills, but not necessarily, for water holes needed to govern the route. Still, it made a dry camp here and early the next morning followed the creek before turning up Sulphur Draw (Tobacco Creek, Nolan called it) to make a difficult climb up the Caprock and onto the high tableland—the Yarner. The men followed the draw in a northwesterly direction, now apparently headed for the Double Lakes area where, according to John R. Cook, a June "waterspout or cloud-burst" had dumped an enormous amount of water "in an amazing short time" and filled the playas to overflowing. After leaving Sulphur Draw, the command on July 21 reached what remained of the largest of the June playas.[23]

Cook remembered that the wet-weather lake was much bigger in early July. Evaporation and absorption, he noted, "had caused the waters to recede," and now, on the twenty-first, it still covered "about five acres of ground." Its depth, Lieutenant Cooper's measurement showed, reached thirty-three inches. The command, which arrived there in the morning, remained until evening.[24]

Here also, the men "witnessed a remarkable sight." As described by Cook, during the mid-afternoon one could see "horses, mules, buffaloes, antelopes, coyotes, wolves, a sand-hill crane, negro soldiers, white men, our part-Cherokee Indian and the Mexican guide, all drinking and bathing" in the lake "at one and the same time." Lieutenant Cooper, who first called Cook's attention to the rare event, suggested "that outside of a tented circus, it" represented one of the greatest "aggregations of the animal kingdom ever witnessed" in so small a place.[25]

Cook also wondered about water quality. He noted that the shallow little lake was exposed to a ceaseless sun in "far above 100 degrees Fahrenheit, [with] an occasional herd of buffalo standing and wallowing in it." As he pointed out as well, pronghorns, "wolves, snipes, curlews, cranes, [and] the wild mustang" all visited the lake. "And yet," he said, "we mixed bread, made coffee, and filled our canteens from it." Seven days later, he concluded, the men "would have sold their birthright for" a chance to drink "in this same decoction."[26]

About four o'clock, Nolan reported, Quanah, a Kwahada leader, and two old Comanche couples rode into camp. Riding in from the north, Quanah held a pass, contained in a large official envelope and signed by both the Indian agent at Fort Sill, J. M. Haworth, and the post commander, Colonel Ranald S. Mackenzie of the Fourth Cavalry. The pass, significantly dated July 12 (only two days after Nolan had left Fort Concho), allowed Quanah and his companions a forty-day leave from the reservation and authorized them to seek out, find, and bring back the large band that had been dodging the bison hunters all summer. It also warned against molesting them. Quanah's group rode army-issued horses and carried, in Nolan's words, a liberal supply of government equipment, arms, ammunition, and rations.[27]

Nolan accepted the pass as genuine, which indeed it was, but he was angry. He swore and let loose a long series of invectives against Mackenzie, Haworth, Quanah, Native Americans in general, and others who had displeased him recently. Nolan reasoned, correctly it seems, that Mackenzie had encouraged Quanah's efforts so that the Comanches would surrender to him (Mackenzie) at Fort Sill rather than to Nolan, Lee, or anyone else. Mackenzie wanted credit for bringing peace, credit that Nolan hoped would be his for striking the Comanches in their camps. Military rivalry was an old shibboleth.[28]

When they left, Quanah and his Comanches rode south. They were heading to such places as Cedar Lake, Sulphur Springs, and Mustang Springs, watering holes that were all favorite Indian camping sites. Quanah, in fact, may have been born on the southern edge of Cedar Lake, and he knew the region well. The bison hunters thought he went south not so much to find his Comanche band as to lead the soldiers away from them, since Quanah knew they were in the sand hills.

At 7:30 P.M., after an eventful day, Nolan started his command for Cedar Lake, a place that he estimated was fifty miles away. It was not. The command arrived, Nolan reported, at 8:00 in the morning, July 22, and went into camp on the same ground on the north side that Nolan and some of the black troops with him on this expedition had visited in 1875 with Lieutenant Colonel William R. Shafter, Twenty-fourth Infantry. Two years earlier, Cedar Lake, four miles wide and six miles long, had been full, the ground muddy, and good, fresh water readily available. Now, in 1877, Nolan "found great difficulty in obtaining water for the command." His men dug holes and dipped out the water with small cups. They poured it into kettles and cooking utensils to provide drinking water for both men and animals. The job was slow and tedious; it filled the long, hot day.[29]

Early on the twenty-third José Tafoya, Jim Harvey, and Johnny Cook left to scout the region south and west of Cedar Lake. They searched for Comanches at Five Wells, twenty-five miles south of Cedar Lake, and rode west from there to Seminole Draw and Ward's Well before returning. They found little water at Five Wells and afterward went thirty hours without water, but about twenty miles west of Cedar Lake, they discovered an Indian trail headed northeast toward Double Lakes. They headed back to Cedar Lake with the news.[30]

Meanwhile, about 11:00 A.M., also on the twenty-third, Quanah and his companions came a second time to Nolan's camp—this one, of course, at Cedar Lake. They rested, watered their horses, visited with the officers and

Fort Concho in the 1870s. Courtesy West Texas Collection, Angelo State University.

bison hunters, and hung around for six hours before departing in a westerly direction. Quanah, the record suggests, wanted to lay a trail that would lead the buffalo soldiers away from the Comanches in the Blue Sand Hills.

Quanah, perhaps, had more sinister plans. He knew José Tafoya from the comenchero trade and had exchanged goods with the former New Mexican businessman in Quitaque Canyon, a deep gulf cut from one of the head streams of the Pease River and located along the Llano Estacado's eastern edge in modern Floyd County. Tafoya had used the canyon for trading from a time before 1868. But Quanah also believed that Tafoya back in 1874 during the Red River War had betrayed the Comanches, Kiowas, and Cheyennes by telling—under threat of death, granted—Colonel Ranald Mackenzie of the Fourth Cavalry that the Kwahadas and others were camping in Palo Duro Canyon. Quanah, according to Charles Goodnight, who knew both the Comanche leader and the former comenchero, swore that "if he ever met [Tafoya] again, "he would broil the old Mexican alive. . . ." If Goodnight is correct, maybe Quanah spent six hours in Nolan's camp waiting for Tafoya's return or gathering information useful in hunting down Mackenzie's reluctant former guide.[31]

The next morning—the day after Quanah left—Tafoya, Harvey, and Cook returned with their report. The trail they had discovered may have been that of Quanah, who, having learned from Nolan that Tafoya and the others were out to the southwest, headed in that direction. There is no way of knowing whether Quanah was searching for his betrayer or laying a trail that the scouts would find and follow. He and his companions rode west and then back northeast.

Tafoya and the others had picked up a fresh "trail of a few Indians." It pointed, they told Nolan, northeasterly toward Double Lakes. In response to the report, Nolan, late in the afternoon, started his command back to the north, to Double Lakes.

About noon on July 25 Nolan's group reached Double Lakes. The men threw up their tents on the same ground where Nolan in 1875 had camped with Shafter. The results were much the same as at Cedar Lake: where plenty of water had existed two years before, this time the men had to dig for water and carefully dole it out for themselves and their animals. There was no indication that Quanah had been there, and they discovered no fresh signs of Indian people at the place. Nolan was becoming anxious and impatient.

Tafoya, George Cornett (one of the better trackers), and a few other hunters rode west seventeen miles to Rich Lake (Laguna Rica, sometimes called Salt Lake, or Dry Lake, as Nolan called it) to search for fresh Indian trails. Located in modern Terry County, northeast of Brownfield, Rich Lake was almost directly west of Double Lakes. The hunters who joined the search were, like Nolan, becoming impatient. And, because they knew the Comanches were in the sand hills, they wanted (at least, some of them wanted) to break from Nolan and on their own strike for the illusive Indian camp. The growing impatience explains, perhaps, why a larger number of hunters went on this scout to search for fresh trails than on previous ones.

By this time, too, other problems had arisen. Because William L. Umbles had displeased him, Nolan demoted Umbles from first sergeant. Umbles was an experienced soldier who had served five years in the Twenty-fifth Infantry before joining the Tenth in the summer of 1876. Resenting the demotion, the sergeant remained angry, and, when the difficulties over the lack of water developed, he rebelled. His resentment may have played a role in his actions during the coming days.

Spotted Jack and his companions, who had showed up at Cedar Lake and followed the command to Double Lakes, now pulled out. In a droughty year such as this one, they refused to go deeper onto the Yarner. Pointing out that most of the bison and pronghorns had quit the country, they argued that "if the rest [of the hunters] had good sense they wouldn't [go with Nolan] either."[32]

Spotted Jack and his men retreated to the supply camp on Bull Creek. There they split up. While Mr. Perkins stayed behind at the supply station to serve as a guide for Sergeant Thomas Allsup and the federal troops, Spotted Jack and the others rode north. They followed the Caprock to a bison hunter camp near the mouth of Yellow House Canyon. A day or so afterward they stopped for a bit with the Mooar brothers, bison hunters who were in the vicinity. Then, they overtook Captain Philip Lee's command—Troop G, Tenth Cavalry, on the High Plains looking for Nolan and the Comanches—from Fort Griffin, and pointed it in the direction of Double Lakes.

Meanwhile, at Double Lakes other developments occurred. About 11:00 A.M. on July 26, Cornett and another hunter raced into Nolan's camp with news that Comanches had been sighted. A large band of warriors, perhaps forty, they said, had passed within three miles of Rich Lake at 8:30. No water existed at the lake, they reported, but the Kwahadas were moving at such a leisurely pace that the Comanches could not have suspected the presence of soldiers in the vicinity. The Indian band rode northwest, hunting game as they went.

As soon as Cornett reported his news, the bugler, "fight-brittle" Private Alexander "Alex" Nolan, twenty-two years old and a December 1876 recruit who was also a member of the regimental band, sounded "Boots and Saddles." Immediately the camp became alive with preparations. The men struck their tents and stowed equipment and supplies in the packs. Gaddie and Thompson for the soldiers and Wilkinson for the hunters supervised the packing of mules. The hunters filled their canteens and watercans, but some of the soldiers, busy with army details, forgot, or had no chance.

Three to four hours later the command started. Nolan blamed the long delay on George Cornett and his fellow scout. Needing to rest their mounts and themselves, refill their water containers—a slow process, remember, that was done by one cupful at a time—and get something to eat, they were tardy by two hours. Nolan chose not to leave without them.

For whatever reason, Nolan did not see to filling his men's canteens, and, although the temperature was above one hundred degrees, some of the buffalo soldiers left with half-filled or perhaps even empty water containers. It was between two and three in the afternoon. The thirsting time had begun.

Chapter 6

The Thirsting Time

In our "troubled" sleep, remembered Mortimer "Wild Bill" Kress, a tall, usually jovial bison hunter, "thirst ever haunted us." On that July 28 evening "it was *thirst,* water, thirst and water, until it was all gone, and still we were all in a horrible condition." Earlier, Sergeant William L. Umbles, Troop A, Tenth Cavalry, upon learning that no water existed at the main soldier camp, had said, "My God, we'll die before morning." Kress, Umbles, and the other buffalo soldiers and bison hunters in the oppressive desert-like heat of the Llano Estacado had been without water for more than two days. They were desperately thirsty.[1]

The thirsting time began a little before 3:00 P.M. on July 26. For many soldiers it did not end until after 5:00 A.M. on July 30—eighty-six hours later. Most bison hunters got to water late on the evening of July 28, but one of them, white-haired Bill Benson, went four full days without water, not reaching the precious resource before mid-afternoon on the thirtieth of July.

DAY ONE—JULY 26—MID-AFTERNOON

The thirsting time started when Captain Nicholas M. Nolan led his Tenth Cavalry buffalo soldiers and the bison hunters under Jim Harvey westward out of Double Lakes in modern Lynn County. Moving out as a result of George Cornett's report that the trail of a party of perhaps forty Comanches had been found, the men headed toward Rich Lake, arriving there about sundown. They found José Tafoya, the chief guide, and several other bison hunters, who now stated that there were only eight Comanches, not the forty that Cornett earlier in the day at Double Lakes had reported.

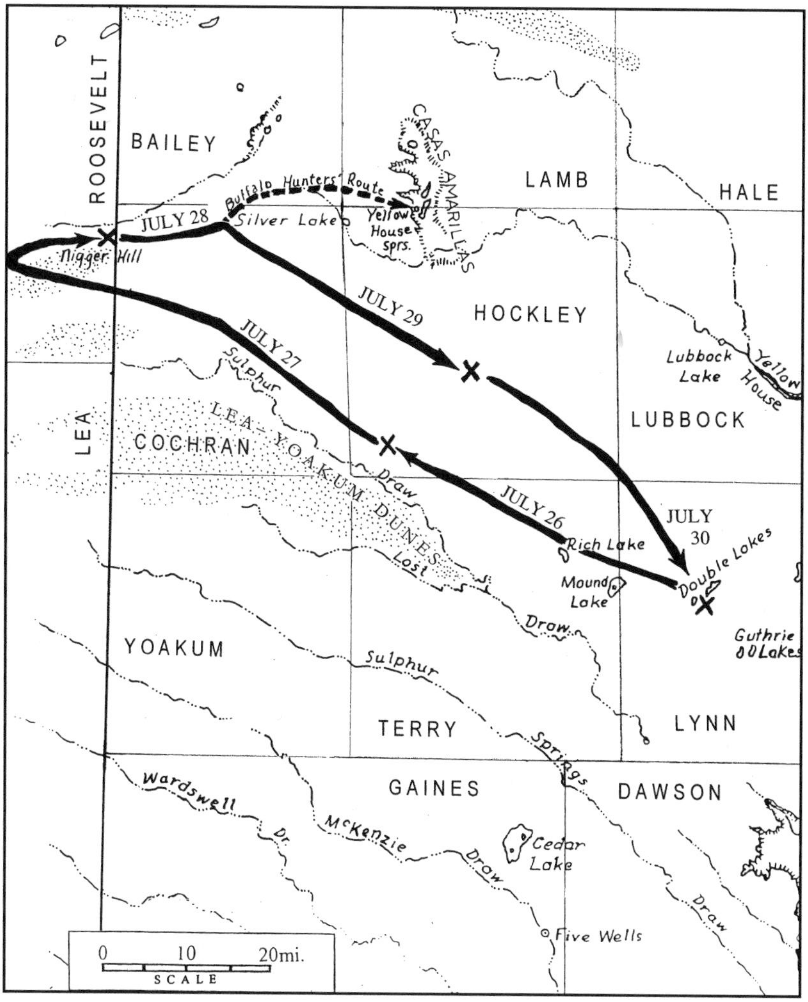

Map 5. Shown here is the route taken by the lost troop expedition from Double Lakes to New Mexico and back again. Courtesy Michael Harter.

Nolan and his command also discovered that no water existed at the lake. Thus, after a seventeen-mile march in the afternoon heat of July 26, fresh water, as Cornett had correctly reported, was not available for either men or animals; the lake was dry, crested over with salt. Moreover, some of the inexperienced soldiers—"recruits" they were called—had already emptied their canteens.

For unexplained reasons, water management was careless. "The soldiers," remembered John Cook, "were out of water, and our boys dividing with them." Tafoya, Nolan wrote, said that water was available about fifteen or twenty miles to the northwest. Hoping to find both the water and the Indian trail, Nolan set off in that direction, but darkness settled over the plains before he located either. Since it was too dark to trail, he called a halt and his command made a dry camp—probably in the southwestern corner of modern Hockley County.[2]

DAY TWO—JULY 27—DAYLIGHT

At daylight, Nolan's command saddled up. It left camp in a northwesterly direction. To its left was Sulphur Draw, shallow here but easily discernible, and beyond the draw stretched the Lea-Yoakum Sand Dunes in their northwest-southeast alignment. Of the command, W. Curtis Nunn wrote, its course "lay over a gently undulating country, the soil dry, mostly of a reddish color, covered with bunches of short grass, here and there a stunted mesquite bush, ten or fifteen inches high." Scrub oak could also be found. As the command moved northwest, the land grew progressively sandy, the travel more difficult.[3]

Over patches of grass in the increasingly sandy country, the men dragged blankets, hoping, as William H. Leckie writes, to obtain from the morning dew "a bit of moisture for their parched throats." It didn't work, and the suffering increased.[4]

By nine that morning the Comanches had discovered the soldiers. Planning to weaken their pursuers, the Kwahadas turned west. The morning became "furiously hot," and temperatures continued to climb. At noon the trail turned northwest and in the afternoon west again. The Kwahadas, in their zigzag course, stayed away from waterholes, remained on the north side of Sulphur Draw and the sand hills, and crossed through the very heart of modern Cochran County. Johnny Cook reasoned that the Indians "were giving us a dry trail; they would finish us with thirst." To prevent that, Nolan had thrown men out on the flanks to seek water, and with the guide they checked "every valley and depression in view."[5]

Betweeen 2:00 and 3:00 P.M. the command halted. It had covered twenty-five miles of twisting trails, and, wrote Nolan, Tafoya's horse as well as those of the "citizens were giving out." He said nothing about the condition of the army horses, most of which were old, grain-fed animals that now had difficulty maintaining their strength on grass only. Besides, as the Comanches had scattered in several directions, there was no single trail to follow, and the men needed a rest.

While the men rested, Tafoya, Cook, Sol Rees ("one of the hottest Indian trailers" in the command, according to Cook), and a few others, including some of the troopers, searched for the main route or the point at which the various tracks came together. When, "after some time," they found it, Nolan started the hot, thirsty, and trail-warn company on its way again. The course pointed west, and the troops headed in that direction for fifteen miles, a route that took them into heavy sands in modern Roosevelt County, New Mexico.

Everyone suffered desperately from lack of water. The horses, too, needed moisture as much as the men. Joseph H. T. King, the post surgeon, reported that "matters were assuming a grave aspect; many were faint and exhausted." One of the troopers, Private Isaac Derwin, who later died during the march, fell from his horse, the result of sunstroke, and Johnny Cook, out ahead of the command with Tafoya, remembered that he and the guide both ached with "physical torture." His "system rejected tobacco," Cook wrote, "the saliva in my throat and mouth had dried up; my jaws would not stay closed."[6]

Nolan sent a trooper out to Cook and Tafoya, asking them to wait. Then, upon reaching the two men with his main force, Nolan halted the command briefly to consult with the guide. If Cook is correct, the meeting was dramatic—perhaps melodramatic. Tafoya, at least according to Cook, indicated that water could be found at Lost Lake (near modern Dora, New Mexico) about six or seven miles to the north, but, believing that the Kwahadas were there, he suggested that the men might have to drive the Comanches from it. The bison hunters were game for a fight; they could see the outlines of the Blue Sand Hills in the distance to the west, and they believed that water was there also.

The buffalo soldiers were not in condition to fight, and Nolan, with at least twenty-five prostrate men, knew it. He preferred to find water elsewhere. He asked Tafoya if he could find water at Silver Lake back to the northeast. If he could find it, how long to get there and back? Tafoya thought he could do it by midnight—way too hopeful, as it turned out. Jim Harvey, the captain of the hunters, countered by suggesting that ten still-strong hunters get water at Silver Lake if Nolan would trust the guide and with both hunters and troopers go for the water in the Blue Sand Hills to the west, only seven miles away.[7]

Nolan refused. Then—again if Cook is correct—the stubborn Troop A captain in an angry but defensive outburst harangued the hunters, especially Cook, Tafoya, and Harvey. Nolan pointed to his many sick men, wrote

Cook, and then Nolan yelled at Jim Harvey: "Look at your own men, suffering the tortures of the d—d. . . . [Soon] we will each be dethroned of his reason, and be a wandering lot of maniacs." Tears coursed down Nolan's cheeks, Cook remembered, and Captain Nolan "captured our sympathy." We "consented to his plan" to head northeast to Silver Lake, "thereby doing him and ourselves an injustice, and adding more horrors to our Forlorn Hope."[8]

Nolan's version is a bit different. His report agreed that water could be had six or seven miles ahead. But it also indicated that Nolan gave one of his fresh—and private—horses to Tafoya that he might move ahead rapidly to find the water; the command would follow at the rate the exhausted horses would allow. Nolan did not mention his angry outburst, if there was one, or the tears. And Tafoya—he headed west about two miles, Nolan wrote, "when [he] suddenly changed his course to a North Easterly direction." With Tafoya on a fresh mount and sick troopers and hunters delaying the force, the others could not keep up. Nolan followed the guide west and then back northeast, he reported, "as fast as I could, but being continually detained by sick [troopers] was unable to keep up with him, without abandoning the sick men."[9]

Lieutenant Charles L. Cooper thought the expedition was lost. He remembered the shifting directions of the march and in a letter to his father afterward wrote about it. Tafoya, he indicated in the August 30 missive, "as well as all of us, was lost on the Staked Plains, without water and no prospects of getting any, as we did not know which way to go for it."[10]

Still, the command plodded forward, the bison hunters in the lead. It marched east-northeast, following the guide. But under a "broiling sun" and over the "barren sandy plain," its members sickened, fell behind, and fell out. "A great portion of the command being recruits," Nolan reported, the men "commenced to give out, continually falling from their horses." Cooper remembered that he himself during the late afternoon "came near to giving up with sunstroke." The command began to stretch back on the trail.

Each time a man went down, Nolan designated a stronger man to stay with him until such time as the sick trooper could be brought up. When Private Rose fainted with sunstroke, for example, the farrier Steven Floyd stayed with him. When Private Stephen Baldwin fell out, Sergeant William L. Umbles stopped, with instructions to bring the sick man up as soon as he was able to travel. Umbles ordered Private John A. Gaddie, one of the chief packers, to stay back as well.

The west lake of Double Lakes. Courtesy Bryan Edwards.

Nolan's plan sounds easy enough, but it did not work. Members of the expedition suffered desperately, and as evening approached on July 27, the men—all sixty-four of them—scattered back on the trail for two or more miles. Lieutenant Cooper at times was with Cook a mile ahead of the center, and at times he was behind the core of the column. The men on weaker horses fell far behind the main body. Thus, men could and did fall out without Nolan's being aware of their plight; unless they had a riding companion, they were on their own. When he was "taken sick with a cramp," for example, Private Isaac Thompson, the other chief packer, dismounted, tied his horse to a bush, lay down under a scrub tree, and waited for the sick men and their assistants, including William Umbles, behind him to catch up. The men not only caught up, said Thompson, but also passed him by, and then his horse ran off ahead toward them. Umbles and the others caught the tired mount and held it for Thompson. Private (Lance Corporal) George W. Fremont, who was the librarian at Fort Concho, and Corporal William Barney, although not sick, had also fallen to the extreme rear.[11]

The bison hunters endured similar pains. Sam Carr, the fleshy and overweight but brilliant horse trainer, dropped from his big powerful animal and fell behind sick. Alt Waite, lean as a greyhound, stayed with him. As the sun was sinking, Johnny Cook rode back down the trail to help get Carr moving again. After some difficulty in getting the heavy Carr onto his horse, all three men headed back. Because Carr again dropped off his horse, saying he could go no farther, Cook and Waite a second time coaxed, fanned, and finally lifted the big stout man onto his horse. The three of them, along with some of the ailing soldiers, were among the last of the men to reach the command.

After nine miles on the march, Nolan called a halt. It was nearly dark, and the exhausted men—both hunters and troopers—had covered some forty-nine miles in temperatures over one hundred degrees without water. Now realizing that he was not going to keep up with Tafoya, Nolan decided on another plan—one Jim Harvey had suggested earlier. He assigned Private Smith Johnson, a veteran who had been on the Llano Estacado with Nolan and Lieutenant Colonel William R. Shafter in 1875, to lead the water detail. With seven others, mostly recruits, Johnson was to take nearly all the remaining canteens plus the hunters' water cans and to follow José Tafoya to Silver Lake and return with water. The men included Privates John Peterson, Henry C. Miller, Blacksmith Carson, Jerry R. Freeman, Pierce Kuston, and two others. The Boston boy, who was accompanying the expedition for the thrill and excitement of the chase, went with them. The men disappeared into the night, and Nolan did not see them again until August 6, when he arrived at the supply camp. He never again saw Tafoya or his horse.[12]

Nolan rode six more miles in the dark and stopped. He and his men, he reported, had marched during the day "about fifty five miles under a broiling sun over a barren sandy plain without a drop of water." Here, "owing to the exhausted condition of the men," Nolan determined to wait for the return of the guide and the men he had detailed to help bring the water. He expected Tafoya to rejoin the command shortly, but in part because the next day Nolan would change directions again, no connection occurred.[13]

Nolan's command was now at the unfortunately titled Nigger Hill. Named for the buffalo soldiers by their weary white hunting companions, the low mound, which rises just a few yards above the surrounding land, is about a mile in diameter and located in Roosevelt County, New Mexico. It is a mile west of the Texas state line. Elvis Fleming writes that it provided "a sharp contrast to the level" land around it. The troopers made a dry camp. They lit no fires. Because there was no water, there was no coffee or cooking. No one could eat anyway, for their mouths and throats were too dry. They fell exhausted and, wrote Cooper, "endeavored to forget in sleep the sufferings we all endured."[14]

The bison hunters stopped about twenty-five to fifty yards ahead (northeast) in the direction of Silver Lake. They sat or lay down in little groups, one of which may have built a fire. They talked in low tones, bemoaned their situation, and, particularly the "Johnny Rebs," cursed Nolan and his black troops. Some must have thought of Spotted Jack, who had refused to join them on the high Yarner in a drought year such as this one, and wished they had listened to him. Others sought sleep, and in fact some were snoring.

The late evening was starlit and clear with no wind. Voices traveled easily through the crisp night air. The moon rose very late, and after midnight, breezes picked up. As they usually do on the Llano Estacado after the sun sets, temperatures dropped sharply, and the cooler nighttime weather served to revive both men and animals. When several of Nolan's pack mules, perhaps smelling water, wandered off, some of the hunters noticed, and one of them, Cook, yelled over to the troopers, but no one went in pursuit of the deserting animals.

Some troopers also abandoned the command. They deserted, Nolan said, but the circumstances are muddled, the reports conflicting. Johnny Cook, writing thirty years later, suggested and testimony at the courts-martial corroborated that once the command had halted for the night of July 27, "Captain Nolan was lying upon the ground, and said that he was too much exhausted to proceed . . . until he could get some sleep." Nolan waved an arm to dismiss the men, and some believed that his action meant, in Cook's words, that "it was every fellow for himself." Nolan, at the court-martial of William L. Umbles, denied that he did or said any such things, but other testimony disagreed—although the dates differed. The testimony of Lieutenant Robert G. Smither, the white officer who had remained in charge at Fort Concho during the thirsting time, indicated that Nolan made the statement and gestures the following day, the twenty-eighth. Smither was quoting Private Stephen Baldwin, one of the first men to get sick from too much heat and sun. Private Steven Floyd, quoting a soldier of similar rank, testified that Lieutenant Cooper had said "to go and find water."[15]

Whatever the case, in the cool, crisp air of the evening Sergeant Umbles along with the sick and straggling men made their way toward the bivouac site on Nigger Hill. Captain Nolan and a few of the troopers could hear the sick men talking and shouted for them to come in. Nolan ordered shots fired to signal the location of the camp, and then he instructed Private Alex Nolan, the bugler from Missouri, to mount his big gray horse and ride out to help the men find their way to camp. But four of the men, including the bugler, did not return.

Nigger Hill. Courtesy Bryan Edwards.

Instead, Isaac Thompson later testified, "by order of Sergeant Umbles," we had "all mounted our horses . . . and started on to retake the command." Umbles, Thompson reported, said "to follow him . . . he knew where [the camp] was though [in the dark] we could not see the trail." Because of the weak conditions of the horses, only Thompson and Floyd could keep up, thus leaving Privates Barney, Gaddie, Rose, and Baldwin, Corporal Gilmore, and Lance Corporal Fremont to follow Louis Keyes, the mixed-blood Anglo-Cherokee-Hispanic bison hunter (a "Mexican guide" the soldiers called him), back to the command. They met Corporal Elias Roberts and five other soldiers plus three bison Hunters—Cook, Carr, and Waite—and together rejoined the soldiers and hunters.

The three others—Umbles, Thompson, and Floyd—went in another direction. They heard shots from the command, and when they "got opposite" the campsite, Private Alex Nolan appeared. Upon inquiry from Sergeant Umbles, Nolan described his view of the situation in camp, which was about two hundred yards away. He indicated that no water was available there but that some of the pack mules had been down in a draw and had returned with mud on their legs. He further indicated that Captain Nicholas Nolan had given the men a free hand to find water. In response, Umbles considered leading his men to water rather than to the camp, and, when Private Nolan "got bewildered and lost [his] right mind and could not find [his] way back" to the command, Umbles determined to strike for water. He convinced (or ordered) the others—Thompson, Floyd, and Nolan—to go with him.[16]

Not two hundred yards farther, the four black troopers ran into Dick Wilkinson. The hunter was on foot chasing his horse and some of his pack mules. He joined the black regulars, and with Wilkinson as the guide the little group of five headed off in the direction of Silver Lake. In the dark, they traveled about six miles before stopping.

DAY THREE—JULY 28—AFTER MIDNIGHT

In the meantime, shortly after midnight more shooting occurred. At the main camp everyone awoke from the sounds. Some men thought the Comanches had attacked. Most, however, thought the shots—and there were a lot of them—came from José Tafoya, Smith Johnson, and the returning water detail. In response, many in the command fired their weapons into the air to signal the guide, for, as Cook wrote, it "was now the darkest part of the night. Objects could not be distinguished at 100 feet." Because a thin film of clouds had rolled in, the "sky was somewhat overcast." The hunters noticed that Dick Wilkinson was missing, but it was too dark to do anything but wait for Tafoya and daylight. As Tafoya did not return that night, the shots may well have come from Comanches, who were camped in fingers of sand dunes (the Lea-Yoakum Dunes) a few miles to the south.[17]

At daybreak on July 28, conditions did not improve. Although somewhat better after a night of rest in the cool air of the Llano Estacado, the hunters and soldiers were still without water and they still could not eat. Their horses were also exhausted and thirsty; the mules—those which had not walked away—were not much better off. Because his chief packers, John A. Gaddie who was ill and in the rear and Isaac Thompson who was with Umbles, were not available, Captain Nolan packed the mules himself.

The combined command started eastward once more for Silver Lake. Then, after traveling about fifteen miles toward the lake, Captain Nolan set a new course. Although a foolhardy decision, he seemed to have no other choice. Tafoya was lost, or so Nolan reasoned, and the bison hunters, he mistakenly believed, could not find the way to either Silver Lake or Casas Amarillas.

Nolan, therefore, instructed Lieutenant Cooper "to set his compass for the Double Lakes." The decision, he later reported, "was based upon the fact that I was now between my trail of the previous day, which lay to the west, and that of Colonel [William R.] Shafter of 1875, which was to the east." Consequently, he concluded, he "could not possibly miss the Lakes." Doubles Lakes was at least fifty-five miles away and toward the southeast, but it was a place he could find—if, in fact, he could reach it before succumbing from lack of water.[18]

Johnny Cook, if we can trust his memory, was one of several bison hunters who tried to change Nolan's mind. The men, including Jim Harvey and Bill Benson, indicated that if the command "kept on the northeast course [it] would . . . get water that day." Nolan, who was lying on the ground, shrugged them off. "Yes, captain," Cook replied, "follow us now and we will lead you to water."

Nolan, according to Cook, responded: "If you men are thinking of going to the [Silver Lake], you are going to your destruction. You don't know where it is, nor how far. If it were within my authority I would prevent your going, only with me." Nolan's report does not mention such an exchange.[19]

The buffalo soldiers and the bison hunters now parted. It was midmorning, July 28, and they were in modern Cochran County perhaps a few miles from present Morton. Silver Lake located to the east-northeast was less than twenty miles away. A march to Double Lakes in modern Lynn County to the southeast meant for the buffalo soldiers a journey to water about three times the distance to Silver Lake.

The hunters continued east-northeast for Silver Lake, but they did not stay together. Three of them—Jim Harvey, Frank Perry, and George Williams, on foot because their horses had wandered away—fell far behind. With Mortimer "Wild Bill" Kress, who was also walking but leading his horse, they drifted off course. The four men followed a route that would take them below the lake—the mysterious "drift" of the Llano pulled them southward away from the east-northeast direction to Silver Lake.

Exhausted and terribly weak, Frank Perry and George Williams were on the verge of giving up. They could barely walk. And Bill Benson—well, after going about two miles, the tired but wise old bison hunter decided to rejoin the troopers, apparently hoping that he might change Nolan's stubborn mind.

After Benson's departure, the hunters plodded on for a short distance and halted again. In the main party, the men who were on foot leading their horses asked that the mounted hunters rush ahead and when they found water return; the walkers would follow as best they could. Because the canteens and powder cans were with the water detail, pint "and quart cups were the only vessels [they] had to bring the water back." Nonetheless, the men with horses, together with the hunters' two remaining pack mules, moved ahead, promising to return with water or news of it as soon as possible.[20]

Johnny Cook described the events that followed. As they rode ahead, he said, the mounted hunters watched from a distance as Benson joined the buffalo soldiers. After that unhappy event, they continued for about four difficult miles through wavy, sandy, slightly undulating land and halted again. "At this stage of our suffering," Cook remembered, "our eyes had sunken back in their sockets; the saliva had dried in our mouths and throats." At this stopping place, Sol Rees, who was in charge of medical supplies, said, "Boys, we have our medicine kit on the black mule, and if you will let me have my way about it I will help you all go ahead."

Rees, according to Cook, took from the black mule two quart bottles of "high-proof brandy." One bottle he set aside with markers and instructions for the hunters on foot, including a note that said, "For God's sake, boys, don't drink it." After opening the second bottle and cutting a piece from his shirt sleeve, he soaked the cloth with brandy and "moistened each man's lips, and had him inhale it through his nostrils." The effort revived the men for a time and allowed them to make some progress. When a sense of exhaustion again appeared, "Rees repeated the operation."

About noon, Cook remembered, "the heat was more intense than it had been at any time during [the] summer." The men had used up all the brandy, and many of them could barely keep up. Rees suggested that Cook (on his big chestnut horse) and rail-thin Alt Waite ride ahead and, when they "saw any favorable signs" of water, signal the hunters, who would continue on the trail as best they could. The two men spurred their mounts and moved out but never separated themselves by more than two miles from Rees and the others. They were in Cochran County, closing in on Silver Lake.[21]

The buffalo soldiers, in the meantime, although still in Cochran County, headed southeast toward Double Lakes. As most of the men had preferred to go with the bison hunters toward Silver Lake or Casas Amarillas, grumbling among the troops—some of it loud—occurred.

Indeed, Captain Nolan's force was breaking up. A few men, including Corporal Charles H. Gilmore and slow-talking Private Walter Cox (both of whom were sick), left the command or fell far behind as Nolan's troopers in effect left them. About noon, Private Johnson Graves seemed ready to give up. His horse was dead and he was lying down a short distance away from the animal. Graves displayed no sign of life. Although few men were strong enough to offer help, someone did (perhaps powerfully built James Jackson, one of Troop A's blacksmiths), and with help Graves managed to get through.

In the afternoon conditions worsened. Additional soldiers fainted in the burning heat and fell from their horses, and Nolan, as he had the day before, detailed stronger men to stay with the stricken ones, ordering the men to bring the sick troopers up as soon as they seemed able to travel. Soldiers, like the hunters heading for Silver Lake, straggled and fell behind the main party.[22]

Sergeant William Umbles and his disparate party, which had gone off with Dick Wilkinson the night before, also split up. Most likely they were near the northern edge of modern Cochran County west of the far upper end of Yellow House Draw. Here they separated. Private Nolan and Wilkinson rode east-northeast toward Casas Amarillas. Umbles, Steven Floyd, and Isaac Thompson headed directly east for Silver Lake. A couple of hours later, however, Floyd, now apparently planning to rejoin the military force, turned back west. Some time later, having spied not the command but the main party of hunters off to his right (north), he joined the bison hunters and rode with them eastward toward Casas Amarillas. Apparently having ridden too far north, the hidemen were in line to miss Silver Lake but strike the upper end of Casas Amarillas.

Umbles and Thompson continued toward Silver Lake. Shortly after noon (July 28) and just a half-mile from their destination, they met Tafoya and four troopers (Privates Henry Miller, Blacksmith Carson, Jerry Freeman, and an unnamed soldier) with twenty-seven filled canteens. As expected, the water detail had found Silver Lake (although many hours later than planned) and was returning with water to the command. The troopers with the water explained that four other men from the detail were waiting at Silver Lake but that one of their party, Private John Peterson, was missing. The two thirsty soldiers each got a canteen and proceeded to the lake, where they found Privates Smith Johnson and Pierce Kuston, the Boston boy, and one other member of the water detail. Tafoya and his group headed for the command.[23]

At nearly the same time (a bit after noon), Private Alex Nolan and Dick Wilkinson reached the breaks of Casas Amarillas. There they met Private Peterson, who in the darkness of the previous night had become separated from others in the water detail. His horse had brought him to the Casas Amarillas breaks, where he arrived about noon, not long before Nolan and Wilkinson showed up.

The afternoon turned hot. The sun beat down in almost "tropical heat causing great suffering." For the men—both hunters and soldiers—out on the trail, the "desire for water now became uncontrollable." Their mouths and throats were parched. They could not swallow; indeed, according to the surgeon Joseph H. T. King, "they could not perceive when anything was in their mouths." The hours passed, the condition of the men and animals deteriorated, and among both the bison hunters and Nolan's troopers weary companions separated from the main party and fell back.[24]

Thus, about two o'clock on the afternoon of July 28 soldiers and hunters were badly scattered. Sergeant Umbles was at Silver Lake with Isaac Thompson, Smith Johnson, Pierce Kuston, the Boston boy, and one other soldier. José Tafoya, Privates Henry C. Miller, Blacksmith Carson, Jerry R. Freeman, and another trooper of the water detail were southwest of Silver Lake, trying to locate the command. Privates Peterson and Nolan were at Casas Amarillas with bison hunter Dick Wilkinson.

At the same time Captain Nolan's command was marching southeastward for the Double Lakes. In the terrible hot weather, the "desire for water now became uncontrollable," and as Surgeon King noted, the "most loathsome fluid" became acceptable "to moisten their swollen tongues and supply their inward craving." In fact, some troopers now drank their own urine and that of their horses. They caught the heavy dark fluid in cups and kettles, and Nolan, "having sugar along . . . issued a liberal supply, . . . which tended to make the Urine palatable." The men also provided small amounts of urine for the horses and mules to drink.[25]

The experience sickened the soldiers. Most of them became nauseous from the odious fluid, and some of them spewed out the liquid. The troopers survived the repulsive drink, however, and it probably brought some slight immediate relief. But in the longer term it did them little good, for urine, which is sterile unless bladder infection is present, contains a high concentration of salt and other electrolytes. Thus, over time urine consumption added significantly to their increasing thirst and dehydration.

Nonetheless, through the long hot afternoon the black regulars pushed ahead, stopping frequently to attend to men who fell from their horses. As a result, Nolan's command made only slow, difficult progress.

At two o'clock the bison hunters were likewise scattered and in poor shape. As noted, Wilkinson was at Casas Amarillas. Bill Benson was still with the soldiers. The main body of hunters was moving eastward slowly and with difficulty toward the wide, north-south–aligned basin at Casas Amarillas. They had missed Silver Lake, apparently passing the lake on its north side. On foot and far behind them to the southwest Jim Harvey, Bill Kress, Frank Perry, and George Williams followed, but they were heading east off the main trail, taking a route that would carry them below Silver Lake.[26]

Finally, some relief came. Just before 3:00 P.M., Johnny Cook and Alt Waite, only two miles ahead of the main party of hunters and still about three miles from water, sighted the breaks of Casas Amarillas in modern Hockley County. As they had agreed around noon when they had parted from the main party, the two men fired their guns to let the trailing hunters, who were scattered and prostrate, know that water had at long last been spotted. Then, the two men separated. Waite turned left, or north, and struck the upper water hole (Yellow Lake). Cook continued straight ahead, rode "down from the plateau into the basin," rounded a little point, and saw on the bluff above the clear Yellow House water hole the little "stone pyramid and flag" the hunters had erected back on July 4.[27]

As Cook rounded the point, his big chestnut-colored horse picked up the scent of water. The horse gave a low whinny, "started into a trot, and finally broke into a gallop." Cook could not hold him, and the horse, "a headstrong animal" so gaunt from lack of water that "he looked like a wasp," bolted off a twelve-foot bluff into the water hole. "He surged into the water," Cook noted, "groaning as if he were dying." The horse drank until Cook, thinking that the animal needed a brief rest from water, struck "him over the head with the bridle-bits before [he] could drive him out and away from the water."

Cook got his own refreshment. "I think no mortal ever experienced more sudden relief from intense suffering, both in body and mind," he wrote, "than I did at that time." He drank what he could and bathed his face and neck as he watched the horse return to drink more water. As Cook bathed, rested, and refreshed himself, the horse left the water on his own account and turned to grazing on the short grass nearby.

Nigger Hill from the southwest, viewing northeast from Highway 114. Courtesy David J. Murrah.

At that time, a little after three, Private John Peterson of the buffalo soldiers came riding out of the draw from the upper water hole. He held "seven canteens full of water," and he told Cook his tale of becoming lost from the water detail the night before and arriving at the upper water hole about noon on July 28. He indicated that both Dick Wilkinson and Alt Waite were resting at the "big Dripping Spring proper," but no mention was made of Private Alex Nolan, who had come in with Wilkinson.

Cook now planned to use Peterson's horse and the canteens to carry water back to his companions. After requesting permission for its use, he took the man's horse, and he and Peterson exchanged weapons: Cook giving the soldier his huge Creedmoor (a favorite bison-hunting rifle) and receiving Peterson's smaller military carbine (a Model 1873 Springfield) in return. Both men were pleased.

Then Cook started back. He found Sol Rees and Jim Foley first. They had split from the main party and, pulled by the Llano Estacado's "drift," had moved away from the generally northeast course to a directly eastern one. Now they were coming back. He gave them water; they hurried him on his way to Louie Keyes, George Cornett, and Charles "Squirrel-eye"

Emory, whose "left eye was gradually covering with a film," for the three men had pretty much "given up the struggle." He met affable and clarioned-voiced John Mathias, who was on foot. Mathias took no water (he said he knew now where it was and would get to it soon enough), but, like Rees and Foley, he told Cook to hurry to the others, especially Keyes, Cornett, and Emory, who were off course a couple of miles back.[28]

A half-mile farther on the trail, Cook met the main group of hunters and Steven Floyd of the Tenth Cavalry. He left them with three canteens of water, not much for six or seven very thirsty men, including at least Powderface Hudson, the two "Englishmen" (Harry Burns and Harold Bradstreet), Joe Freed, Tom Sherman, and Henry Deacon. The hunters also hurried him on to the three prostrate men.

When Cook found them, Emory, Keyes, and Cornett "were lying down, side by side, having been very methodical about it." Expecting to die, they were on their sides with their backs facing east and they had written their names on their saddles. About twenty feet away Emory's horse was dead, its throat cut, for the men had drunk its blood. Cook indicated that "dried blood was on their lips and mustaches. Their lower jaws had dropped. [Keyes's] tongue was swollen and protruding . . . they were all in a comatose condition." With a dampened cloth, Cook rubbed their faces, lips, and necks and cleaned off the dried blood. As he talked loudly to them, he administered a few drops of water and then in turn got each man revived, giving each a good drink from the canteens.

Just as the men regained their consciousness, Sol Rees came up. He took over care of the men, saying that he would get them to water, and hurried Cook away, for Sam Carr had disappeared somewhere west of Casas Amarillas and Cook needed to find him. Cook, on Private Peterson's fresh army horse, rode "for several miles around the Casa Amarilla." About a mile west of the upper water hole, he found Carr and the man's well-trained horse, an animal Carr called Prince. Cook wiped the man's face and gave him a good, long drink from his last canteen and, turning to Prince, moistened the animal's nose and lips. He got Carr onto Prince, mounted his own horse, and together they rode into Yellow Lake (the upper water hole), where they found Dick Wilkinson's pack animals, which had disappeared the night before.

As these developments evolved in the late afternoon near the Casas Amarillas basin, Jim Harvey, Frank Perry, Bill Kress, and George Williams endured similar difficulties. Kress reported the experiences. He told John R. Cook that about mid-morning of July 28 he had tried to convince Bill Benson not to go with the Tenth Cavalry troops, but the unsuccessful effort only got him separated from the other bison hunters. While trying to catch up, his horse played out and he met Harvey, who told him that Perry and Williams had quit—"he could not get them to walk." The two of them, with Kress leading his horse, walked back to the prostrate men.

There, in the northwestern part of modern Cochran County, Kress and Harvey built a sunshade. After using their knives to dig holes, they set the stock ends of their big-fifty Sharps buffalo guns into the shallow pits. They stretched a lariat between the upright gun barrels and placed saddle blankets over the rope. In this fashion they constructed a fine shade for themselves and the sick men. It was about noon "and very hot."

About two hours later, George Williams, who now felt encouraged, and Jim Harvey started out, but Bill Kress some thirty minutes later still could not get Frank Perry, who was very weak, onto Kress's horse. Ahead of them, Williams, exhausted, fell again, and Harvey determined to go alone for water. Within another thirty minutes, two members of the water detail, probably Harry Miller and Blacksmith Carson, showed up. They gave Harvey a canteen before riding to Williams and giving him water. The two black soldiers then rode to Kress and Perry. "The soldiers, who had several canteens," reported Kress, "divided with us," before continuing their search for the military command.

The four hidemen came together again about three o'clock. A bit refreshed from the water, they thought they were moving in an east-northeast direction toward Silver Lake and Casas Amarillas, but apparently they "drifted" east-southeast. Because of the extreme heat, however, they stopped often to rest as the long afternoon and early evening wore on. As the sun set a couple of hours later, they halted again, made note of a storm rolling in to their north and west and, as darkness approached, quickly dropped off to a troubled sleep, dreaming of water and thirst.[29]

About the same time—before sunset on July 28—Captain Nicholas Nolan, seeing his troops stretched back over several miles with some of the men "Completely Exhausted" and unable to keep up in the suffocating heat, called a halt. Our "men were almost completely used up," Lieutenant Charles L. Cooper later wrote to his father; "their tongues and throats were swollen, and they were unable even to swallow their saliva—in fact they had no saliva to swallow." His own mouth was so dry, he said, that when he "put a few morsels of brown sugar . . . into my mouth, I was unable to dissolve it."[30]

Nolan's command was probably in the far western portions of modern Hockley County, possibly west or just northwest of present Levelland. Nolan planned now to wait for darkness, a rising moon to light the way, and cooler nighttime temperatures before continuing toward the Double Lakes. The men and animals by this time were so dehydrated that they could not urinate—there were no body fluids to eliminate.

Here, with no urine or other liquids available, the men killed an exhausted private horse belonging to Lieutenant Cooper. Then they distributed its blood for drinking—which, because the horse had been deprived of fluid, "was thick and coagulated instantly on exposure." The horse blood, or so Surgeon King reasoned, saved their lives, and both the men and officers eagerly took it. The small amount of liquid in the concentrated blood, however, would help only to a limited degree, for the blood's solutes (such as sodium, potassium, and chlorides) would draw fluid from the body and, thus, add to the problem of thirst and dehydration. In other words, while it might have brought some slight immediate relief, drinking blood served only the same limited purpose for the soldiers that consuming salty seawater served persons marooned on a ocean raft; in a short time it complicated the severity of their condition.[31]

Here also, some men simply walked away from Nolan's troubled little force. Among these were Lance Corporal George W. Fremont and Privates John A. Gaddie and Isaac Derwin. They took their horses and two pack mules and headed east after Corporal Charles H. Gilmore and Private Walter Cox. Cooper indicated that "we had now reduced our little party to eighteen men, two officers and one buffalo-hunter."[32]

Meanwhile, the sun was down—or nearly so—on July 28 when Johnny Cook and Sam Carr got to Yellow Lake. Dick Wilkinson had killed a pronghorn and from its hide had fashioned a water container that held forty-two quarts of liquid. His plan was to carry water to his companions, but by this time all but eight of them and the guide José Tafoya were down the basin either at the big Dripping Spring or where Cook had entered the wide depression. Still out on the plains, somewhere west of Casas Amarillas, were two groups of hunters. In one, located above and east of Silver Lake, Sol Rees was doing the best he could to get Squirrel-eye Emory, Louie Keyes, and George Cornett to Casas Amarilla. In the other party, located south and west of Silver Lake, Jim Harvey, Bill Kress, George Williams, and Frank Perry were already asleep or trying to be.

The men at Casas Amarillas, including the black troopers Privates John Peterson and Alex Nolan, gathered at Yellow House Springs. There, with one of the African American soldiers—probably Peterson—taking the lead, most of them roasted the pronghorn, boiled coffee, ate army hardtack bread, and rested and watered their horses. A couple of men headed back up the basin to retrieve the pack mules.[33]

As darkness settled in, others headed for the plains to find the eight missing hunters. Dick Wilkinson with his skin-pouch water container and Alt Waite started first; they rode west toward Silver Lake looking for Jim Harvey's group. At the lake they found Sergeant William L. Umbles, Privates Smith Johnson, Pierce Kuston, and Isaac Thompson, the Boston boy, and the other trooper. Using their knives and hands, they had "dug a place large enough to hold twenty barrels of water." Not knowing that Troop A had changed directions, Umbles and his group thought they would provide fresh water for the command when it came to the lake. Both Umbles and Johnson later claimed that Waite and Wilkinson said "the command had turned back and taken a South Easterly course" and that the hunters "believed that all would perish before they reached water in the direction they had taken." Because the night was late and the weather threatened rain, the hunters stopped there until the first fingers of light appeared in the morning.[34]

Also as darkness settled in, John Cook, taking six filled canteens, headed for Sol Rees and the others who were above and east of Silver Lake. Although it was dark, a flashing thunderstorm was moving across the drought-stricken Llano Estacado. Located off to the west and south, its lightning provided some sense of direction, and Cook fired Private Peterson's carbine. Rees answered by shooting his gun, and Cook, upon seeing the flash, headed in that direction. The four weary men—Rees, Emory, Keyes, and Cornett—emptied the six water containers, but with Cook leading the way in the dark they walked and rode to Casas Amarillas, where a late-night supper of pronghorn, bread, and coffee was ready. Cook wrote that "some of the men could not eat. . . . It was water, *water*, water, they wanted first."[35]

DAY FOUR—JULY 29—TOWARD MORNING

Toward morning on July 29, bison hunters and buffalo soldiers remained scattered. While most of the hunters rested at Casas Amarillas, Bill Kress, Frank Perry, George Williams, and Jim Harvey waited south and west of Silver Lake and hoped for rain from the late-night storm. In fact, some rain fell where they were, said Kress, and they "spread out the blanket and caught a few sips of water," but they knew that earlier heavy rains had fallen north of them. At daylight, Kress, leaving the others to walk, rode north looking for a playa (wet-weather) lake that must have filled during the storm. He found one. Then, a long way off toward the east, he saw two men on horseback—Alt Waite and Dick Wilkinson, as it turned out, coming from Silver Lake. Kress fired his gun three times before attracting their attention.

Conditions now improved. Kress, Wilkinson, and Waite rode into the playa, drank plenty of fresh rainwater, and let their horses drink. Wilkinson emptied his skin water pouch and refilled it with fresh rainwater from the playa. Then he hurried to the three men—Frank Perry, George Williams, and Jim Harvey—who were still on foot and still waiting for Kress to return. He led the three men back to the playa.

Not long afterward, a hard rain began. When Frank Perry complained about getting wet, Wild Bill Kress threw Perry in the lake. After the rain let up, the six men made coffee, ate the hardtack bread and pronghorn meat that Waite and Wilkinson had carried with them, and rested until early afternoon. Then all of them headed again for Casas Amarillas, reaching their companions in the wide basin at nightfall.[36]

Also in the morning of July 29, shortly after Waite and Wilkinson had departed, Sergeant Umbles prepared to leave Silver Lake. At a conspicuous place, he "posted a notice containing directions to any soldiers" who might find their way to the lake. The directions indicated that he and the five others there were headed to Casas Amarillas. They filled the canteens they had with them and started east, arriving at their destination a couple of hours later.[37]

At Casas Amarillas that evening, Jim Harvey asked Umbles to let the hunters have the best of their horses. Because he and his men were personally responsible for the army-issued animals, Umbles declined, and the hunters interpreted the decision as a refusal "to go back to the relief of his officers and comrades." Umbles would not allow the other soldiers to give up their horses, and the hunters read the stance—incorrectly, as it turns out—as an order to "his squad *not to return*" to Nolan's command.[38]

Angry with Umbles, the hunters informed the black soldiers that they "would have to look out for [their] chuck somewhere else." With that, the troopers "moved away a short distance" and camped. "That evening," Umbles said later, the four troopers—Privates Henry Miller, Jerry Freeman, Blacksmith Carson, and one other—from the water detail and José Tafoya "who had gone out" from Silver Lake "to carry water to the command came in." They had returned to Silver Lake, found Umbles's note, filled their canteens, watered their horses, and, following the directions that Umbles had left at the lake, headed for Casas Amarillas. With Private Nolan and the Boston boy, Umbles's little squad, counting himself, contained twelve men. Private John Peterson stayed with the bison hunters.[39]

Very early on July 29, Captain Nicholas Nolan, still in Hockley County, started again for Double Lakes. To take advantage of the cooler night temperatures and the strong moonlight, his command moved out at 2:00 A.M. He had planned to leave earlier, "but owing to the exhausted condition of the men," it had taken three difficult hours to pack, saddle up, and prepare for the start. He abandoned a large portion of the rations, for the men could not eat, and he left behind a horse that had staggered and fallen and "was unable to move." Although his report does not say so, the men probably cut its throat, drained its blood into cups, and drank the warm, wet but coagulating fluid.

The little force, still including Bill Benson, marched through the early morning darkness. They followed Cooper's compass as best they could and kept in the right direction, but the going was slow, as both men and animals struggled to move in any direction. They alternately rode and, to rest the horses, walked. Nonetheless, during the march, Nolan reported, they lost (or perhaps killed) a horse and abandoned additional equipment. Surely they stopped from time to time, but the command, wanting to cover as much ground as possible before the sun worked its heated misery, pushed hard over the waterless stretch toward Double Lakes. Compounding their mental and emotional anguish was the thunderstorm behind them, the same one the hunters watched. The soldiers could see the lightning and hear the thunder, but, like the hunters on the plains west of Casas Amarillas, they had no rain to provide a few sips of moisture.

Lieutenant Cooper noted that the command—or what was left of it—stopped for an hour or so about mid-morning. The men then left their resting place about 11:00 A.M., he wrote to his father, and rode through the noontime heat. Sometime in the afternoon, Nolan reported, "owing to the intense heat and the fearful condition of the men," they halted at a scrub mesquite flat. If Nolan is correct, they had covered twenty-five miles, placing their location near the boundary (toward the north) separating modern Terry and Lynn Counties, southeast of present Ropesville.

Here, the men got a long, but troubled, rest. They spread saddle blankets across the short mesquite bushes to provide shade and lay down beneath them. Some fell asleep, but, according to Surgeon King, their sleep "was disturbed with ever recurring dreams of banquets, feasts, and similar scenes in which they were enjoying every kind of dainty food and delicious drink." They abandoned a second of Lieutenant Cooper's horses and four of the Tenth Cavalry animals. Two of the mules walked away.[40]

Here also, Bill Benson rode away. Disgusted with Nolan's leadership and the direction of the march, Benson determined to rejoin his companions of the Forlorn Hope. He rode northeastward, planning to strike the Yellow House Canyon where he knew he could find water. Because he lost his horse during the night, he walked a good portion of the twenty-five tormenting miles, reaching water below Punta del Agua in modern Lubbock about 3:00 P.M. on July 30, or some ninety-six hours after leaving Double Lakes.[41]

As Benson walked and rode toward Yellow House Canyon, Captain Nolan and his black troopers, at different times during the day (July 29), killed three horses for the animals' blood. They cut open the dead mounts, removed the heart and other viscera, and sucked on the wet organs to secure what precious moisture they could. King noted that the blood, which coagulated quickly, had to be moved in their mouths "to and fro between the teeth until it became somewhat broken up, after which they" could "force it down their parched throats." Still, he wrote, "at the time it appeared more delicious than anything they had ever tasted."

The reports of Surgeon King and Lieutenant Cooper concerning this day—July 29—are far more depressing than that of Captain Nolan. It was a day of agony, said Cooper; the men were thirsty but could not drink, famished but could not eat, although they had plenty of food. Cooper tried to eat "by soaking a hard tack in horse's blood, and masticate it that way, but I nearly strangled in the attempt." He had to remove the bread from his mouth with his fingers.

King, more clinical in his report, said that vertigo "and dimness of vision affected all." The men could hardly speak, with "voices weak and strange sounding." Deafness was a problem, and the men appeared "stupid to each other, questions having to be repeated several times before they could be understood." The men were "very feeble and had a tottering gait. Many were delirious." They also were dehydrated. In such a state, blood does not circulate as freely as it normally does, a situation that in part produced the aphonic and obtuse conditions.[42]

While their reports agree on the sorry condition of the men of Troop A, King and Cooper differ on what level of military order and discipline prevailed. King wrote that "everyone was so eager to obtain [blood] that discipline alone prevented [the men] from struggling for more than the stinted share allowable to each."[43]

Lieutenant Cooper, however, reported that "the crazed survivors of our men" were "fighting each his neighbor for the blood of the horses as the animals' throats were cut." He told his father that prayers, "curses, and howls of anguish intermingled" and came "from every direction." They had, he said, "eighteen madmen" on their hands.[44]

Several men were missing. Not all forty African American troopers who had left Double Lakes some three days earlier could be accounted for. Eighteen men camped with Nolan and Cooper. Sergeant Umbles had twelve men in his command, including himself. Corporal Charles Gilmore and Private Walter Cox were heading for Punta del Agua. Corporal George Fremont and Privates Isaac Derwin and John Gaddie had ridden eastward away from the command. Private Peterson remained with the bison hunters. Five men, then, were unaccountably absent from the command; they had deserted, or more likely fallen behind from sunstroke and the effects of dehydration. Privates John Bonds, John Gordon, and John Isaacs, each of whom died during the scout, may have been among the missing five.

During the day, Captain Nolan and Lieutenant Cooper decided on a new course. And, if he is correct, Nolan ordered Acting First Sergeant Jim Thompson and six men on the strongest horses to head immediately for Double Lakes. Cooper's letter suggests that the seven men simply rode away and were missing. Thompson and the others reached the lake, probably late in the evening or early the next morning, but not before five of their horses had died.

Meanwhile, toward evening—July 29—Cooper gave a short speech about their new course. He told the eleven men still with the command that the plan now was "to drive the two remaining horses as far as [they] could," and kill "them for their blood when required." They would travel by night, rest during the day, and "endeavor to reach some of the streams to the east of us." In their delirious conditions, apparently only "some of the men" understood him.

The officers and eleven men of Troop A left camp about eight o'clock that evening. They abandoned all the food, equipment, and unnecessary articles, taking only their weapons for protection or perchance for shooting a bison for its blood. Cooper and Nolan, their own horses gone and the other two very weak, mounted the last two pack mules. The men walked behind. It was a tired, dirty, bedraggled group that stumbled into the night, but, because of what Cooper's letter says, it is not clear if they continued southeast or marched in a more easterly direction.

In either case, Cooper took the lead. Nolan followed on muleback, and the men walked behind, but half of them could not keep up. They fell out ("straggled," in Nolan's words) as the brutal nature of the Llano Estacado crushed their weary bodies. Still, they walked and rode into the night.

DAY FIVE—JULY 30—AFTER MIDNIGHT

The little party of two officers and eleven men struggled forward, even as more men fell behind or drifted off course. They traveled, Cooper wrote, until about three the next morning, July 30, "when, as we were marching along, we came across what seemed an old wagon-trail." After following it a short distance, Cooper surmised that the ruts, probably from comanchero carts, represented William R. Shater's 1875 trail from Double Lakes north to Punta del Agua.

Because he now knew his location, Cooper "at once made the good news known to all, and such wild hurrahs and firing of guns you never heard in your life." Cooper and Nolan rode to Double Lakes, arriving there about 5:00 A.M. Most of their eleven remaining men, whose spirits had been lifted by Cooper's report a couple of hours earlier, followed slowly behind them. For most of the command, whether its men were at Casas Amarillas or Double Lakes, the thirsting time was over.[45]

Nolan's work was not done. Even as he refreshed himself, Nolan ordered two men of Sergeant Jim Thompson's squad, which had arrived several hours earlier, on their weak but refreshed horses back on the trail. In seven canteens, they carried water for the stragglers but were unable to find some of them. The missing men, it seems, were so exhausted, both physically and mentally, that they could not recognize the wagon ruts, as Cooper had done, for trail markers, and they stumbled away from the trail apparently not knowing in what direction they were headed.

Nolan kept up the search. As the early morning sun rose, he sent in different directions other rested men on three of the hunters' horses, horses that had walked away from Jim Harvey, Frank Perry, and George Williams in the predawn hours of July 28 and had found their way to Double Lakes. The black regulars, he reported, made a "diligent search" for their Troop A companions but with limited success.[46]

As the day wore on, Nolan must have reassessed the failed scout. Several men were missing, but no one was as yet reported dead. That sad news would come over the next couple of days. He did not know the condition or fate of Private Smith Johnson's water detail, Sergeant William Umbles and his squad, the bison hunters, or the other men still missing. He had started from Double Lakes with forty-four horses and eight mules. Back at Double Lakes eighty-six hours later he had four horses and two mules, although (unknown to Nolan) Umbles and his squad, increased by the arrival of Charles Gilmore and Walter Cox on foot, had twelve horses. Tafoya had one of Nolan's private mounts. Later one of the stragglers would bring in an animal, but another horse would die; the loss of at least twenty-nine horses and either four or six mules was not a good record. Nolan had caught no Kwahadas, and in fact the only Comanches he had seen were Quanah's small parties with whom he had talked on two occasions. Rations, equipment, other supplies, and even weapons had been abandoned and sat scattered over some twenty-five or more miles back on the trail. In a military unit that seldom experienced desertion, he counted—reluctantly—several men who had walked away from his command.

Nonetheless, about sunrise on July 30, 1877, the thirsting time was over. For both bison hunters and buffalo soldiers, it had been an adventure in courage and fortitude, a testament to human will and determination. The tired but angry and disgusted hidemen, except perhaps for the missing Bill Benson, still wanted their horses. And the black regulars, well, as quickly as possible, Captain Nolan, Lieutenant Cooper, and the healthy men of Troop A, Tenth Cavalry, needed to find the stragglers, gather the abandoned equipment and supplies, reorganize the command, and get down off the High Yarner.

Chapter 7

Down off the High Yarner

"It is [ascertained] that a disastrous encounter was had on the Staked Plains, in which there were two officers and 26 enlisted soldiers killed." Thus read the first official army communication about the black troop tragedy. Dated August 8, 1877, the notice came from military personnel at the headquarters of the Division of the Missouri in Chicago. Although they had very little news to report, and nearly all of it in error, officers released the eighteen-line statement in response to dozens of excited inquires from around the country. "Information . . . confirming the rumor received here a few days since," the bulletin said, indicates that a "remnant of the party continued its march having suffered their loss and since reached Fort [Concho]." They hoped that "full details [might] be received in the course of a few days."[1]

"Full details"—whatever that might mean—of Captain Nicholas Nolan's lost troop expedition did not arrive in a few days. The men, both bison hunters and black regulars, first needed water, food, and rest. They were dehydrated and famished. Their skin was gray-colored, their eyes bloodshot and sunken. They needed to regain not only their physical well-being but also their mental and emotional stability. They needed to get back to their home stations and down off the high Yarner.

The Comanches, likewise, needed to get down off the High Plains. They had not suffered from thirst or lack of food—they knew the Llano Estacado too well for that—but they needed rest from the hide hunters and the two-months-long chase the hunters had been giving them. Plus, as we have seen, at the end of July the buffalo soldiers had joined the hated bison hunters in pursuit. The Kwahadas were tired.

Accordingly, many of Red Young Man's band welcomed the news that Quanah, the government's emissary from Fort Sill, was on his way with four companions to the Llano Estacado. In fact, the "runners" or scouts who had brought the news to the Comanche camp in the Blue Sand Hills had met Quanah in Yellow House Canyon, probably at the long water hole in modern Lubbock, the site of the battle of Yellow House Canyon the previous March. The runners, if John Cook is correct, told Quanah where the bison hunters and buffalo soldiers could be found and where he could find the Comanches in the Blue Sand Hills.[2]

Using the information, Quanah and his four companions headed south. On July 21, he found the soldiers and hunters in their Tobacco Creek camp and told them—incorrectly, of course—that the Indian people they sought were to the southwest in the upper Mustang Draw area. Quanah then headed in that direction, hoping to draw the pursuers away from the Comanches he had come to get, Indians he knew were in the Blue Sand Hills to the west. Two days later Quanah again rode into Nolan's camp, now at Cedar Lake (Laguna Sabinas), and spent six hours with the soldiers and hunters. He left in the early evening "taking a westerly direction."[3]

Johnny Cook saw two reasons for Quanah's going "out of his way some forty miles in all to reach our camp and then get back again to the Indians." Cook, who got his information afterwards from Four Feathers, one of the warriors in the Blue Sand Hills, said Quanah wanted first, to "show his commission and orders, thus hoping to allay the vengeance of the hunters, and check the movement of the soldiers against their camp." Second, he wanted to "get us as far south as possible, when he would, under cover of night, turn and hurry to the sand-hills and get the . . . [Comanches] moving to Fort Sill."[4]

With their supplies on three pack animals, Quanah and his companions, upon leaving Nolan's camp, hurried to reach their friends in the Blue Sand Hills. Perhaps they had been joined by a few additional warriors and perhaps they were the Indians that José Piedad Tafoya, the hunters' guide, and the other scouts had seen on July 26, the chance sighting west of Rich Lake that started the black troop tragedy.

Among the supplies and equipment that Quanah carried with him was "a pair of army field-glasses," issued to him at Fort Sill. Using the field glasses, the Kwahadas at the end of July kept a close eye on the bison hunters and the buffalo soldiers. Indeed, the Comanches must have wondered at the men who chased them, for their pursuers were never far from water. Tafoya, the guide, knew water existed in the Blue Sand Hills, and, while the hunters and soldiers may not have known it, many water holes—some, such as Monument Lake, quite large—existed just to their north in modern Bailey County. In some ways, in fact, water surrounded the bison hunters and buffalo soldiers.

But the Comanches were also "surrounded." Settlers, including both livestockmen and farmers, were moving in from the north, east, and southeast; and hide hunters—those not pursuing them—edged toward the Staked Plains. Besides Nolan's troops, Captain Phillip L. Lee with Troop G of the Tenth Cavalry from Fort Griffin, as he had in April and May, approached from the east. Texas Rangers would soon be stationed at Saint Angela (modern San Angelo). For the Comanches there was no place to go, and as the summer drought of 1877 worsened, game animals, including the bison, vacated the region.

Quanah understood the Kwahadas' plight. About July 25 or 26, when he and his four companions arrived at the Kwahada camp in the Blue Sand Hills, Quanah "told us," remembered Herman Lehmann, "that it was useless for us to fight longer, for the white people would kill all of us if we kept on fighting." Quanah indicated that "the white men had us completely surrounded; that they would come in on us from every side." He wanted the Comanches to return to the reservation and promised "that if we would go to Fort Sill we would not be punished or hurt in any way." After four days of talk in council, the band agreed to return, and on July 29, seeing that the soldiers and hunters had parted and gone separate ways, the Comanches made a run eastward between their now-divided pursuers and across the Llano Estacado.[5]

The flight was not easy. Cook wrote that according to Four Feathers, when they saw the hunters approach their camp on July 28, the Comanches, leaving behind many horses and supplies, pulled out to the east, "keeping in the basins of the sand-hills." They knew that the hunters and soldiers suffered from lack of water on Nigger Hill during the night. Then, on July 29, when they saw the military command "turn toward [Silver Lake], following the water party, they halted and camped." They watched as the command separated that morning, and that evening "they started to run the [gauntlet] between" the soldiers and hunters.[6]

The Comanches knew the Llano Estacado, some of them since childhood. Thus, "they could safely anticipate," wrote Cook, "where each party was that night [the 29th]." They kept "a course as far from [the] hunters as possible, and [crossed] Nolan's trail well in his rear." Quanah and the Comanches "got through to the eastern breaks of the Staked Plains without being seen," and stopped for a brief rest on July 30 "in the rough broken

Silver Lake, on the north edge of the Hockley-Cochran county line, was a popular camping place and water source for Native Americans, Federal troopers, and bison hunters. Courtesy Bryan Edwards.

country" upstream from where the battle in March at the long water hole (present Lubbock) had occurred. "They were so scared and in such a hurry," wrote Cook, that they "left more than one hundred head of stock here in these breaks." They moved east off the Yarner, perhaps to Silver Falls, and then rode north along the Caprock escarpment, stopping at Roaring Springs before following the Pease River valley through modern Cottle, Foard, and Hardeman Counties. They crossed the Red River near the future site of Doan's Store, the trading post on the cattle trail to Dodge City, north of modern Vernon, and hurried east from there to Fort Sill. The route they followed had become, for Comanches and Kiowas, a familiar one connecting Fort Sill and the southern Llano Estacado.[7]

Captain Nolan's official report indicated that the Comanches took a different route off the Llano Estacado. Nolan stated that the Kwahadas must have followed the Lea-Yoakum sand dunes in a southeasterly direction, for he wrote that on August 4 Tonkawa scouts had seen Comanche camps at Cedar Lake, a place far to the south of his back trail. Such a circuitous route seems unlikely, for it eventually would have brought them past the black soldier supply camp at Bull Creek, something the Kwahadas wanted to avoid.[8]

Some Comanches only reluctantly left the High Plains. The group included Hishorty, Cotopah, Esatema, Watsacatova, and Herman Lehmann. The fate of Red Young Man remains unknown, but presumably he too followed Quanah to Fort Sill. Once down off the high Yarner, said Lehmann, "Quanah sent scouts ahead to notify the soldiers at Fort Sill that we were coming in." They wanted protection. "In a few days," noted Lehmann, "we began to meet white people everywhere, but" because Quanah "could speak English we got along all right." A few days later, in early August, they arrived at Fort Sill.[9]

In the meantime, Sergeant William L. Umbles and his squad of Tenth Cavalry soldiers at Casas Amarillas sought to rejoin Nolan's command. On the evening of July 29, the Umbles party consisted of twelve men, and as a result of a disagreement over horses the soldiers camped a short distance away from the bison hunters—who were also at Casas Amarillas. The Troop A squad included Umbles, Privates Isaac Thompson, Alexander Nolan, and Steven Floyd, plus seven men from the water detail (Privates Smith Johnson, Blacksmith Carson, Henry C. Miller, Jerry R. Freeman, Pierce Kuston, and two others). Probably it included the Boston boy—if, in fact, the boy had not joined the hunters as John R. Cook claimed. That leaves Private John Peterson or another soldier of the water detail unaccounted for.[10]

Records at Fort Concho suggest that the Boston youth returned to the post. Alice Grierson, for example, wife of the Tenth Cavalry's colonel, wrote to her husband that the boy while on the Llano Estacado "was quite brave and plucky." Susan Miles indicated that on August 23, 1877, "Young Boston" left Fort Concho in a wagon for San Antonio, a place where his father had sent money for the boy's return.[11]

Private John Peterson may have been the soldier who, Cook claimed, joined the hunters. A soldier was counted among the missing, but Nolan indicated that on August 6 he saw all eight men of the water detail at the Bull Creek supply camp. Obviously, either Nolan or Cook is in error about a soldier having joined the bison hunters.[12]

In any case, early the next morning, Monday, July 30, Umbles's party left Casas Amarillas for Punta del Agua. The black troopers went down Yellow House Draw, taking a trail Lieutenant Colonel William R. Shafter's command had made in 1875, a command that had included Privates Smith Johnson and Isaac Thompson. They arrived that evening and to their great enjoyment found a tiny bison herd grazing along the headwaters of the

Brazos River. They fired into the herd, killing an animal and making him their supper.[13]

Not long afterward, Corporal Charles H. Gilmore and Private Walter Cox walked into camp. They had left Nolan's command in the afternoon of July 28, they reported, and headed east. The next day they had found water in a playa lake. The previous night, rain from the elusive thunderstorm, which in its narrow path had missed both the hunters and soldiers, had partly filled the little lake. Gilmore and Cox left their horses at the top edge of the playa (or so they claimed) and walked down for a long-sought drink.

As fate would have it, at just that moment Quanah and Red Young Man's Comanches were rushing through the region on their way back to Fort Sill. A couple of the young Kwahada warriors, who had seen Gilmore and Cox picket their animals, rode over to the shallow lake, took a shot at the soldiers, and knocked a drinking cup from Gilmore's mouth. When the soldiers returned the fire, the warriors took the horses and hurried to rejoin the departing Comanches. The two troopers, now refreshed but very hungry, walked to Punta del Agua, arriving there just in time to enjoy the bison meat that Umbles and the others were preparing.[14]

At Punta del Agua, Sergeant Umbles gave orders. He sent Private Smith Johnson to find Lieutenant Colonel Shafter's trail to Double Lakes and directed preparations to rejoin Nolan's command. Accordingly, when the group found a rusty old shovel, Umbles wrote a note and attached the note to the spade advising any who found the missive to head for the command by following the trail he and his men were taking to Double Lakes.

Private Johnson found Shafter's trail, or thought he did, and in the morning Umbles and his men climbed out of the Brazos breaks. After following the tracks a short distance, they realized that they were on the wrong route. Now Umbles determined to follow his own map, one that the bison hunters had prepared for him. The map pointed them in the direction of the Bull Creek supply camp rather than to Double Lakes. While some men objected, particularly Privates Johnson and Thompson who had been on the Llano two years earlier, Umbles demanded that they follow him. The new route carried them quickly down Yellow House Canyon to near its mouth and than south to Bull Creek. They reached the supply camp early on August 1.[15]

After the arrival of Umbles's fourteen-man squad in the supply camp, confusion reigned. Nervousness and fear for the welfare of Nolan, Cooper, and the men of Troop A added to the confusion. Plus a question over who was the ranking officer—Umbles, who had been set back from first sergeant, or First Sergeant Thomas H. Allsup, who was in charge of the supply camp—complicated the discussions. Unnecessary infighting and intrigue resulted. While Umbles and Allsup conferred, Barney Howard, the quartermaster sergeant, organized breakfast for Umbles's men, and Sergeant John Fry, one of Allsup's aides, distributed tobacco to the men.

As they smoked and ate, the men related their tales and debated the course of action. Umbles, suggesting that Captain Nolan and his men probably were dead, wanted to go to Fort Concho where they might organize a relief party and find a commissioned officer to take command of the foundering expedition. Allsup wanted to hurry to Double Lakes and from there search for Nolan.

The men did both. Sergeant Allsup tended to the needs of the men in camp and organized a relief expedition. After conferring with Hi Bickerdyke and Billy Devins, the bison hunters who had remained at the supply camp, Allsup took one of their wagons, loaded it with barrels of water, and made other plans to find Nolan's party or what remained of it. Then, taking fifteen men with water and several days' rations, Allsup headed overland to Tobacco Creek. He moved up the creek, climbed the caprock, and pushed toward Double Lakes, reaching the place on August 4 and finding, happily, that his captain, Lieutenant Cooper, and many of the men were alive and safe and recuperating.

Sergeant Umbles, in the meantime, headed for Fort Concho. Taking Corporal Charles Gilmore, Private Smith Johnson, and a guide known only as Mr. Perkins (the same Perkins who had been with Spotted Jack), he hurried away from the supply camp at Bull Creek. Mounted on fresh horses and with plenty of water and two days' rations, the four men raced south. Some forty miles from their destination, however, Perkins, not wanting to continue, stopped. He would, he said, await any relief party that might be formed and guide it back to Bull Creek. The three others continued to Fort Concho and in the early evening of August 3 rode onto the post.[16]

William Umbles's arrival at the post shocked Fort Concho's residents. Umbles, Gilmore, and Johnson "spilled [a] frightful and incredible . . . tale of sufferings." They reported to Lieutenant Robert Smither, in charge at the post, and others "that Captain Nolan's command was lost and probably perishing . . . on the Staked Plains." The "garrison reeled in the news." One woman fell faint, others hustled children to homes, rumors spread about an impending Indian attack on Concho, and a pervading sense of uncertainty and fear—gloom and doom—spread through the compound.[17]

But now events moved quickly. Smither suggested that Chaplain George W. Dunbar talk with Mrs. Charles Cooper and break the delicate news to her about the possible fate of her husband. The Nolan children went to Captain Nathaniel S. Constable's home to be with his children, where Mrs. Constable would "tell them the news." Smither ordered telegrams of explanation sent to neighboring posts and to department headquarters in San Antonio, and he organized a relief expedition, planning for it to get under way before dark. He also requested that troops be sent from Fort McKavett, as his relief party, when it departed, would empty Fort Concho of soldiers.[18]

Then Smither, leading Surgeon Joseph H. T. King and ten men of the cavalry's band and two army ambulances, raced up the North Concho River. The next afternoon about forty-five miles from the post the men met their waiting guide, Mr. Perkins. They hurried northward from there along the Caprock for two days and arrived at Bull Creek late on August 6. Here, to their great and happy surprise, they found Captain Nolan and Lieutenant Cooper with twenty-two men of Troop A. They also discovered Captain Phillip L. Lee with a group of black regulars and Tonkawa scouts of Troop G. Nolan, Lee, and their men had ridden in from Double Lakes a few hours earlier.

Lieutenant Smither reported on the arrival at Fort Concho of Sergeant Umbles and the others. He indicated that he had asked—but not ordered—Umbles to guide him back to the Bull Creek supply camp, but that Umbles, protesting that he needed to rest until morning, begged off. Smither, therefore, left the three men behind.[19]

Captain Nolan described his company's status. He indicated that through much of the morning of July 30, his healthy men, seven of them led by Sergeant Jim Thompson, searched for stragglers and supplies but with little success. The others, about fifteen soldiers, drank water—large amounts of it—slept, rested, and swam in the lake. Nolan washed his clothes and, once some of the supplies had been retrieved on July 31, shaved.

On July 31, Nolan remained in camp at Double Lakes. He sent search parties back up the trail to retrieve supplies and find the men who were still missing. About eleven o'clock, he noted, Captain Phillip Lee with Troop G, buffalo soldiers who had been scouting from Fort Griffin along the forks of the Brazos River before moving to the High Plains, rode into camp. Lee's command had met Spotted Jack and his two companions on July 29 near Yellow House Canyon and had learned from them that Nolan may have been at Double Lakes, to which Lee then directed his command.

Lee's men, including some Tonkawa scouts led by Tonkawa (or Chief) Johnson, went back on the trail to gather supplies and seek the missing soldiers. Lee, reported Nolan, gave the scouts "instructions to scatter and use all possible means to find lost men and property." They were not successful in finding Troop A soldiers, but they ran into some of the hidemen, led by Johnny Cook, who had determined to go back to the Blue Sand Hills to find their horses.[20]

On August 1, Lee's men, including the scouts, returned to Double Lakes. One party of the soldiers about ten miles from camp had found Lance Corporal George W. Fremont and Private John A. Gaddie, the men who had ridden away from the command on the twenty-eighth with Private Isaac Derwin. Derwin, reported Fremont, had died. Their horses were also dead. The scouts indicated that near Rich Lake they had discovered the body of a soldier, "which proved to be that of Private [John T.] Gordon." They carried Gordon's body back to Double Lakes and buried it there.[21]

For two more days, men searched without success for missing troopers—John Isaacs and John Bond, both of whom Captain Nolan reported dead. Others rested and regained their health; they drank plenty of water. Captain Lee sent his Tonkawa scouts south to Cedar Lake "to search for signs of Indians." They reported back on August 4, and Nolan said that the scouts had seen "signs of Indians, which was supposed to be that of [Quanah] and Party returning to Fort Sill." Nolan was incorrect, as we have seen, for the Kwahadas had crossed the Llano Estacado, according to Herman Lehmann who was with them, well to the north of Double Lakes.[22]

Also on August 4, Sergeant Thomas H. Allsup and fifteen men from the supply camp at Bull Creek arrived at Double Lakes. They carried additional supplies and barrels of water. They indicated that Sergeant Umbles's squad "had reached the supply camp in safety" but had reported that Nolan, Lieutenant Cooper, and the other men were lost and presumed dead. Captain Nolan immediately "sent two couriers to Fort Concho by way of supply camp, with a penciled communication" to Lieutenant Robert Smither. The note gave "a rough statement as to the condition" of Nolan's command and suggested that any statements by Umbles, Corporal Charles H. Gilmore, and Private Smith Johnson "would be false."[23]

The departure of the couriers left Captain Nicholas Nolan with less than half of his original command. Forty black troopers had started from Double Lakes on July 26. Nine days later on August 4, not counting those who had just arrived with Sergeant Allsup, Nolan led nineteen men. Private Peterson, if John Cook is correct, was with the bison hunters. Troopers Umbles,

Gilmore, and Johnson were at Fort Concho explaining their versions of the scout to Lieutenant Robert Smither. Four men were dead. Eleven men (twelve, if the Boston boy is included) who had come in with Sergeant Umbles waited at the Bull Creek supply camp.

By most measures, Nolan's scout was a failed campaign. Other expeditions to the Llano Estacado had experienced a lack of water, but none had suffered as much in terms of privation and death. In 1875, for example, Lieutenant Colonel Shafter's men marched two days from Silver Lake southwestward to the Pecos River before reaching water. Shafter tied some of his men to their horses to keep them in their saddles. Also in 1875, Captain Theodore A. Baldwin with 120 men of the Tenth Cavalry went thirty-eight hours without water. Clearly, then, on the Staked Plains going for long stretches without water was not unusual. Neither Shafter nor Baldwin had lost a man. This time tragedy resulted.

Meanwhile, on the next day, August 5, the soldiers and scouts, including Captain Lee's Troop G, left Double Lakes for the supply camp. They traveled east-southeast, climbed down off the high Yarner at the breaks of the South Fork of the Double Mountain Fork of the Brazos (probably in modern southwest Garza County), and made in this droughty season a dry camp—bad luck had not yet slipped Nolan. Early on August 6 they left again and moved south, arriving that afternoon at the supply camp on Bull Creek.[24]

Some seventy miles to the northwest, the bison hunters also moved to get down off the high Yarner. At Casas Amarillas, having separated from Sergeant William Umbles and his small group of Tenth Cavalry troopers, the hidemen rested a bit and on July 31 started for the long water hole in modern Lubbock, site of the March 19 bison hunter battle with Comanches. With them now, remembered Cook some thirty years later, was Private John Peterson, one of the buffalo soldiers who having become disgusted with Umbles joined the hunters as they headed down Yellow House draw.[25]

About August 1, the bison hunters, still officially led by Jim Harvey, reached the long water hole. At the popular old camping site they found some of their missing pack mules.

Here also the hunters found Bill Benson, their companion who for a time had remained with Nolan and the buffalo soldiers. Benson, they learned, had left the soldiers on the twenty-ninth and made his way to Punta del Agua in modern Lubbock. Having been ninety-six hours without water, the white-bearded Benson when they found him, wrote Cook, "was crazy as a bug." Delusional, sick, and unsure of himself, Benson did not recover his senses or regain his mental health for nearly a month. From the happy, but anxious, moment that they found their hallucinating companion, the hunters affectionately referred to him as "Old" Bill Benson.[26]

Benson had reached Punta del Agua in the frightful condition about three o'clock on the afternoon of July 30. Because he had lost his horse during the previous night, he had walked most of the distance to Yellow House Canyon. His tongue had become swollen so large it hung from his mouth. Although delirious, Benson understood, writes J. Evetts Haley, "that if he lay down to drink, as an outdoor man usually does, he might faint when he touched the water" and drown. Accordingly, the seasoned plainsman "sat down, stuck his feet into the [water], scooped up a double handful" of the precious liquid, and, while leaning backward, splashed the water on his face. He fainted, but as explained by Haley, "instead of falling forward into the pool and drowning, he fell on his back." As he regained consciousness, his feet and lower legs soaked up water, and as he continued to drink, "his swollen tongue subsided." The bison hunters found him two days later.[27]

"After leaving the old battle-ground, where [they] found Benson," remembered Cook, the hunters moved down the canyon in "easy stages." They took their time, moving only a few miles each day. They camped at Buffalo Springs in southeastern Lubbock County and from there followed the permanent stream, the North Fork of the Double Mountain Fork of the Brazos River, toward the mouth of the canyon. In some places the stream reached three feet deep and five feet wide, but in some stretches the hunters encountered, as described by O. W. Williams, "dry ponds choked with the skeletons of buffaloes." They found springs of water feeding the riverbed and saw "a great abundance of small catfish." Undoubtedly, they recognized fresh wagon tracks in the valley, and near the canyon's mouth, in fact, about noon on August 3, they "ran onto a large surveying party."[28]

The surveyors saw the hunters approach. Fearing the riders were Comanches, they prepared for battle. "We promptly unhitched our animals," remembered O. W. Williams, "got out arms and cartridges, and under our wagon lined our guns on the spokes of the wheels." They were "ready for good shooting," but then, largely because Johnny Cook in a red undershirt at the head of the riders was yelling "friends," they recognized that the horsemen were not Indians.

Upon arrival in the camp, the hunters turned to rest. They staked their horses on a glade of good grass and settled in for some hot coffee. The cook "began to prepare a large dinner," and the surveyors gathered around to listen to the dramatic story the hunters had to tell. The chief narrator, remembered Williams, was Johnny Cook, "the red shirted horseman who . . . later gave the story in book form under the title *The Border and the Buffalo.*" The surveyors also had a tale to tell: on July 30 they had seen the Comanches at a spot up the canyon with a large number of horses. The next morning, however, the Kwahadas had been gone and had left behind many of their animals.[29]

Intrigued with the tale, the hunters on August 4—the day following their meeting with the surveyors—scoured the area where the Comanches had camped. They went looking for horses and in fact gathered some 136 head. A few of the animals belonged to the hunters and had been taken from Rath City back in early May—the daring Comanche raid that had started the "Forlorn Hope" on its long, tragic adventure to the Llano Estacado in the first place. There were horses in the herd that belonged to John Mathias, Harry Burns, George Williams, Billy Devins, Joe Freed, and others, and some of the stock they recognized as belonging to bison hunters who had not participated in the pursuit of Red Young Man's Comanches.

During breakfast on the morning of August 5, the hunters determined to divide their command into three units. One, led by Jim Harvey, would head straight for Rath City. It included Benson—whom the hunters kept close tabs on for he wanted to wander off to "find the boys"—Sam Carr, Louis Keyes, George Cornett, Charles "Squirrel Eye" Emory, Harry Burns, and Harold Bradstreet. They drove the recaptured horses with them.

A second party followed the Kwahadas toward Fort Sill, hoping that they might find additional horses left behind. They crossed the Salt Fork of the Brazos and then moved up Blanco Canyon and passed the stone house—"Tasker's Ranche"—that now belonged to Hank Smith, a friend and businessman from Fort Griffin. They rode along the Indian route as it passed Roaring Springs and then turned eastward down the Middle Pease River Valley until they came to Rath's Trail in modern Cottle County. Once they struck the north-south trail that connected Fort Elliott with Rath City, they turned south and followed it back to the busy trade center below the Double Mountain, which they reached in mid-August without having found additional horses.

The third group headed back to the Blue Sand Hills. Following the back trail the Comanches had made in their flight to Fort Sill, they climbed out of Yellow House Canyon and back onto the Llano Estacado. "On top of the 'yarner,'" wrote John Cook, and a fair distance out from the canyon breaks, they met Tonkawa (Chief) Johnson, the scout attached to Captain Philip Lee's Troop G of the Tenth Cavalry and five of his Tonkawa companions. Johnson told the hunters about the condition of Nolan's men and indicated that he and the Tonkawas were looking for missing pack mules, discarded supplies and equipment, and some soldiers, including Privates John Bonds, John T. Gordon, and John Isaacs, who could not be found. They also reported that Isaac Derwin had died.

After the brief meeting, the bison hunters continued toward the Blue Sand Hills, taking two days to reach their destination. They entered the hills at the point the Comanches had left them in modern Roosevelt County, New Mexico. According to Johnny Cook, the hunters followed the Indian "trail about seven miles" through the sands. They "passed by horses, mules and ponies for two miles" and arrived at a place they believed was the main Kwahada camp from early May, when Captain Lee had driven the Comanches from Silver Lake, to the end of July, when the Indians had fled to Fort Sill. The campsite, noted Cook and apparently the others, with a certain wonderment at the fickleness of fate, was precisely seven miles from where on July 28 the bison hunters and black soldiers had abandoned their failed pursuit of the Comanches. It was, in other words, precisely where José Piedad Tafoya had said they would find it.[30]

The bison hunters rounded up 107 horses in the sand dunes and returned with the animals to Rath City. They arrived at the trade center after mid-August, two days later than the men who had taken the Indian trail toward Fort Sill had reached the place. They moved all the horses, ponies, and mules into a common herd, sent messengers to hunters and ranchers notifying them that the stock was at Rath City, and settled in for some rest and recuperation. Charles Rath boarded the hunters at his restaurant, said Cook, "until we got our outfits rigged up for the fall and winter hunt."[31]

Hiram Bickerdyke and Billy Devins, the bison hunters who had remained at Bull Creek to protect supplies and equipment, also returned to Rath City. The details of their return are not recorded, but presumably early on August 2 they left the supply camp with rations on a mule and plenty of ammunition (as they did not know the fate of the Comanches). They followed the Caprock north to the mouth of Yellow House Canyon. They may have rejoined their fellow hunters about August 4 and, if so, may have been part of the group that returned to the Blue Sand Hills. Or, they may have talked to the surveyors or found the Mooar brothers, J. Wright and John Wesley, who were hunting for lost horses in the region. Whatever their story may have been, Bickerdyke and Devins in mid-August enjoyed the comforts of Rath City.

By mid-August, 1877, the Comanches, the buffalo soldiers, and the bison hunters had all returned to their home stations. For the Kwahadas, adjusting to life on the reservation around Fort Sill was not easy, and partly as a result many of the younger warriors continued to seek permission to hunt or trade on the Llano Estacado. For the hidemen, life on the great southern bison range suddenly had become less dangerous; they no longer had to fear Indian attacks. Partly as a result the fall and winter of 1877–78 produced a huge number of hides—the largest number taken in Texas during any one season.

For Captain Nolan, Lieutenant Cooper, their men of Troop A, and the people at the post, mid-August at Fort Concho was a perplexing and ambivalent time. Sadly and disappointingly, on one hand, four men of the troop were in jail awaiting court-martial for desertion and related crimes associated with the recent expedition, and citizens and soldiers mourned the loss of four men who had died on the failed scout. On the other hand, everyone at the post celebrated the return of those men who had made it "back from the dead."

Chapter 8

Back from the Dead

On Tuesday morning, August 7, 1877, couriers from Double Lakes, high up on the Llano Estacado, arrived at Fort Concho. Sent ahead by Captain Nicholas M. Nolan to counter the reports of his own and Lieutenant Charles L. Cooper's probable death, the couriers brought exciting news. They assured everyone at the post that not only were Nolan and Cooper alive but also most men of Troop A were recovering and making their way down off the Llano Estacado to the supply camp at Bull Creek. They were, in effect, back from the dead.

For several days the post had been a place of "gloom and depression." The despair had begun on August 3 with the arrival of Sergeant William L. Umbles, Corporal Charles H. Gilmore, and Private Smith Johnson and their reports that Nolan, Cooper, and the buffalo soldiers had become lost and had likely perished from lack of water. Women and children were consumed with worry. Residents of officers' row closed the drapes, talked in hushed tones, and avoided afternoon teas. They whispered about the fate of the Nolan children and fretted for Mrs. Cooper. Realizing that the men and officers of Troop A might have died from want of water, the women believed that taking a bath or even getting a drink of water was something akin to sin. The post was a dismal place.[1]

Lieutenant Robert G. Smither, as we have seen, organized a rescue party. Knowing that a guide (Mr. Perkins) was waiting about forty-five miles away, he left the post with Surgeon Joseph H. T. King and ten members of the Tenth Cavalry band. They headed for the supply camp on Bull Creek.[2]

About two hours later Sergeant Umbles headed for Saint Angela, the tiny village of "miserable hovels" along the north bank of the North Concho River. Because the sutler's store on the post was closed and he wanted a bottle of brandy, he went to Wilson's Saloon, a combination barroom and dance hall. Although too worn and tired to dance, he got his brandy and at the same time became the center of attention. Over the next few hours, he related tales of the pain and thirst endured recently by both buffalo soldiers and bison hunters. He returned to the garrison a little after one o'clock in the morning. Apparently neither Gilmore nor Johnson had accompanied him to the saloon.[3]

Two more days passed. The arrival on August 5 of Lieutenant Alured Larke with twenty men of the Tenth Infantry from Fort McKavett improved security at the post, but it did not relieve the concern. Indeed, worry intensified. "Mrs. Cooper," wrote Susan Miles, "walked the floor and wrung her hands." People "tiptoed when passing Mrs. Cooper's quarters, picturing her already in widow's weeds." Several of the women at Fort Concho worried for the future of Katie and little Ned Nolan. Their mother had died in February, and now everyone saw the children as "doubly pitied for their doubly orphaned state."[4]

Then, on August 7, the couriers arrived. Quickly afterward the post's telegrapher wired the good news to Forts Stockton, Griffin, and Richardson. He also sent a similar message to department headquarters in San Antonio. The message, signed by Lieutenant John J. Morrison who was in temporary command of Fort Concho, read in part: "Nolan's command is safe with loss of two men and three missing. Five pack mules and twenty horses lost. Eighty-six hours without water and great suffering."[5]

On the same day, Morrison placed Umbles, Gilmore, and Johnson in the guardhouse. "From the start," writes Susan Miles, he had wondered about their stories. The men, or so Morrison believed, "would have much to explain upon Captain Nolan's return."[6]

Also on August 7, Captain Nolan's command left the supply camp at Bull Creek. Early in the morning Nolan sent Surgeon Joseph H. T. King and Lieutenant Wallace Tear, who had arrived with troops from the Twenty-fifth Infantry out of Fort McKavett, with a four-mule ambulance ahead to Fort Concho, noting that Tear and his troops might be needed at the undermanned post. Then, pursuant to instructions received upon his arrival at the supply camp the day before, Nolan, accompanied by Captain Phillip Lee with Troop G of the Tenth, led his force—with many of the cavalry men on foot or in wagons—south some fifteen miles to the Colorado River. Here the men camped.

On the eighth, Nolan and Lee separated. Lee's Troop G and the Tonkawa scouts with Chief (or Tonkawa) Johnson turned east and headed toward

Fort Griffin. Nolan's Troop A continued south along the Caprock toward Fort Concho. They moved slowly. Six days later, between 8:00 and 9:00 A.M., Nolan, Lieutenant Cooper, and the buffalo soldiers entered their home post. Katie Nolan and her young friend Edith Grierson, daughter of the Tenth Cavalry's colonel, were the first to greet them.[7]

The troopers were "pitiful scarecrows." The men had lost weight, their uniforms (although relatively clean from having been washed a few days previous) were ragged, and they had not recovered fully from the thirsting time. Eyes on some men were still sunken and blood shot, and their skin remained gray colored. They needed rest. Lieutenants Smither and Cooper had not shaved and their "side-whiskers [had] grown out." But the men were back.[8]

Once back, Captain Nolan assumed command of the post. He arrested Sergeant Umbles, Corporal Gilmore, and Privates George W. Fremont and Alexander Nolan and charged them with desertion. He sent Lieutenant Larke with his troops of the Tenth Infantry back to Fort McKavett, and he asked officials at Department of Texas headquarters in San Antonio to plan for the courts-martial of the deserters.

Captain Nolan wanted to press similar charges on other men of his command, including Private Isaac Thompson, but he backed off. Apparently Colonel Benjamin Grierson intervened, and Lieutenant Smither, noting that the troopers' "sufferings must have been terrible," supported the colonel. In a letter to Grierson, Smither reported that "Nolan has released all the men excepting the four mentioned and those he insists upon their being tried."[9]

Private (Lance Corporal) George Fremont, however, insisted the charges against him were unfair. He appealed the charges and asked for a court of inquiry, believing such an action would clear him. Lieutenant Smither indicated that Fremont "does not like to talk on the subject, and feels a little sore over his misfortunes, more than he should." Smither was of the opinion that Fremont ought to have been released from the charges but believed firmly that the others should be tried. Fremont did not get his court of inquiry.[10]

Captain Nolan tried to get the post back to normal. He made sure that his buffalo soldiers got good food and plenty of rest. Quiet and private celebrations occurred, but a failed scouting expedition, one that counted the loss of four men dead and one missing, inspired little cause for public jubilee. Instead, Nolan requested from headquarters horses to replace those lost, gathered evidence and witnesses for a series of courts-martial, attended to the affairs of the post, and prepared his official report of the lost expedition.

In 1978 the group of men shown here, led by Eric Strong, retraced the route taken in 1877 by Troop A of the Tenth Cavalry. Courtesy Lubbock Avalanche-Journal.

At Rath City, in the meantime, the hidemen celebrated. They had returned safely, even Old Bill Benson who was improving and Hi Bickerdyke and Billy Devins who had remained at the supply camp on Bull Creek. They had got their horses back, and the Comanches had returned to the reservation. The bison hunters had accomplished what in May they had set out to do.

In September, as we have seen, the hunters and area cowboys held a large dance, or "ball," to honor their return. "Girls came over from Fort Griffin," writes Naomi H. Kincaid, "riding in the big blue hide wagons." Cadmus Brown provided music with his fiddle, and the hunters and cowboys took turns dancing with the sweet smelling "gals" to such favorite tunes as "Turkey in the Straw" and "Sally Goodins."[11]

Not long afterward, the hidemen, including several who had been with the Forlorn Hope, once again struck out for the bison range. Now, without fear of an Indian attack on their camp sites, they scattered over West Texas from the South Concho River below modern San Angelo northward to the Pease River. Many, in fact, including the famous Mooar brothers, J. Wright and John Wesley, were on the bison range at the very time when Jim Harvey's Forlorn Hope suffered from lack of water.

By late September, perhaps four thousand hunters, skinners, teamsters, and others had scattered over the West Texas plains. Johnny Cook and some of his friends moved to the Big Spring area on the North Concho River and hunted on and east of the Caprock in Howard County. Sam Carr and Thomas L. (George) Causey, the latter one of those who in 1874 had first led hidemen south from Dodge City, moved up Yellow House Canyon to establish a permanent camp in Casas Amarillas. The Englishmen, Harry Burns and Harold Bradstreet, moved south to the painted rocks along the Concho River east of modern San Angelo. Others set up hunting camps along the South Concho, the Double Mountain Forks of the Brazos, and elsewhere south and west of Rath City. Hunters also searched the Texas Panhandle.[12]

For bison hunters on the Southern Plains, the fall and winter of 1877–78 represented the last big hide-gathering season. John R. Cook writes that "during the months of December, 1877, and January, 1878, more than one hundred thousand buffalo-hides" moved through Rath City. Prices dropped. Some hides brought only fifty cents, and as a result Carr and Causey sent some of their hides all the way to Fort Worth in hope of getting better prices.[13]

Nonetheless, Rath City boomed over the winter. "Buffalo hides," writes Jerry Eckhart, "poured into Rath's hideyard until there seemed no end to the prosperity." Perhaps a million dollars' worth of business was done through the winter. "The dancehall rocked to the stomp of the hunters," Eckhart notes with some hyperbole. The "saloons," he mentions, "ran until dawn, and wagon after wagon rolled north to Dodge City" or east to Fort Griffin. It "was a gamy, unwashed place, reeking with the stench of drying buffalo hides . . . but no one minded for the squalor signified money."[14]

By May 1878 conditions had changed. Most bison hunters had abandoned the southern range, and those who remained counted their kills in twos and threes, not the hundreds or even thousands of previous seasons. Some hidemen left for the last bison hunts on the Northern Plains—the lush killing fields west and north of the Black Hills. Some returned east. Some hired themselves out as scouts and guides for the United States Army. Some turned to cattle raising on land they had hunted while gathering bison hides. Some turned to wolf hunting. Some set up small businesses; some became barkeeps.[15]

Rath City's short boom ended. The little supply center and "watering hole" declined rapidly in the late spring of 1878. In the summer, Charles Rath, after a final visit to the place, closed his business and ordered Harvey West to move the remaining stock to Fort Griffin, where Rath and Frank Conrad operated a general merchandise store. Rath himself headed back to Dodge City.

Other businesses closed. George Aiken, one of the saloon owners, freighted his supplies and equipment to Camp Supply in western Indian Territory about one hundred miles south of Dodge City. Others headed for the recently established Mobeetie, located in the Texas Panhandle near Fort Elliott and not far from the abandoned Hide Town (or Sweetwater, as some hunters called it) where Rath and W. M. D. Lee had supplied bison hunters in the eastern Panhandle. Shortly afterward, Rath opened a general merchandise store in Mobeetie. Charlie Sing, the laundryman, was among the last to leave the mesa top community, and, when he and West left the place, "Rath City," writes Jerry Eckhart, "was left to the rain, dust, and wind."[16]

Meanwhile, as the bison hunters in late September 1877 scattered over the Southern Plains, the army court-martialed four men of Captain Nicholas Nolan's lost expedition. Sergeant Umbles, Corporal Gilmore, and Privates Fremont and Nolan, all charged with desertion and related offences, remained in the guardhouse at Fort Concho as Captain Nolan gathered evidence, talked to witnesses, and prepared charges against the men.

The trials occurred at Fort McKavett. Established in 1852 and located near the head of the San Saba River in Menard County, about 75 miles southeast of Fort Concho and 180 miles northwest of San Antonio, the fort was part of a chain of garrisons stretching from the Rio Grande to the Red River. The posts provided safety along the state's western line of settlement. McKavett stood on high ground from which one could observe the surrounding country, and the beautiful upper San Saba provided plenty of fresh water for the post.

In 1877 Fort McKavett, dominated by wood-frame buildings, was a large and busy place. Major Thomas M. Anderson, Tenth Infantry, commanded the garrison. It was headquarters for six companies of the Tenth Infantry, and from time to time troops of the Tenth Cavalry and the Twenty-fifth Infantry also performed duty there.[17]

The trials began on October 15, 1877. Major Anderson served as president of the court, and First Lieutenant E. O. Gibson, Adjutant of the Tenth Infantry, was the court's judge advocate. Members of the court included Captain F. E. Lacey, Lieutenant S. H. Lincoln, and Lieutenant Alured Larke, all of the Tenth Infantry. Two other members, Captains Nathaniel S. Constable and E. B. Atwood, came from the Quartermaster's Department. The officers were all white men. They were trying four African American soldiers, and the black regulars had little influence to ensure a fair trial or to redress their grievances. In the post–Civil War army, as was the case for black soldiers during the war, the "best spokesmen for the black troops," writes Joseph T. Glatthaar, "were their own officers." In this instance, the very officers whose support the four black men needed were the people bringing the charges.[18]

The Tenth Cavalry defendants were a mixed group. William L. Umbles, twenty-seven years old, was an experienced soldier who had served in the Twenty-fifth Infantry for five years before joining the Tenth Cavalry. Just under five feet, seven inches tall and described in his enlistment records as having a "light brown" complexion, Umbles was born in Lynchburg, New York, and worked as a tobacconist before enlisting in the infantry at Cleveland in 1871.[19]

Corporal Charles H. Gilmore and Private (Lance Corporal) George W. Fremont, like Umbles, were experienced soldiers who had been in the service for several years. Described as having black eyes, hair, and complexions and standing under five feet, eight inches tall, they had been day laborers before joining the military. Both had been born in the Upper South but recruited in the North, and both had come to the Tenth Cavalry after serving five years in one of the black infantry regiments. They were in their late twenties. When the expedition had begun back in July, Fremont, who had received an education, was Fort Concho's post librarian. His absence during the month, wrote Susan Miles, inconvenienced "those left behind, for a library was manna to the literate on the frontier."[20]

Private Alexander "Alex" Nolan, from Morgan County, Missouri, joined the Tenth Cavalry in Saint Louis in 1876. Enlistment records, which state that Nolan had black eyes, brown hair, and a "yellow" complexion, show that the twenty-two-year-old recruit was an engineer. At five feet, ten inches in height, he was one of the tallest men in Troop A. He played the bugle and participated in the cavalry band.[21]

The court tried each of the four men separately. Its members questioned witnesses and allowed for cross-examination in one case for a couple of hours, adjourned it until the next day, and moved on to a subsequent case. In such fashion the court moved through six days—Monday through Saturday—of testimony. Witnesses, including Captain Nicholas Nolan, testified in more than one case, and even the defendants testified in one another's trials.

The Umbles and Gilmore trials were the more difficult and complicated. They were also the longer ones, as they required a substantial number of witnesses. Both men faced several charges, each with specifications. The charges and specifications included desertion, lying, theft of government property, and disobedience of orders. Against Private Fremont were charges of theft, absence without leave, and conduct to the prejudice of good order and military discipline. The single charge against Private Nolan was disobedience of orders.[22]

During the trials, First Lieutenant E. O. Gibson, the judge advocate, spoke for the court. He questioned the witnesses and led the cross-examinations. The men on trial handled their own defense, asked questions of the witnesses, and took charge of any cross-examinations. Much of the testimony was repetitious, with each witness giving his own view of the march. In the Umbles trial, for example, both the court and Umbles emphasized events associated with the night of July 27 and the early morning of July 28 at Nigger Hill. Private Isaac Thompson testified that "the Captain said for the men to go and find water if they thought they could find it; . . ." Captain Nolan denied he made such a statement, and the court asked many of the witnesses to describe their own experience that evening, the night of Umbles's and Private Alex Nolan's alleged desertion.

Later in the week, during the defense phase of the trial, Sergeant Umbles placed emphasis on the evening of August 3. Here he called witnesses to testify about his reporting to Fort Concho, his absence to Wilson's saloon and dancehall in Saint Angela, and his request to wait until morning before guiding Lieutenant Robert Smither back to Bull Creek. Umbles, however, admitted that he went to Saint Angela before ten o'clock that evening "and bought a bottle of brandy, took several drinks, and then returned to camp." Leaving the post that night was a bad move, he admitted, but he justified it in his statement by saying he could not sleep and hoped the liquor would relax him.

On Monday, October 22, the seventh and last day of the Umbles trail (the longest trial), the court took a written statement from Sergeant Umbles. The document was a lengthy, but not effective, argument in the sergeant's defense. Lieutenant Gibson, the judge advocate, read the statement and made it part of the court record. Thereupon, Thomas Anderson closed the court and cleared the courtroom for deliberation.

Not long afterward the court presented its decisions. It found the men guilty of nearly all charges and specifications against them. It sentenced each of them to be reduced in rank, to be dishonorably discharged, and to be denied all pay and "allowances due." It also sentenced each man to a lengthy prison term: Umbles to fifteen years, Gilmore to ten, Fremont to eight, and Nolan to four. The sentences, considering the conditions and circumstances of the expedition, seemed far too harsh, or so Brigadier General Edward O. C. Ord, commanding the Department of Texas, reasoned.[23]

Ord on October 26 told the court to "re-assemble." He wanted it to repair "clerical omissions in its records of the cases" of Umbles and Corporal Gilmore. On November 1, the court complied and shortly afterward sent its corrected decisions back to headquarters in San Antonio.[24]

Ord was not finished. During November, with a review board, he further studied the trial transcripts and testimony. In the end, he disapproved some of the court's findings and for each man reduced the prison term. In Fremont's case, for example, Ord reasoned that on at least one specification, "the evidence strongly favors [a different] view." In Umbles's and Gilmore's cases, he argued that for at least one specification in each case, "the findings are not supported by the evidence." Ord reduced the prison terms to two years for Umbles and one year for each of the others. He ordered them to be held in confinement at Fort Concho until such time as they could be moved to Leavenworth Military Prison at Fort Leavenworth, Kansas.[25]

Brigadier General Ord's decision to have a review board study the Fort McKavett trials was not unusual in the Department of Texas. It may have been required. Ord had done it before; he would do it again, most memorably in the 1881 court-martial of Lieutenant Henry O. Flipper, a Tenth Cavalry (Troop A) officer who was the first African American to be graduated from West Point. In the Fort McKavett cases, the uncommon harshness of the original sentences may have triggered Ord's aggressive intervention.

By the time of Ord's directive, dated November 21, 1877, Tenth Cavalry officers had already moved the prisoners back to Fort Concho. Confined to the guardhouse, the four troopers awaited their transfer to Kansas. The courts-martial were over.[26]

With the trial over and the men of Nolan's expedition having recovered, Fort Concho returned to a more normal state. In fact, Lieutenants Robert Smither and Wallace Tear hosted a large party to celebrate the improving conditions. Then, at Thanksgiving, Colonel Benjamin Grierson, who had been gone since early July, returned with his son Charles. It was a happy reunion, not only for the Griersons but also for the entire garrison.[27]

Events in December, perhaps, brought closure to the black troop tragedy. Grierson left for Fort Clark on December 8, and on December 10 the four guardhouse prisoners received their dishonorable discharges. The following day, they began the long journey to Fort Leavenworth, and Mrs. Alice Grierson, writing to her husband, indicated that the men "feel very badly about being dishonorably discharged," but they "don't seem to mind imprisonment so much." Finally, after Christmas, Captain Nicholas Nolan and Lieutenant Charles Cooper with their Troop A completed preparations for leaving the post. They were headed to Fort Sill in Indian Territory. By mid-January 1878, then, nearly everyone associated with the black troop tragedy had left the near-empty post.[28]

As he rode out of Fort Concho in January, Captain Nolan must have been pleased to be leaving the place associated with so much personal and professional pain. His wife's death, his near court-martial in 1875, and the black troop tragedy of 1877 had all centered around the dusty stone and adobe post. As he rode at the head of his command, the route he followed again carried him up the Concho River, along the eastern edge of the Llano Estacado, and past his summer supply camp on Bull Creek. The weather was cooler this time, and little fear existed about water shortages, sunstroke, or Indian attacks.

As he rode north, then, perhaps Nolan pondered his summertime leadership and the choices and decisions that went with it. Or, maybe he didn't. But scholars who have studied Nolan's lost troop expedition, even those afflicted with barely concealed racism, have questioned Nolan's judgment and actions while at the same time finding little fault with the black soldiers of his command.[29]

Others, too, point to problems in Nolan's decision making. J. Evetts Haley, for example, argues that during the scout Nolan made several critical errors in judgment. The first, in Haley's estimation, occurred when Nolan allowed some of his men to leave Double Lakes without filled canteens, "a grievous oversight," writes Haley, "that cannot be attributed to the excitement of leaving. . . ." Among men in the field in 1877, a cardinal rule, one Nolan knew well, prescribed that a man never left a water hole without filling his canteen.[30]

Nolan's second error was his failure after leaving Double Lakes to ration the water. Partly as a result, some of the soldiers were out of water before the first day's march was complete. Official army policy required that men on a march eat and drink sparingly. Nolan knew and understood the policy, but he let his men empty their canteens early.

A third mistake was his decision the next day, July 27, to continue the elusive pursuit of Indians when both his men and their horses were giving out. Haley argues that Nolan "should have headed for water while all were still able to travel and then returned to the trail." Nolan may have known "that he was doing wrong," wrote Alice Grierson to her husband, "but because they court-martialed Capt. [Alexander] Keyes [of Troop D in 1874] for not following Indians, that he went." Perhaps Nolan recalled his own near–court-martial in 1875 for not aggressively giving pursuit while on an Indian trail.[31]

Another error, although it was as much the fault of the bison hunters as the captain, occurred when Nolan refused to strike for the water hole in the Blue Sand Hills because Comanches might be there. Instead, he turned back toward Silver Lake. The hunters should not have submitted to what Cook called Nolan's teary-eyed speech.[32]

Haley, on less solid ground, also faults Nolan for not taking aggressive action against Sergeant Umbles on the night of July 27, the night Umbles and the others passed the command's campsite on Nigger Hill. To Haley the Umbles action represented "open mutiny," and Umbles should have been stopped. Perhaps it was desertion, but at the time Nolan either did not see it that way or was too prostrate to take action.

Besides, Umbles and his group not only rejoined the command at Bull Creek, but they also reached water before Captain Nolan and the main force. In addition, at Silver Lake in preparation for what they thought would be Nolan's arrival, they dug with only knives and their hands a reservoir large enough to hold eight barrels of water. Their actions at Silver Lake and Casas Amarillas do not seem to suggest desertion.

The most fateful error, the most grievous one, was Nolan's insistence on July 28 to abandon the march to Silver Lake for the "new and suicidal course" to Double Lakes. There is no question but that this choice led to disaster. The hidemen knew water could be found at Silver Lake or just beyond at Casas Amarillas, places they had visited previously—especially Casas Amarillas, where they had celebrated Independence Day. But Nolan reasoned—incorrectly, as it turned out—that the guide, José Tafoya, was lost, and he believed that his water detail could not find its way back. Clearly, in this instance, Nolan made the wrong decision.[33]

On the other hand, the surgeon, Joseph King, praised Nolan for getting his men through with a minimum loss of human life. Considering the drought and dry water holes, the extremely hot temperatures, Tafoya's concentration on tracking Comanches at the expense of finding water, and Smith Johnson's failure to get back with water from Silver Lake, Nolan, writes King, had performed satisfactorily. Problems existed, of course, but while they were his responsibility, they were not all always Nolan's fault.[34]

Nonetheless, extant records of the expedition offer additional reasons to question Captain Nolan's leadership. Nolan's official report faults the guide

Tafoya, questions the bison hunters' scouting skills, and blames the command's difficulties on the drought. Nolan, perhaps understandably, admits to no mistakes or weaknesses on his own part—he had, in his view, made all the right decisions.[35]

Conversely, Lieutenant Charles Cooper's letter to his father, written ten days after Nolan had penned his report, admits to being lost, suggests that the command was in disarray, and complains about the changing directions of the scout. Moreover, courts-martial testimony and the reminiscence of John R. Cook suggest that Nolan broke down emotionally and at least temporarily lost control of the command. During the Umbles court-martial, for example, in response to testimony that suggested he was unable to lead, the court asked Nolan about his stability. The court wanted to know if at any time during the scout he was out of his mind from weakness or sickness or if he might have forgotten some of the things he said or did. Nolan, of course, denied such problems.[36]

After reading the Nolan and Cooper versions of the expedition, one gets the impression that during the last leg of the scout, the one beginning at 8:00 P.M. on July 29, Cooper had assumed the dominant role. He rallied the troops and took the lead, and he writes in detail about the last hours. Nolan, after he and Cooper had determined again to march in a new direction (east), writes little. Cook, the bison hunter, writes that about this time one of the buffalo soldiers reassured the troops, inspired Cooper, and harangued Nolan. Neither Cooper nor Nolan mentions the leadership of such a soldier.[37]

One wonders, too, if Nolan and Cooper got along. Trial testimony indicates that at one time during the scout Cooper turned to Nolan and told him the command was lost and it was Nolan's fault. Cooper's letter to his father also indicates that the command was lost and that discipline had broken down. Nolan mentions no such problems. Revealingly, it seems, in his official report of the scout, Nolan speaks well of Captain Phillip Lee, "who rendered me such valuable assistance," and he thanks Surgeon King, Lieutenant Smither, and Lieutenant Tear "for the zeal displayed by them in coming to my relief." He makes no mention of Lieutenant Cooper, the officer who discovered the trail that took the command the last five miles to Double Lakes.[38]

For a twenty-five-year veteran who had been on the Llano Estacado just two years before, Captain Nolan's leadership was hardly sterling. Indeed, had the events of the 1877 expedition occurred in a modern American army, Nolan, rather than his men, might well have been the person court-martialed.

The men, except for those who died and the soldier who went with the bison hunters, all rejoined the command at either Double Lakes or Bull Creek, and court-martial testimony and John Cook's memoir suggest that Nolan had signaled the men to search for water on their own. Clearly, on this scout Nolan was no hero.

If the thirsting time produced a "hero," the person was one of the black regulars. John R. Cook praised a trooper named Barney Howard, but Howard was a quartermaster sergeant who had remained behind at the supply camp on Bull Creek and had not climbed onto the Llano. Cook writes that he got his information from Howard at Fort Concho sometime after the command had returned from its scout. Howard may have been talking about another sergeant, and Cook, writing some thirty years later, may have confused the two. The person about whom Cook wrote may have been Acting First Sergeant Jim Thompson, a dark-skinned trooper who had replaced Umbles as first sergeant. Sergeant Thompson stayed with the command until near its end, when, either under Nolan's orders or on his own account, he and six others took seven of the strongest horses and hurried ahead to Double Lakes. Or, more likely, it was James Jackson, a thirty-one-year-old former laborer from Kentucky who was one of Troop A's blacksmiths. Described as having black eyes, black hair, and a black complexion, he stayed with the command to the end. He was one of only five soldiers who walked in to Double Lakes with Nolan and Cooper.

According to Cook, the real hero, whoever he was, rallied the troops. On the last night out, he reassured Lieutenant Cooper, reminding the lieutenant about "the little black-eyed woman" who waited for him at Fort Concho. He urged Cooper not to peter out, not to worry his wife. He walked "among his weak, discouraged comrades," reported Cook, "and [told] them of the good things in store for them in the future." He cajoled, emboldened, and inspired them. He faced Captain Nolan head on, telling the captain that his constant whining in front of the men did not set a good example.[39]

Extant records do not corroborate Cook's memory about the unknown hero, but neither do they refute it. Surgeon King's report, which is a somewhat strange defense of Nolan—strange because King was not there—and Lieutenant Cooper's letter to his father, which presents a subtly critical view of Nolan, do not help. As noted previously, Nolan wrote little about the last twenty-four hours of the ordeal. Perhaps he could not recall events of that day. Absent records to the contrary, one might assume that a healthy, young trooper remained vigorous enough to rally his fellow soldiers and his commanding officers.

Nicholas M. Nolan remained in command of Troop A for five more years. He moved with his buffalo soldiers from Fort Sill in Indian Territory to Fort Elliott in the Texas Panhandle and then to the Big Bend country of Texas, where he served at Fort Davis. In August of 1878 he married Anne Eleanor Dwyer in San Antonio, and they had one child, a girl. He and Lieutenant Cooper fell out over a long series of minor incidents, including Nolan's denial of leave for Cooper, and in late 1879 Nolan reported Cooper "for failure to forward personal reports." In December 1882 Nolan transferred to the Third Cavalry and received a promotion to major. The transfer took him to Arizona Territory, where in 1883 he died at Holbrook.[40]

Charles L. Cooper, who had participated in the Civil War and joined the Tenth Cavalry in 1870, remained first lieutenant of Troop A until 1882. He then became the regiment's adjutant. A year later he accepted promotion to captain, and in 1898 he transferred to the Fifth Cavalry as major. Not long afterward he became lieutenant colonel of the Fifteenth Cavalry and in 1901 moved to the Fourth Cavalry at the same rank.[41]

The Troop A soldiers had enlisted for five years. Enlistment records for Troop A show that nearly every one of the men who had been on the Llano Estacado during the black troop tragedy served out his full five-year hitch and received an honorable discharge. Records also show that at the end of their service the men received character ratings of "good," "very good," or "excellent." But, few of the men who had been on the 1877 expedition reenlisted. Most who survived the black troop tragedy, in other words, chose to leave military service and seek other employment.

Clearly, the black troop tragedy was a disaster. It cost the lives of four men. It resulted in the loss of nearly thirty horses and mules. Men had scattered supplies, equipment, ammunition, and rations for miles over the trail, and scouting parties never recovered some of the abandoned materials. While the bison hunters, except for Bill Benson, recovered quickly, the black regulars, who had gone longer without water, took longer to regain their health. Weakened from the intense heat and shortage of water, the soldiers, a group of strong, usually disciplined men, became demoralized.

Near the end of the ordeal, the soldiers were in frightful condition and looked awful. Their clothes were dirty and getting ragged. Their faces and clothes were covered with dried blood that they were unable to wash off. Their eyes were sunken and bloodshot, their skin had lost its luster. In addition, their minds had begun to play tricks on them. They could not concentrate, they could barely talk, they could hardly understand others who were talking to them. Many of them struggled to stay on the tracks to Double

Lakes, but some, such as those who died, stumbled, perhaps unknowingly, away from the trail.

The four men who perished were young, recent enlistees with little military experience. John T. Gordon, for example, a twenty-five-year-old recruit who had been born in Norfolk, Virginia, signed up at Baltimore in December 1876. John Isaacs, a twenty-five-year-old former waiter from Baltimore, joined the Tenth in January, 1877. John H. Bonds, a day laborer from Bedford County, Virginia, was twenty-four when in 1876 he enlisted at Washington, D.C. Only Isaac Derwin had been in the army for more than a few months.[42]

The three most recent recruits, none of whom had been on the Llano Estacado previously, probably did not understand as well as the veterans, such as Isaac Thompson and Smith Johnson, the vital need to conserve water in their canteens. If so, they paid a high price for their ignorance—or for the failure of their leaders to ensure that the troops left water sources with full canteens. Isaac Derwin's death may be related to the debilitating sunstroke he suffered, a stroke from which he never fully recovered.

And the Comanches—well, confined to the reservation they shared with the Kiowas and Plains Apaches, they made only a few small raids in 1878, but the government probably blamed them for a few Apache strikes in southwestern Texas. Black Horse, out of prison in Florida, led a hunting party to the Big Spring area, where in late June 1878 trouble occurred between his Comanches and some Texas Rangers. Some of the younger men were able to get passes to hunt for bison on the Llano Estacado, and in June 1878 the Comanches received permission for a large hunt on the Staked Plains. They found a few bison in June, "but subsequent hunts," writes William T. Hagan, "were complete failures." Hagan notes also that in January 1879 federal troops accompanied Comanches on a large hunt in the Texas Panhandle, but it went badly enough that supplies from the reservation and from Fort Elliott had to be sent to the Indian hunting parties.[43]

Quanah, however, was already on his way to dominating Comanche politics. He soon took his mother's family name, and on the reservation he quickly grasped the idea of balancing his Comanche traditions with the dominating power of the federal presence. He "succeeded as chief," writes Hagan, "because of his remarkable talent for seeking out the middle ground." He cultivated white favor without giving up in any fundamental way his Indian heritage, and in turn government agents and Texas cattlemen who wanted to place their longhorns on reservation land sought his support, bribed him with gifts, and encouraged his ascendancy.[44]

In the larger picture of American military action in the Southwest, the black troop tragedy of 1877 made little lasting impact. Its raw brutality and its agonizing, sensational story of survival against great odds captured national interest. In Texas, stories about the expedition appeared in San Antonio, Houston, and Galveston newspapers. Nationally, papers in New York, Saint Louis, Chicago, and elsewhere, carried pieces on the tragedy. The *Atlanta Daily Constitution* covered it under a small banner that read, "A Captain, Lieutenant and Twenty Soldiers Lost."[45]

Soon, though, Americans focused their concerns elsewhere. The Nez Perce difficulties in Idaho and Montana, for example, received nationally much more space than did the black troop tragedy. And in Texas federal troops scoured the Rio Grande border, and several times in 1877 and 1878 they crossed into Mexico, turning everyone's attention in that direction, especially after Congressmen in the nation's capital accused Department of Texas military leaders of trying to start a war with Mexico.[46]

About the same time, Apache activities in the Southwest led the army to concentrate large numbers of troops in Arizona and New Mexico. The action further drained the great Texas interior of government soldiers, and soon, except along the Rio Grande, the state became something of a military backwater.

The black troop tragedy receives little attention in the larger histories. It is not mentioned in Comanche histories or even biographies of Quanah Parker. Military histories that include events in West Texas give it only passing attention, and no biography of Nicholas Nolan has appeared. Some histories of the Texas bison hunter experience cover it, granted, but they follow John R. Cook's flawed memoirs. Neither Billy Dixon nor Frank Collinson, who wrote about it as if they had participated, was part of the Forlorn Hope. W. S. Glenn, another bison hunter turned author, also knew of it only secondhand.

On a more local level, the black troop tragedy gets some, but not much, attention in the better county histories. As a result, many modern residents of areas through which the hunters and soldiers passed in 1877 remain only vaguely aware of the tragedy's history. Besides, cattlemen, who dominate the interest and the histories of West Texans, came hard on the heels of the bison hunters, driving their large longhorn herds onto the high tableland. Settlers were not far behind. Towns, such as Estacado on the Crosby-Lubbock County line, appeared, and soon freighting and stage coaching operations crisscrossed West Texas and pushed up against the Llano Estacado's eastern Caprock. In the excitement of other developments, then, Captain Nolan's expedition got brushed aside.

Still, the black troop tragedy was high drama. And it is remembered in the legends and folklore of the Llano Estacado. In July of 1978, for example, eight African American men, led by Eric Strong from the Lubbock-based Roots Historical Committee, commemorated the event. The enterprising young men gathered supplies and equipment, gained permission from landowners to cross private property, and as best they could retraced the route that one hundred years earlier Captain Nolan and his buffalo soldiers had followed. They camped each night at a spot, including Nigger Hill, as close as they could determine to where the black soldiers had stopped a century earlier.[47]

Traveling briefly with Strong and the others was Elmer Kelton, one of America's finest western writers. At the time, Kelton was working on *The Wolf and the Buffalo,* his majestic western novel that wrestles with fate, chance meetings, and the differing world views that influence a young Comanche warrior and a Tenth Cavalry soldier as their cultures cross in the West. For Kelton, it was a research trip, and the experiences became lessons for use in crafting at least two exciting chapters—both remarkably faithful to the expedition's history—in the highly acclaimed book.

In the end, events associated with the black troop tragedy mattered to few people. Pressed by food and material shortages, the Comanches, after the Red River War of 1874–75, bent to agency and government wishes. Most of them stayed on the reservation. Except for a few groups, such as Troop A, black regulars in 1877 engaged in activities far more dangerous and significant than chasing Comanches on the Llano Estacado should have been. With an estimated four thousand hidemen, skinners, teamsters, and others on the bison ranges of the Southern Plains in late 1877, the twenty-four members of Jim Harvey's Forlorn Hope represented only a fraction of all hide-gathering activity.

Finally, then, while it was a dramatic affair, the black troop tragedy—the Staked Plains Horror, as newspapers called it—was not a turning point of any time-honored kind. For several days, nonetheless, it captured national attention, and in that sense it became a national tragedy. In many ways, moreover, it was unique. During a few days in July, it brought Comanches, bison hunters, and buffalo soldiers together in ways that had not occurred previously and would not—could not—occur again.

Dramatis Personae

Sources: John R. Cook, *The Border and the Buffalo* (Topeka, Kans.: Crane & Co., 1907); Registers of Enlistments in the United States Army, 1798–1914, Volumes 76–77, 1871–1877, Roll 40, Microcopy No. 233; Records of United States Army Commands, Record Group, 98, National Archives.

BISON HUNTERS: "THE FORLORN HOPE"

Jim Harvey—captain of the bison hunter group; veteran of the Fourth Cavalry

Bill Benson—stayed with buffalo soldiers; went ninety-six hours without water; later a wolf hunter in New Mexico

Harry Burns—Scotsman, poet; hunters thought him related to the poet Robert Burns

Harold Bradstreet—Englishman

Samuel Carr—big, stout fellow; excellent horse trainer

John R. Cook—assistant guide and interpreter; historian of the "Forlorn Hope"

George Cornett—a Texan, "raised on the northern frontier"; excellent tracker; one of the "Johnny Rebs"

Henry Deacon—a bison-hunting partner of Hi Bickerdyke

Charles "Squirrel-eye" Emory—a Texan and former Confederate soldier; his left eye was clouded over

Joe Freed—third in command in the Yellow House Canyon fight

Jim Foley—former Union soldier; rode out to greet the soldiers on July 17 at the Bull Creek camp site

Powderface Hudson—a good singer

Mortimer N. "Wild Bill" Kress—big, generous, warm-hearted; was judge at the July 4 celebration at Casas Amarillas; went to 1876 Philadelphia world fair with Sol Rees

Louis Keyes—part-Cherokee, part-Mexican, part-Anglo; troopers called him "a Mexican guide"; served as interpreter

John "Jack" Mathias—humorous, cheerful; a "clarion voice"

Frank Perry—lost his horse and with Kress, Harvey, and Williams on July 28 drifted southeast, nearly missing Casas Amarillas

Solomon "Sol" Rees—in charge of medical supplies; excellent Indian tracker; later became a successful rancher; went to the 1876 Philadelphia world fair with Bill Kress

Tom Sherman—a young, lovesick "womanizer"

José Piedad Tafoya—guide and former comanchero who knew the Llano Estacado's trails and waterholes

Alfred "Alt" Waite—tall, thin

Dick Wilkinson—the chief packer, in charge of the mules

George Williams—lost his horse, drifted southeast

Hiram "Hi" Bickerdyke—remained at supply camp along Bull Creek to guard the wagons and supplies

Billy Devins—remained at the supply camp with Bickerdyke and twenty black regulars led by Sergeant Thomas Allsup

BUFFALO SOLDIERS

Black regulars of Troop A, Tenth Cavalry, known to be members of the forty-man troop that left Bull Creek supply camp on July 19.

Noncommissioned Officers

First Sergeant William L. Umbles—court-martialed

Acting First Sergeant James Thompson—on last night out, led six other men away from command to Double Lakes

Corporal William H. Barney—one of the straggling soldiers on the night of July 27

Corporal Charles H. Gilmore—court-martialed, went with William Umbles to Fort Concho

Corporal Elias Roberts—one of the straggling soldiers on the night of July 27

Lance Corporal George W. Fremont—court-martialed

Privates

Stephen Baldwin—one of the troopers who got sick on the night of July 27 and later left the command with Private Cox

John H. Bonds—died

Blacksmith Carson—on water detail, with Henry Miller brought water to bison hunters Harvey, Kress, Perry, and Williams, thereby perhaps saving their lives

Walter D. Cox—rode away from command with Private Baldwin and joined Umbles at Punta del Agua

William Davis—deserted in 1879

Isaac Derwin—died after leaving command with Corporal Fremont and Private Gaddie

William A. Dobbin—later promoted to corporal

William Fletcher—"very good" character

Stephen Floyd—blacksmith; straggled on night of July 27

Jerry R. Freeman—on water detail; thirty-six years old, but a recent recruit to the Tenth Cavalry

John A. Gaddie—one of the chief packers; one of the soldiers who fell behind on the night of July 27; later left the command with Private Derwin and Corporal Fremont

John T. Gordon—died

Johnson Graves—one of many soldiers who suffered from sunstroke; his life perhaps saved by Private James Jackson

Higgins—one of many soldiers who suffered from sunstroke

John Isaacs—died

James Jackson—blacksmith; may have been the hero who rallied the men and officers on the last leg of the expedition

Dover Johnson

Smith Johnson—led water detail; had been on Llano Estacado in 1875; went with William Umbles to Fort Concho

William Johnson—thirty-three years old when he joined Tenth in 1877

Pierce Kuston—on water detail

Henry C. Miller—on water detail; with Blacksmith Carson provided water to bison hunters Harvey, Kress, Perry, and Williams, thereby perhaps saving their lives

Frank Neal

Jerry Nichols

Alexander Nolan—court-martialed; bugler

John Peterson—on water detail; may have split off with the bison hunters
Rose—one of many soldiers who suffered from sunstroke
Isaac Thompson—one of the two chief packers; with Umbles, had been on Llano Estacado in 1875
Edward T. Western

Troopers known to have been at the Bull Creek supply camp

First Sergeant Thomas Allsup
Quartermaster Sergeant Barney Howard
Sergeant John Fry
Private Green Johnson

Troop A, Tenth Cavalry, soldiers who may have been members of either the 40-man expedition or assigned to the supply camp at Bull Creek

Noncommissioned Officers
Sergeant George W. Ford—a "most excellent" character
Sergeant Richard L. Johnson—a "good" character
Corporal Isaac Fry—a "good" character

Privates
Charles Dixon, James Davel, John F. Dorsey, Thomas C. Dyson, John W. Fields, William Freeman, Frank Fry, Robert Guggs, Joshua Inglis, Frank Johnson, Thomas Johnson, Charles Lyles, Taylor Nichols, Samuel Poke, Thomas Smith, Aaron Walker, and Robert Young

(Privates Nichols and Young were in the hospital on July 10 and may not have reported out in time to join Captain Nolan's sixty-man squad that left Fort Concho that day.)

Band Members (all privates)

Rodolphus Boom, David Dillon, William Freeman, Jefferson Fuller, John Gaddis, and Charles Person

Notes

CHAPTER 1. LAND OF SUNSHINE AND SPACE

1. C. U. Connellee, "Some Experiences of a Pioneer Surveyor," *West Texas Historical Association Year Book* 6 (1930): 93.
2. See, for example, the *Galveston Daily News,* Aug. 9, 1877; *New York Times,* Aug. 9, 1877; *Saint Louis Globe-Democrat,* Aug. 9, 1877; *Atlanta Daily Constitution,* Aug. 7, 1877; *San Antonio Herald,* Aug. 7, 1877; and New York *Daily Tribune,* September 8, 1877.
3. William R. Shafter to J. H. Taylor, Asst. Adj. Gen., Dept. of Texas, Jan. 4, 1876, in M. L. Crimmins, ed. "Shafter's Exploration in Western Texas, 1875," *West Texas Historical Association Year Book* 9 (Oct., 1933): 82–96. See also William Curry Holden, *Rollie Burns,* 134–35; and W. C. Holden, "The Land," in Lawrence Graves, ed., *A History of Lubbock,* I: 36.
4. See, for example, Fayette Copeland, *Kendall of the Picayune,* 75; Connellee, "Some Experiences of a Pioneer Surveyor," 91–94.
5. John R. Cook, *The Border and the Buffalo,* 252; Connellee, "Some Experiences of a Pioneer Surveyor," 93.
6. See, for example, Holden, *Rollie Burns,* 168–70; and Dan Flores, *Horizontal Yellow: Nature and History in the Near Southwest,* 259–60.
7. Quoted in Lan Franks (Don H. Biggers), *History That Will Never be Repeated,* 69–70. See also Historical marker, Canyon View Road, Buddy Holly Recreation Area, Lubbock, Texas; Dan Flores, *Caprock Canyonlands: Journeys into the Heart of the Southern Plains,* 58; Rex Strickland, ed., "The Recollections of W. S. Glenn, Buffalo Hunter," *Panhandle-Plains Historical Review* 22 (1949): 15–64; Walter Posey and J. Evetts Haley, interview with W. C. Holden, July 21, 1949, transcript in Southwest Collection, Texas Tech University; Connellee, "Some Experiences of a Pioneer Surveyor," 92.
8. See Holden, "The Land," 13; Connellee, "Some Experiences of a Pioneer Surveyor," 93.
9. Holden, "The Land," 11–12; Shafter to Taylor, Jan. 4, 1876, in Crimmins, ed., "Shafter's Exploration in Western Texas, 1875," 82–96; Albert Pike, *Prose Sketches and Poems Written in the Western Country,* 53. George Wilkins Kendall of the Texan-Santa Fe expedition in 1842 made note of a large "prairie-dog town" on the Llano, and other early travelers likewise reported the presence of the busy little animal. See, for example, Copeland, *Kendall of the Picayune,* 72.
10. Shafter to Taylor, Jan. 4, 1876, in Crimmins, ed., "Shafter's Exploration in Western Texas, 1875," 82–96.
11. See Frederick W. Rathjen, *The Texas Panhandle Frontier,* 2–6; and John Miller Morris, *El Llano Estacado: Exploration and Imagination on the High Plains of Texas and New Mexico, 1536–1860,* 28, 47–49, 53–54.

12. Elvis E. Fleming, "'Buffalo Soldiers' and Buffalo Hunters: The Story of 'Nigger Hill,'" *Southwest Heritage* 3 (1973): 26; U.S. Dept. of War, "Map of the Country Scouted by Colonels Mackenzie and Shafter, Capt. R. P. Wilson and Others in the Years 1874 and 1875," drawn by Alex. L. Lucas, 2832 Adjutant General's Office 1876, Record Group 94, National Archives (hereafter Lucas Map). See also Vance T. Holliday, *Paleoindian: Geoarchaeology of the Southern High Plains,* 2–3.
13. Shafter to Taylor, Jan. 4, 1876, in Crimmins, ed., "Shafter's Explorations in Western Texas, 1875," 87, 91.
14. Holden quotes from Holden, "The Land," 7–8; Shafter to Taylor, Jan. 4, 1876, in Crimmins, ed., "Shafter's Explorations in Western Texas, 1875," 86, 87, 91, 93.
15. Holden, "The Land," 7.
16. O. W. Williams, "From Dallas to the Site of Lubbock in 1877," *West Texas Historical Association Year Book* 15 (1939): 11; Ernest Wallace, *Ranald S. Mackenzie on the Texas Frontier,* 69–72.
17. Shafter to Taylor, Jan. 4, 1876, in Crimmins, ed., "Shafter's Explorations in Western Texas, 1875," 92.
18. Ibid.
19. Ibid., 87; Baldwin quote in L. F. Sheffy, ed., "Letters and Reminiscences of General Theodore A. Baldwin: Scouting after Indians on the Plains of West Texas," *Panhandle-Plains Historical Review* 11 (1938): 7–30; Cook quote from Cook, *The Border and the Buffalo,* 208; Collinson quote from Frank Collinson, *Life in the Saddle,* 110. Casas Amarillas also gave its name to the shallow draw (Yellow House) that, downstream at Mackenzie Park in Lubbock, joined Blackwater Draw (but variously called Cañon del Rescate and Thompson's Canyon). Such early travelers as Albert Pike and such military maps as the 1876 Lucas Map refer to the wide, deep gulf that extends from Mackenzie Park to its mouth near Post as Cañon del Rescate, but most people today call it Yellow House Canyon.
20. Shafter to Taylor, Jan. 4, 1876, in Crimmins, ed., "Shafter's Explorations in Western Texas, 1875," 87. See also Collinson, *Life in the Saddle,* 110.
21. Shafter to Taylor, Jan. 4, 1876, in Crimmins, ed., "Shafter's Explorations in Western Texas, 1875," 86–87; Lucas Map; Officer's quote in Sheffy, ed., "Letters and Reminiscences of General Theodore A. Baldwin: Scouting after Indians on the Plains of West Texas," 8–12.
22. Shafter to Taylor, Jan. 4, 1876, in Crimmins, ed., "Shafter's Explorations in Western Texas, 1875," 88.
23. Ibid.
24. Edna Clark Miller, "Mushaway (Mucha-Que) Peak," *Permian Historical Annual* 15 (1975): 7–14; David J. Murrah, "Mushaway or Muchaque? A Hill by Any Other Name. . . ," *The Cyclone,* Newsletter of the West Texas Historical Association 7, August 15, 2000, 1–2.
25. Shafter to Taylor, Jan. 4, 1876, in Crimmins, ed., "Shafter's Explorations in Western Texas, 1875," 91.
26. The official itinerary of the scout is in Shafter to J. H. Taylor, Asst. Adj. Gen. Dept. of Texas, Sept. 29, 1875, Selected Letters Received Relating to Texas, 1875–76, Adjuntant General's Office, National Archives (photocopy in William R. Shafter Papers, Southwest Collection, Texas Tech University). But see also William H. Leckie, *The Buffalo Soldiers: A Narrative of the Negro Cavalry in the West,* 143–46; Paul H. Carlson, *"Pecos Bill": A Military Biography of William R. Shafter,* 1, 79–82; Sheffy, ed., "Letters and Reminiscences of General Baldwin," 11–16.
27. Shafter to Taylor, Jan. 4, 1876, in Crimmins, ed., "Shafter's Explorations in West-

ern Texas, 1875," 95; Testimony of Private Isaac Thompson, Tenth Cavalry, in Proceedings of a General Court Martial (Sergeant William Umbles, Tenth Cavalry) convened at Fort McKavitt, Texas, October 15, 1877, by virtue of Special Orders No. 169, September 26, 1877, Headquarters, Department of Texsas, San Antonio, Texas; Lucas Map.

28. Shafter to Taylor, Jan. 4, 1876, in Cimmins, ed., "Shafter's Explorations in Western Texas, 1875," 90; Flores, *Caprock Canyonlands,* 89; Miller, "Mushaway (Mucha–Que) Peak," 7–14; Murrah, "Mushaway or Muchaque?" 1–2.
29. Early maps, including the Lucas Map, show Cañon del Rescate extending from its mouth near modern Post, through Buffalo Springs to modern Lubbock (where it is joined by Yellow House draw in Mackenzie Park), and then north and west up Blackwater Draw. In 1877, however, the bison hunters knew the lower Rescate, including the modern community of Ransom Canyon, as Yellow House Canyon, and they referred to Blackwater Draw as Thompson's Canyon. See Lucas Map; Cook *The Border and the Buffalo,* 208–209, 225; Pike, *Prose Sketches,* 40–57.
30. See, for example, Flores, *Caprock Canyonlands,* 49.
31. See, for example, Morris, *El Llano Estacado,* 4–5; and Rathjen, *The Texas Panhandle Frontier,* 15–18.

CHAPTER 2. BISON HUNTERS AND RATH CITY IN 1877

1. J. Wright Mooar, "Frontier Experiences of J. Wright Mooar," *West Texas Historical Association Year Book* 4 (1929): 91–92. Among the audience in Abilene's Carnegie Library that March 14 afternoon were Walter Prescott Webb, Rupert N. Richardson, Carl Coke Rister, William Curry Holden, Albert B. Thomas, Charles W. Ramsdell, J. Marvin Hunter, and R. C. Crane, all of whom became published and highly respected historians.
2. Dodge quote in E. Douglas Branch, *The Hunting of the Buffalo,* 196–97; Jim McIntire, *Early Days in Texas: A Trip to Hell and Heaven,* 224, but also see 103; Herman Lehmann, *Nine Years with the Indians, 1870–1879: The Story of the Captivity and Life of a Texan Among the Indians,* 170–71.
3. J. Wright Mooar to John Wesley Mooar, Feb. 22, 1872, in John Wesley Mooar Papers (Mooar Papers), Box 1, Correspondence, Notes, etc., 1871–1879 (Correspondence), Southwest Collection (SWC), Texas Tech University (TTU). See also John W. Combs to John Wesley Mooar, Jan. 29, 1872, in the same collection.
4. Frederick W. Rathjen, *The Texas Panhandle Frontier,* 121–22; Ty Cashion, *A Texas Frontier: The Clear Fork Country and Fort Griffin, 1849–1887,* 114–15; C. Robert Haywood, *Trails South: The Wagon-Road Economy in the Dodge City-Panhandle Region,* 129; Mari Sandoz, *The Buffalo Hunters,* 88–89; Andrew C. Isenberg, *The Destruction of the Bison,* 132–34; Branch, *The Hunting of the Buffalo,* 151–53; James Winford Hunt, ed., "Buffalo Days: The Chronicle of an Old Buffalo Hunter, J. Wright Mooar," *Holland's: The Magazine of the South* 52 (January 1933): 13, 24; Carl Coke Rister, *Fort Griffin on the Texas Frontier,* 166–67; Wayne Gard, *The Great Buffalo Hunt,* 90–91, 96–97.
5. John Wesley Mooar to "Sister," July 7, 1874, in Mooar Papers, Correspondence, SWC, TTU; Mooar, "Frontier Experiences of J. Wright Mooar," 89–92; Rathjen, *The Texas Panhandle Frontier,* 123–25, 131–32; Gard, *The Great Buffalo Hunt,* 133–35, 138–40.
6. Mooar to "Sister," July 7, 1874, in Mooar Papers, SWC, TTU; Cashion, *A Texas Frontier,* 90, 165–67; Rister, *Fort Griffin on the Texas Frontier,* 170–71.

7. Mooar, "Frontier Experiences of J. Wright Mooar," 90–91.
8. Donald F. Schofield, *Indians, Cattle, Ships and Oil: The Story of W. M. D. Lee,* 39–40.
9. R. C. Crane, "King of Them All," *Amarillo Sunday News-Globe,* Golden Anniversary Edition, Aug. 14, 1938, Sec. D, 1; J. Evetts Haley, "The Rath Trail," *San Angelo Standard-Times,* May 16, 1948. Willis Glenn, a bison hunter, said "some forty women" followed Rath south, but that is unlikely. See Rex Strickland, ed., "The Recollections of W. S. Glenn, Buffalo Hunter," 45, 50. See also Naomi H. Kincaid, "Rath City," *West Texas Historical Association Year Book* 24 (1948): 40–41, 44; Rister, *Fort Griffin on the Texas Frontier,* 172–73; Cashion, *A Texas Frontier,* 176–77; and Haywood, *Trails South,* 130.
10. For first-hand descriptions of Rath City see John R. Cook, *The Border and the Buffalo,* 188, 242; O. W. Williams, "From Dallas to the Site of Lubbock in 1877," *West Texas Historical Association Year Book* 15 (1939): 20; and Kincaid, "Rath City," 40, 44. See also Sandoz, *The Buffalo Hunters,* 289–90; Jerry Eckhart, "Rath City: Texas Hide Town," *True West* 39 (September 1992): 42–45; Gary Ford, "Rath City: A Brief but Important Time in History," *"Back to Rath's Trail" Souvenir Section 2000,* June 2–4, 2000, 2–3; and Cashion, *A Texas Frontier,* 167–77.
11. See for example, Kincaid, "Rath City," 46; and Rister, *Fort Griffin on the Texas Frontier,* 174.
12. Quote in Kincaid, "Rath City," 40–41. See also Eckhart, "Rath City: Texas Hide Town," 42; Ford, "Rath City: A Brief but Important Time in History," 2; and Rister, *Fort Griffin on the Texas Frontier,* 173–74.
13. Rister, *Fort Griffin on the Texas Frontier,* 174. For a different version, see Kincaid, "Rath City," 46. See also Sandoz, *The Buffalo Hunters,* 315.
14. Bryan cited in Kincaid, "Rath City," 46.
15. Quote in McIntire, *Early Days in Texas,* 60; Cashion, *A Texas Frontier,* 177–78.
16. Cook refers to the store manager as George West, but this is an error of memory. West had been associated with W. M. D. Lee in Mobeetie and Camp Supply. See Cook, *The Border and the Buffalo,* 180, 190, 239, 244; Schofield, *Indians, Cattle, Ships, and Oil,* 40.
17. Eckhart, "Rath City: Texas Hide Town," 43; Cashion, *A Texas Frontier,* 182–83.
18. John Wesley Mooar to J. Wright Mooar, July 15, 1879, in Louise Mooar, "The Mooar Brothers and Adobe Walls," 7–8, typescript in Miss Lydia Louise Mooar Collection, Mooar Family Papers, Box 2, Correspondence, 1971, Literary Productions, undated (Mooar Collection), SWC, TTU; Cashion, *A Texas Frontier,* 182–83.
19. Louise Mooar, "The Mooar Brothers and Adobe Walls," 51, typescript in Mooar Collection, SWC, TTU; Cashion, *A Texas Frontier,* 181.
20. For first-hand accounts of the Yellow House Canyon fight see Frank Collinson, *Life in the Saddle,* 101–106; Strickland, ed., "The Recollections of W. S. Glenn, Buffalo Hunter," 42–63; and Cook, *The Border and the Buffalo,* 205–232. See also Rathjen, *The Texas Panhandle Frontier,* 135–36, 224n. 95. Perhaps the best brief accounts are William C. Griggs, "The Battle of Yellowhouse Canyon in 1877," *West Texas Historical Association Year Book* 51 (1975): 37–50; and Preston Lewis, "Bluster's Last Stand: The Battle of Yellowhouse Canyon," *True West* 39, Part I (April 1992): 14–18; Part II (May 1992): 20–25.
21. Cook, *The Border and the Buffalo,* 201, 233–34.
22. Ibid., 232–34. Most accounts of the affair follow Cook; see, for example, Sandoz, *The Buffalo Hunters,* 280–81. For a different version of Lumpkin's death, see

Kincaid, "Rath City," 46, whose source is the diary of Sam Allen, which, in turn, suggests that Lumpkin died in a gun fight with a bison hunter named Murphy, a fight that resulted after a poker game went sour. For the name "Lumpkin" see Karen Keeley, a Lumpkin relative, to Bob Johnson, January 13, 2000, in Records, Back to Rath's Trail Museum, Hamlin, Texas.

23. See Leckie, *The Buffalo Soldiers*, 155–56.
24. Thomas T. Smith, *The Old Army in Texas: A Research Guide to the U.S. Army in Nineteenth-Century Texas*, 161; Regimental Returns, Tenth Cavalry, May–June, 1877, Adjutant General's Office (AGO), Department of War, Record Group (RG) 94, National Archives (NA); Leckie, *The Buffalo Soldiers*, 155–56; Cook, *The Border and the Buffalo*, 232–40.
25. Cook does not always have his dates correct or facts in order and sometimes—probably often—he exaggerates. See Wilbur S. Nye, *Carbine and Lance: The Story of Old Fort Sill*, 117 and 235; J. Evetts Haley, *Fort Concho and the Texas Frontier*, 327–28; Ernest Wallace and E. Adamson Hoebel, *Comanches: Lords of the South Plains*, 328; Arrell Morgan Gibson, "The St. Augustine Prisoners," *Red River Valley Historical Review* 3 (Spring 1978): 259, 265, 268, 270.
26. Cook, *The Border and the Buffalo*, 241–46.
27. Ibid., 246; Ernest Wallace, ed., "The Journal of Ranald S. Mackenzie's Messenger to the Kwahadi Comanches," *Red River Valley Historical Review* 3 (Spring 1978): 235, 235n 16; Ernest Wallace, *Ranald S. Mackenzie on the Texas Frontier*, 67, 130, 147 n7, map facing 66, map facing 146; U.S. Department of War, "Map of the Country Scouted by Colonels Mackenzie and Shafter, Capt. R. P. Wilson and others in the Years 1874 and 1875," drawn by Alex.L. Lucas, 2832 AGO 1876, RG 94, NA. See also post cards, photocopies, and miscellaneous materials in Silver Falls, Reference File, SWC, TTU.
28. Cook, *The Border and the Buffalo*, 246–47.
29. Ibid., 248–49.
30. Ibid., 248, 293.

CHAPTER 3. COMANCHES AND SETTLERS IN 1877

1. Belknap quote cited in Ty Cashion, *A Texas Frontier*, 26; other quotes in William Curry Holden, *Alkali Trails or Social and Economic Movements of the Texas Frontier, 1846–1900*, 228–229. See also T. R. Fehrenbach, *Lone Star: A History of Texas and Texans*, 555, 565, 605, 611.
2. "Treaty with the Comanche and Kiowa, 1865," in Charles J. Kappler, comp., *Indian Affairs: Laws and Treaties*, II: 893.
3. "Treaty with the Comanche and Kiowa, 1867," in Ibid., II: 980; Thomas W. Kavanagh, *Comanche Political History: An Ethnohistorical Perspective, 1706–1875*, 464. For a different view, see Rathjen, *The Texas Panhandle Frontier*, 122.
4. W. S. Nye, *Carbine and Lance: The Story of Old Fort Sill*, 190; Kavanagh, *Comanche Political History*, 437, 448, 472, 476.
5. Nye, *Carbine and Lance*, 177, 235, 238; Haley, *Fort Concho and the Texas Frontier*, 327–28.
6. Rupert Norval Richardson, *Comanche Barrier to South Plains Settlement*, 190–92; Nye, *Carbine and Lance*, 189–91; Kavanagh, *Comanche Political History*, 445–46; Rathjen, *The Texas Panhandle Frontier*, 127.
7. See Rathjen, *The Texas Panhandle Frontier*, 127–31; T. Lindsay Baker and Billy R. Harrison, *Adobe Walls: The History and Archeology of the 1874 Trading Post*, 50–

74; Wallace, *Ranald S. Mackenzie on the Texas Frontier,* 120–22; Kavanagh, *Comanche Political History,* 446–47; William T. Hagan, *Quanah Parker, Comanche Chief,* 12–13.

8. Wallace, *Ranald S. Mackenzie on the Texas Frontier,* 138–46; Robert M. Utley, *Frontier Regulars: The United States Army and the Indian, 1866–1890,* 219–33; William T. Hagan, *United States—Comanche Relations: The Reservation Years,* 108–19; James L. Haley, *The Buffalo War: The History of the Red River Indian Uprising of 1874,* 178–83.
9. Richardson, *Comanche Barrier to South Plains Settlement,* 197–201; Ernest Wallace, ed., "The Journal of Ranald S. Mackenzie's Messenger to the Kwahadi Comanches," *Red River Valley Historical Review* 3 (Spring, 1978): 227–46; Hagan, *United States-Comanche Relations,* 112–13; Hagan, *Quanah Parker, Comanche Chief,* 12–15.
10. "Report of P. H. Hunt, August 30, 1879," in *Annual Report of the Commissioner of Indian Affairs, 1879,* 171, as cited in Charles L. Kenner, *The Comanchero Frontier: A History of New Mexican-Plains Indian Relations,* 209; Hagan, *United States Comanche Relations,* 124.
11. Hagan, *United States Comanche Relations,* 122.
12. Ibid., 133. See also Kavanagh, *Comanche Political History,* 472–73.
13. The number who left the reservation is unknown. There may have been some twenty-five Comanche warriors with their familes plus some Cheyenne warriors with their familes who, once on the Llano Estacado, were joined by some Mescalero Apaches from New Mexico who were there to find comancheros. The total may have reached 170 Indian people, but the figure comes from John R. Cook, who did not always remember details correctly. Cook, in fact, wrote that 170 warriors with their families had left the reservation, a figure far too high. See Lewis, "Bluster's Last Stand," Part I, 14–18; Cook, *The Border and the Buffalo,* 181, 183.
14. Lehmann, *Nine Years with the Indians,* 171; Cook, *The Border and the Buffalo,* 181–83, 188.
15. Quote in Lehmann, *Nine Years with the Indians,* 171; Cook, *The Border and the Buffalo,* 181–83, 192–95. See also Sandoz, *The Buffalo Hunters,* 265–71; and for a slightly different version see Griggs, "The Battle of Yellowhouse Canyon in 1877," 38–39.
16. Lehmann, *Nine Years with the Indians,* 171–72.
17. Ibid.; Cook, *The Border and the Buffalo,* 204.
18. Lehmann, *Nine Years with the Indians,* 173.
19. Ibid., 173–74. For the hunters' point of view see Cook, *The Border and the Buffalo,* 204–32; Frank Collinson, *Life in the Saddle,* 101–106; Rex W. Strickland, ed., "The Recollections of W. S. Glenn, Buffalo Hunter," 42–63. See also Griggs, "The Battle of Yellowhouse Canyon in 1877," 37–50; Lewis, "Bluster's Last Stand," Part I, 14–18, Part II, 20–25; and Rathjen, *The Texas Panhandle Frontier,* 224, n95.
20. Lehmann, *Nine Years with the Indians,* 174–75.
21. Ibid., 185.
22. Ibid., 185–86; Leckie, *The Buffalo Soldiers,* 156; Cook, *The Border and the Buffalo,* 235–39; Thomas T. Smith, *The Old Army in Texas: A Research Guide to the U.S. Army in Nineteenth-Century Texas,* 161. Captain Lee reported four Indians dead.
23. Lehmann, *Nine Years with the Indians,* 185–86.
24. Quote in Wallace and Hoebel, *The Comanches,* 328. See also Keith R. Owen,

"Doans: The Birth and Death of a Frontier Town," *West Texas Historical Association Year Book* 71 (1995): 84–95.

25. Roy Riddle, "Casimero Romero Reigned as Benevolent Don in Brief Pastoral Era," *Amarillo Sunday Globe-News,* Golden Anniversary Edition, Aug. 14, 1938, Section C, 29; Jose Ynocencio Romero, "Spanish Sheepmen on the Canadian at Old Tascosa," ed. Ernest R. Archambeau, *Panhandle-Plains Historical Review* 19 (1946): 46–48; Edward N. Wentworth, *America's Sheep Trails: History, Personalities,* 118–20.
26. Rathjen, *The Texas Panhandle Frontier,* 80–82. One of the ranchers who followed Goodnight was W. M. D. Lee, the wealthy freighter and bison hide buyer who had been a partner with Charles Rath. In 1882, Lee, with plenty of money in his pocket, rode down the river and bought out one pastore after another to establish his own ranches across the Canadian River Valley. See Schofield, *Indians, Cattle, Ships and Oil,* 53.
27. O. W. Williams, "From Dallas to the Site of Lubbock in 1877," *West Texas Historical Association Year Book* 15 (1939): 3, 6, 10–11; For Hank Smith's story see W. Hubert Curry, *Sun Rising on the West: The Saga of Henry Clay and Elizabeth Smith,* 1–3, 141–62.
28. Williams, "From Dallas to the Site of Lubbock in 1877,", 8; Owen, "Doans," 85–94.
29. Williams, "From Dallas to the Site of Lubbock in 1877," 9, 10.
30. Ibid., 11.
31. Ibid.
32. Ibid., 13.
33. Ibid., 14; Cook, *The Border and the Buffalo,* 287. See also S. D. Myers, ed. *Pioneer Surveyor—Frontier Lawyer: The Personal Narrative of O. W. Williams, 1877–1902,* 41, 44–46.
34. Scholars and others continue to argue over the place of Quanah's birth, most suggesting that it was in the Wichita Mountains of western Oklahoma. Others maintain that in was on the southern edge of Cedar Lake. Quanah, while passing through Lubbock in a large touring car in 1909, told Walter Posey that he was on his way to his birth place at Cedar Lake. See Walter Posey, interview with Seymour V. Connor, July 24, 1956, and Walter Posey and J. Evetts Haley, interview with W. C. Holden, July 21, 1949, transcripts of both in Southwest Collection, Texas Tech University.
35. Lehmann, *Nine Years with the Indians,* 185–86.

CHAPTER 4. BUFFALO SOLDIERS AND THE ARMY IN 1877

1. Comanches and whites used the term "buffalo soldiers"; the black regulars did not. The black troopers may have seen the term as an insult. See William A. Dobak and Thomas D. Phillips, *The Black Regulars, 1866–1898,* xvii.
2. William H. Leckie's classic *The Buffalo Soldiers: A Narrative of the Negro Cavalry in the West* remains the best history of the black cavalry regiments; for the early history of the Tenth Cavalry, see pp. 3–7. Herschel V. Cashin, *Under Fire with the Tenth Cavalry* treats mainly the black regiment in Cuba during the Spanish-American War, and Edward L. N. Glass, *The History of the Tenth Cavalry,* has very little on the Texas years. For a more recent study, see Dobak and Phillips, *The Black Regulars.*
3. Francis B. Heitman, *Historical Register and Dictionary of the United States Army,* I: 355–56; Leckie, *The Buffalo Soldiers,* 69 & n.

4. Leckie, *The Buffalo Soldiers,* 152.
5. Ibid., 9.
6. Quote in Ibid., 12.
7. Quote in Ibid., 15, 71–72. For a different view see Dobak and Phillips, *The Black Regulars,* xvi, 106–107.
8. See Don Rickey, Jr., *Forty Miles a Day on Beans and Hay: The Enlisted Soldier Fighting the Indian Wars,* 56–57.
9. Leckie, *The Buffalo Soldiers,* 163–64. See also Arlen L. Fowler, *The Black Infantry in the West, 1861–1891,* 25–26.
10. Leckie, *The Buffalo Soldiers,* 164.
11. Cashion, *A Texas Frontier,* 205.
12. Lecky, *The Buffalo Soldiers,* 34–37.
13. For a thorough and engaging discussion of post life in Texas, see Robert Wooster, *Soldiers, Sutlers, and Settlers: Garrison Life on the Texas Frontier,* 83–102, 163–201.
14. U.S. Congress, House, Exec. Doc. No. 1, *Report of the Secretary of War,* 45th Cong., 2d Sess., 1878, pt. 2: 49; Leckie, *The Buffalo Soldiers,* 163 & n, 178 & n.
15. See Clarence C. Clendenen, *Blood on the Border: The United States Army and the Mexican Irregulars,* 46, 50–54, 56–59; Henry Bamford Parkes, *A History of Mexico,* 259–74.
16. See Jeffrey M. Roth, "Civil War Frontier Defense Challenger in Northwest Texas," *Military History of the West* 30 (Spring 2000): 22–23, 40–41, 43; David Paul Smith, *Frontier Defense in the Civil War: Texas Rangers and the Rebels,* 168–74; and Cashion, *A Texas Frontier,* 86–87, 89, 94, 305–307.
17. Variously called "the Salt Creek massacre" or "the Warren Wagon Train massacre," the attack led to the arrest of such powerful Kiowa leaders as Satank, Big Tree, and Satanta. See Benjamin Capps, *The Warren Wagon Train Raid,* for the most detailed account of the affair and the trial of Big Tree and Satanta afterward. See also Cashion, *A Texas Frontier,* 108–110; and Wallace, *Ranald S. Mackenzie on the Texas Frontier,* 30–31. For Sherman's response, see William T. Sherman to Col. Ranald S. Mackenzie, May 19, 1871, Sherman to Col. William H. Wood, May 19, 1871, and Sherman to General John Pope, May 24, 1871, all in Ernest Wallace, ed., *Ranald S. Mackenzie's Official Correspondence Relating to Texas, 1871–1873,* 23–27.
18. Wallace, *Ranald S. Mackenzie on the Texas Frontier,* 4; Michael Pierce, *The Most Promising Young Officer: A Life of Ranald Slidell Mackenzie,* 28–52, esp., 52.
19. Wallace, *Ranald S. Mackenzie on the Texas Frontier,* 40–56; Ranald S. Mackenzie to H. Clay Wood, Asst. Adj. Gen., Dept. of Texas, November 15, 1871, in Wallace, ed., *Ranald S. Mackenzie's Official Correspondence Relating to Texas, 1871–1873,* 41–42.
20. William R. Shafter to H. Clay Wood, Asst. Adj. Gen., Dept. of Texas, July 15, 1871, United States Army Commands, Record Group 94, National Archives (NA); U.S. Dept. of War, Returns from United States Military Posts, 1800–1916, Fort Davis, June-July, 1871, Roll 297, Microcopy No. 617, NA; U.S. Dept. of War, Post Medical Reports, Fort Davis, June-July, 1871, Books No. 7–9–12, Old Records Division, Adj. Gen. Office, NA. See also Thomas T. Smith, *The Old Army in Texas,* 153; Haley, *Fort Concho and the Texas Frontier,* 163–67.
21. Wallace, *Ranald S. Mackenzie on the Texas Frontier,* 64–89; Carlson, "*Pecos Bill,*" 63–67; Ranald S. Mackenzie to H. Clay Wood, Asst. Adj. Gen., Dept. of Texas,

October 12, 1872, in Wallace, ed., *Ranald S. Mackenzie's Official Correspondence Relating to Texas, 1871–1873*, 141–45.

22. Clendenen, *Blood on the Border*, 62–71; Wallace, *Ranald S. Mackenzie on the Texas Frontier*, 92–111.
23. Rathjen, *The Texas Panhandle Frontier*, 77–80; Baker and Harrison, *Adobe Walls: The History and Archeology of the 1874 Trading Post*, 50–74; John Wesley Mooar to "Sister," July 7, 1874, in John Wesley Mooar Papers, Box 1, Correspondence, Notes, etc., 1871–1879, Southwest Collection, Texas Tech University.
24. T. R. Fehrenbach, *Comanches: The Destruction of a People*, 539–47; Hagan, *United States–Comanche Relations*, 108–15; Rathjen, *The Texas Panhandle Frontier*, 164–79; Wallace, *Ranald S. Mackenzie on the Texas Frontier*, 128–46, 150–66; Leckie, *The Buffalo Soldiers*, 113–33.
25. William R. Shafter to J. H. Taylor, Asst. Adj. Gen., Dept. of Texas, Jan. 4, 1876 in M.L. Crimmins, ed., "Shafter's Exploration in Western Texas, 1875," *West Texas Historical Association Year Book* 9 (Oct., 1933): 82–96; Fowler, *The Black Infantry in the West*, 32–33; Leckie, *The Buffalo Soldiers*, 143–48; J. Evetts Haley, *Fort Concho and the Texas Frontier*, 227–43.
26. Testimony of Private Isaac Thompson, Company A, Tenth Cavalry, October 16, 1877, Proceedings of a General Court Martial, Fort McKavett, Texas; Special Orders No. 169, Headquarters, Department of Texas, San Antonio, September 26, 1877, trial of Sergeant William L. Umbles, convened on October 15, 1877, photocopy in Museum Research Library and Archives, Fort Concho National Historic Landmark, San Angelo, Texas.
27. *Special Committee of the House of Representatives to Investigate Texas Frontier Troubles*, 44th Cong., 1st sess., 1876, H. Report. 343, pp. 73–74; Bernarr Cresap, *Appomattox Commander: The Story of General E. O. C. Ord*, 306–15; Utley, *Frontier Regulars*, 349–51; Robert M. Utley, "'Pecos Bill' on the Texas Frontier," *The American West*, 6 (Jan., 1969): 4–13.
28. William R. Shafter testimony, Jan. 6, 7, 8, 1878, in *Testimony Taken by Committee on Military Affairs in Relation to Texas Border Troubles*, 45th Cong., 2d sess., 1879, H. Misc. Doc. 64, pp. 152–87; Utley, *Frontier Regulars*, 350–54.
29. J. H. Taylor, Asst. Adj. Gen., Dept. of Texas, to William R. Shafter, October 27, 1876, in William R. Shafter Papers, Stanford University Library, Stanford, Calif., photocopy in Southwest Collection, Texas Tech University; Smith, *The Old Army in Texas*, 116–17; Carlson, *"Pecos Bill,"* 96–99; Utley, *Frontier Regulars*, 351–53; Leckie, *The Buffalo Soldiers*, 149–55; Clendenen, *Blood on the Border*, 77–83.
30. U.S. Dept. of War, Returns from United States Military Posts, 1800–1916, Fort Concho, Jan.–July, 1877, Roll 241, Microfilm No. M617, NA; Susan Miles, "Fort Concho in 1877," *West Texas Historical Association Year Book* 35 (1959): 29–36.

CHAPTER 5. ONTO THE HIGH YARNER

1. Charles L. Cooper, letter to his father, August 30, 1877, as cited in *Lynn County News*, Tahoka, Texas, Oct. 19, 1933. Copies of the letter also appeared in the New York *Daily Tribune*, Sept. 8, 1877, and in W. Curtis Nunn, "Eighty-six Hours without Water on the Texas Plains," *Southwestern Historical Quarterly* 43 (Jan., 1940): 360–64 (hereafter Cooper to his father, August 30, 1877).
2. Testimony of Thomas L. Allsup, October 17, 1877, Proceedings of a General Court Martial, Fort McKavett, Texas; Special Orders No. 169, Headquarters,

Department of Texas, San Antonio, September 26, 1877, trial of Sergeant William L. Umbles, convened on October 15, 1877, photocopy in Museum Research Library and Archives, Fort Concho National Historic Landmark, San Angelo, Texas (hereafter Umbles Court-martial).

3. Leckie, *The Buffalo Soldiers,* 155–57; Elvis E. Fleming, "'Buffalo Soldiers' and Buffalo Hunters: The Story of 'Nigger Hill,'" *Southwest Heritage* 3 (Mar. 1973): 13–15; Elvis Eugene Fleming, "Captain Nicholas Nolan: Lost on the Staked Plains," *Texana* 4 (Spring 1966): 1–5; Cook, *The Border and the Buffalo,* 180–253, 261; H. Bailey Carroll, "Nolan's 'Lost Nigger' Expedition of 1877," *Southwestern Historical Quarterly* 44 (July 1940): 55–57.
4. Col. Benjamin H. Grierson, Post Commander, to Capt. Nicholas Nolan, Troop A, Tenth Cavalry, July 4, 1877, Records of U. S. Army Continental Commands, Fort Concho, Texas, Letters Sent, Record Group 393, National Archives; Cook, *The Border and the Buffalo,* 248, 261, 293; Utley, *Frontier Regulars,* 218–33, 344–55.
5. Susan Miles, "Fort Concho in 1877," *West Texas Historical Association Year Book* 35 (1959): 29, 32.
6. Ibid., 30–31; Smith, *The Old Army in Texas,* 60, 116.
7. Miles, "Fort Concho in 1877," 30–31.
8. Ibid., 33.
9. Mrs. Nolan's death was attributed to "quick consumption," or perhaps a form of pulmonary tuberculosis, ibid., 29; quotes in ibid., 29, 33, 34. See also Francis B. Heitman, *Historical Register and Dictionary of the United States Army,* I: 750; Leckie, *The Buffalo Soldiers,* 144, 157; Carlson, *"Pecos Bill,"* 77, 79; Cook, *The Border and the Buffalo,* 261.
10. Nicholas Nolan to J. H. Taylor, Asst. Adj. Gen., Department of Texas, August 20, 1877, Letters Received (LR), Department of Texas, 1877, Adjutant General's Office (AGO), Record Group (RG) 94, National Archives (copy in Carroll, "Nolan's 'Lost Nigger' Expedition of 1877," 55–75); Cooper to his father, August 30, 1877; Miles, "Fort Concho in 1877," 43; Cook, *The Border and the Buffalo,* 269.
11. Nolan to Taylor, August 20, 1877, LR, Dept. of Texas, 1877, AGO, RG 94, NA.
12. See Sandoz, *The Buffalo Hunters,* 295. Some writers claim that Spotted Jack died in an Indian attack near the town on June 14, 1877, and the gravestone there so indicates. See, for example, Eckhert, "Rath City," 44. Willis S. Glenn, a bison hunter who was in the Yellow House Canyon fight, writes that Spotted Jack was one of the bison hunters who "took part in the dry march." See Strickland, ed., "The Recollections of W. S. Glenn, Buffalo Hunter," 63–64; Testimony of Sergeant Thomas H. Allsup, October 18, 1877, in Umbles Court-martial.
13. Nolan to Taylor, August 20, 1877, LR, Dept. of Texas, 1877, AGO, RG 94, NA.
14. Dorothy H. Dennis, "Historic Pecan Tree," typescript in Nicholas M. Nolan, Papers, box 1, folder 14, Southwest Collection, Texas Tech University.
15. Cook, *The Border and the Buffalo,* 260.
16. Quote in Sandoz, *The Buffalo Hunters,* 295.
17. Cook, *The Border and the Buffalo,* 261–62; Nolan to Taylor, August 20, 1877, LR, Dept. of Texas, 1877, AGO, G 94, NA.
18. Quote in Cooper to father, August 30, 1877; Nolan to Taylor, August 20, 1877, LR, Dept. of Texas, 1877, AGO, RG 94, NA; Cook, *The Border and the Buffalo,* 260–61. See also Haley, *Fort Concho and the Texas Frontier,* 246–47; Fleming, "Captain Nicholas Nolan, 5; Leckie, *The Buffalo Soldiers,* 157; and J. Evetts Haley, *Charles Goodnight: Cowman and Plainsman,* 190–91.

19. Compare Nolan to Taylor, August 20, 1877, LR, Dept. of Texas, 1877, AGO, RG 94, NA, with Cook, *The Border and the Buffalo,* 261–62.
20. The only other extant records that add to the discussion are the medical report of post surgeon Joseph Henry Thomas King and a brief statement Mortimer N. Kress, a buffalo hunter, made to John R. Cook. King's report was filed with the Adjutant General's Office in the War Department and published in 1877 as *A Brief Account of the Sufferings of a Detachment of United States Cavalry from Deprivation of Water during a Period of Eighty-six Hours while Scouting on the Staked Plains of Texas* (hereafter King Medical Report). The same year, and probably the same month, King's report was also published—and by the same printer—as *Experience of Troop A, 10th Cavalry, on the "Staked Plains," Texas, July 1877.* Cook included the Kress statement in a separate section of his book *The Border and the Buffalo.* There are extant telegrams, letters, and newspaper accounts, of course, but they follow Nolan and Cooper.
21. Nolan to Taylor, August 20, 1877, LR, Dept. of Texas, 1877, AGO, RG 94, NA; Testimony of Private John A. Gaddie, October 18, 1877, in Umbles Court martial.
22. Nolan and Cooper reported twenty-eight bison hunters in the camp when the soldiers arrived on July 17; Cook writes that twenty-two men were there, but that two more, absent on a scout, were expected back shortly. The Nolan-Cooper numbers may come from the appearance of Spotted Jack and his companions who a few days later showed up at one of Nolan's camps—without their cattle. What happened, one wonders, to the longhorns they were herding?
23. Again, compare Nolan to Taylor, August 20, 1877, LR, Dept. of Texas, 1877, AGO, RG 94, NA, and Cook, *The Border and the Buffalo,* 262–63. Clearly, Cook has the days wrong, but just as clearly Nolan has the miles and directions wrong. Cedar Lake is not fifty-five or even fifty miles from the head of Tobacco Creek; it is just over thirty miles distant. The distance from the waterspout lake that Cook describes is a bit closer to the fifty miles that Nolan cites.
24. Cook, *The Border and the Buffalo,* 262–63.
25. Ibid., 263.
26. Ibid.
27. Nolan to Taylor, August 20, 1877, LR, Dept. of Texas, 1877, AGO, RG 94, NA; Cook, *The Border and the Buffalo,* 265. See also Leckie, *The Buffalo Soldiers,* 158; Haley, *Fort Concho and the Texas Frontier,* 247; Fleming, "'Buffalo Soldiers' and Buffalo Hunters," 15; Fleming, "Captain Nicholas Nolan," 6.
28. Nolan to Taylor, August 20, 1877, LR, Dept. of Texas, 1877, AGO, RG 94, NA; Cook, *The Border and the Buffalo,* 265–66.
29. Nolan to Taylor, August 20, 1877, LR, Dept. of Texas, 1877, AGO, RG 94, NA.
30. Ibid. See also Leckie, *The Buffalo Soldiers,* 158.
31. Haley, *Charles Goodnight,* 196–97.
32. Sandoz, *The Buffalo Hunters,* 267; Testimony of Thomas H. Allsup, October 17, 1877, in Umbles Court-martial.

CHAPTER 6. THE THIRSTING TIME

1. Kress quoted in Cook, *The Border and the Buffalo,* 320; Umbles quoted in Testimony of Private Alexander Nolan, Company A, Tenth Cavalry, October 18, 1877, Umbles Court-martial.

2. Cook, *The Border and the Buffalo,* 266; Nicholas Nolan to J. H. Taylor, Asst. Adj. Gen., Dept. of Texas, August 20, 1877, Letters Received (LR), Dept. of Texas, 1877, AGO, RG 94, NA, copy in H. Bailey Carroll, "Nolan's 'Lost Nigger' Expedition of 1877," *Southwestern Historical Quarterly* 44 (July 1940): 55–75; Leckie, *The Buffalo Soldiers,* 158; Haley, *Fort Concho and the Texas Frontier,* 248–49; Fleming, "'Buffalo Soldiers' and Buffalo Hunters," 16.
3. W. Curtis Nunn, "Eighty-six Hours without Water on the Texas Plains," *Southwestern Historical Quarterly* 43 (January 1940): 357; Nolan to Taylor, August 20, 1877, LR, Dept. of Texas, 1877, AGO, RG 94, NA.
4. Leckie, *The Buffalo Soldiers,* 159.
5. Ibid.; Cook, *The Border and the Buffalo,* 266–67; King Medical Report, 4. For a careful, and perhaps the best, delineation of the command's route see Fleming, "'Buffalo Soldiers' and Buffalo Hunters," 16–18, 24–25.
6. King Medical Report, 4; Nolan to Taylor, August 20, 1877, LR, Dept. of Texas, 1877, AGO, RG 94, NA; Cook, *The Border and the Buffalo,* 267; Fleming, "Captain Nicholas Nolan," 7.
7. Cook, *The Border and the Buffalo,* 267–68; Fleming, "Captain Nicholas Nolan," 8.
8. Cook, *The Border and the Buffalo,* 268–69.
9. Nolan to Taylor, August 20, 1877, LR, Dept. of Texas, 1877, AGO, RG 94, NA.
10. Cooper to his father, August 30, 1877.
11. Testimony of Captain Nicholas Nolan, October 15, 1877, Lieutenant Charles L. Cooper, October 15 & 16, 1877, and Private Isaac Thompson, October 16, 1877, all in Umbles Court-martial.
12. Nolan to Taylor, August 30, 1877, LR, Dept. of Texas, 1877, AGO, RG 94, NA; Testimony of Private Isaac Thompson, October 16, 1877, and Private Smith Johnson, October 17, 1877, both in Umbles Court-martial.
13. Nolan to Taylor, August 20, 1877, LR, Dept. of Texas, 1877, AGO, RG 94, NA.
14. Fleming, "'Buffalo Soldiers' and Buffalo Hunters," 13, 17; Cooper to his father, August 30, 1877; Cook, *The Border and the Buffalo,* 269–70; Nolan to Taylor, August 20, 1877, LR, Dept. of Texas, 1877, AGO, RG 94, NA; Leckie, *The Buffalo Soldiers,* 159–60; Fleming, "Captain Nicholas Nolan," 8; Haley, *Fort Concho and the Texas Frontier,* 250–51; Carroll, "Nolan's 'Lost Nigger' Expedition of 1877," 58–59.
15. Cook, *The Border and the Buffalo,* 269–70; Testimony of First Lieutenant Robert G. Smithers, October 18, 1877, Private Steven Floyd, October 16, 1877, both in Umbles Court-martial.
16. See testimony of Privates Steven Floyd, October 16, 1877, Smith Thompson, October 16, 1877, and Alexander Nolan, October 18, 1877, all in Umbles Court-martial.
17. Cook, *The Border and the Buffalo,* 270.
18. Ibid.; Nolan to Taylor, August 20, 1877, LR, Dept. of Texas, 1877, AGO, RG 94, NA. See also Leckie, *The Buffalo Soldiers,* 160; Sandoz, *The Buffalo Hunters,* 303; Haley, *Fort Concho and the Texas Frontier,* 250–51; Fleming, "Captain Nicholas Nolan," 9; Colonel M. L. Crimmins, "Captain Nolan's Lost Troop on the Staked Plains," 70.
19. Cook, *The Border and the Buffalo,* 270–71.
20. Ibid., 271.
21. Ibid., 271–73.
22. Testimony of Private Alexander Nolan, October 18, 1877, in Umbles Court-martial.

23. Testimony of privates Smith Thompson, October 16, 1877, and Pierce Kuston, October 19, 1877, and statement of Sergeant William L. Umbles, October 22, 1877, in Umbles Court-martial.
24. King Medical Report, 2.
25. Nolan to Taylor, August 20, 1877, LR, Dept. of Texas, 1877, AGO, RG 94, NA; King Medical Report, 3; Cooper to his father, August 30, 1877.
26. Cook, *The Border and the Buffalo,* 271–79; Cooper to father, August 30, 1877.
27. Fleming, "'Buffalo Soldiers' and Buffalo Hunters," 18, 24; Cook, *The Border and the Buffalo,* 272–73, 275.
28. Cook, *The Border and the Buffalo,* 171, 273–76.
29. Kress quoted in Cook, *The Border and the Buffalo,* 319–20. On the idea of drift, see Chapter 1.
30. Nolan to Taylor, August 20, 1877, LR, Dept. of Texas, AGO, RG 94, NA; Cooper to his father, August 30, 1877; King Medical Report, 3.
31. Nolan to Taylor, August 20, 1877, LR, Dept. of Texas, AGO, RG 94, NA; King Medical Report, 3; Cooper to his father, August 30, 1877; Robert L. Carr, M.D., memorandum, to Paul Carlson, May 3, 2002, in Folder A, Nicholas M. Nolan Papers, in possession of author.
32. Nolan to Taylor, August 20, 1877, LR, Dept. of Texas, AGO, RG 94, NA; Cooper to his father, August 30, 1877.
33. Ibid., 276–81.
34. Testimony of Private Smith Johnson, October 19, 1877, and statement of Sergeant William L. Umbles, October 22, 1877, in Umbles Court-martial.
35. Cook, *The Border and the Buffalo,* 281.
36. Kress quoted in Cook, *The Border and the Buffalo,* 320–21. If John R. Cook is correct, the downpour on the night of July 28 fell in a strip only two miles wide—fairly typical of rainfall patterns on the Llano Estacado—a few miles south of Casas Amarillas. See Ibid., 282.
37. Statement of Sergeant William L. Umbles, October 22, 1877, and testimony of Private Smith Johnson, October 19, 1877, in Umbles Court-martial.
38. Cook, *The Border and the Buffalo,* 283; Statement of Sergeant William L. Umbles, October 22, 1877, in Umbles Court-martial.
39. Statement of Sergeant William L. Umbles, October 22, 1877, testimony of Privates Smith Johnson, October 19, 1877, and Henry C. Miller, October 20, 1877, in Umbles Court-martial.
40. Nolan to Taylor, August 20, 1877, LR, Dept. of Texas, AGO, RG 94, NA; Cooper to his father, August 30, 1877; King Medical Report, 3–4.
41. Cook, *The Border and the Buffalo,* 283.
42. King Medical Report, 3–5; *Lubbock Avalanche-Journal,* April 20, 2002.
43. King Medical Report, 3–5.
44. Cooper to his father, August 30, 1877. See also Nolan to Taylor, August 20, 1877, LR, Dept. of Texas, AGO, RG 94, NA.
45. Nolan to Taylor, August 20, 1877, LR, Dept. of Texas, AGO, RG 94, NA; Cooper to his father, August 30, 1877. See also King Medical Report, 4–5; Leckie, *The Buffalo Soldiers,* 161; Haley, *Fort Concho and the Texas Frontier,* 256–57; Crimmins, "Captain Nolan's Lost Troop on the Staked Plains," 71–72; Fleming, "Captain Nicholas Nolan," 10–11; Fleming, "Buffalo Soldiers and Buffalo Hunters," 24–26.
46. Nolan to Taylor, August 20, 1877, LR, Dept. of Texas, AGO, RG 94, NA.

CHAPTER 7. DOWN OFF THE HIGH YARNER

1. Newspaper clipping, dated August 8, 1877, in Nicholas M. Nolan, Papers, box 1, folder 1, Southwest Collection, Texas Tech University.
2. Cook, *The Border and the Buffalo,* 285–86.
3. Nicholas Nolan to J. H. Taylor, Asst. Adj. Gen., Dept. of Texas, August 20, 1877, Letters Received (LR), Dept. of Texas, 1877, Adjutant General's Office (AGO), Record Group (RG) 94, National Archives (NA), copy in H. Bailey Carroll, "Nolan's 'Lost Nigger' Expedition of 1877," *Southwestern Historical Quarterly* 44 (July 1940): 62–75 (hereafter Nolan to Taylor, August 20, 1877, LR, Dept. of Texas, 1877, AGO, RG 94, NA); Cook, *The Border and the Buffalo,* 285–86.
4. Cook, *The Border and the Buffalo,* 285–286.
5. Herman Lehmann, *Nine Years with the Indians, 1870–1879: The Story of the Captivity and Life of a Texan Among the Indians,* 186–87; Nolan to Taylor, August 20, 1877, LR, Dept. of Texas, 1877, AGO, RG 94, NA; Cook, *The Border and the Buffalo,* 285–87.
6. Cook, *The Border and the Buffalo,* 285–86. See also Fleming, "Captain Nicholas Nolan," 12–13; Carroll, "Nolan 'Lost Nigger' Expedition of 1877," 74–75; Fleming, "'Buffalo Soldiers' and Buffalo Hunters," 26; *The Portales, New Mexico, Tribune,* Historical and Progress Edition, April 1, 1938, 4–5.
7. Cook, *The Border and the Buffalo,* 286–87. See also O. W. Williams, "From Dallas to the Site of Lubbock in 1877," *West Texas Historical Association Year Book* 15 (1939): 13–14, 16; and Ernest Wallace, ed., "The Journal of Ranald S. Mackenzie's Messenger to the Kwahadi Comanches," *Red River Valley Historical Review* 3 (Spring 1978): 230, 232; Owen, "Doans," 84–95.
8. See Nolan to Taylor, August 20, 1877, LR, Dept. of Texas, 1877, AGO, RG 94, NA. See also Fleming, "Captain Nicholas Nolan," 13.
9. Lehmann, *Nine Years with the Indians,* 187.
10. Cook, *The Border and the Buffalo,* 289.
11. Alice Grierson to Benjamin Grierson, n.d., as cited in Susan Miles, "Fort Concho in 1877," *West Texas Historical Association Year Book* 35 (1959): 43, 45.
12. Nolan's report of the expedition and testimony at the courts-martial make no mention of Private Peterson or anyone else joining the bison hunters. At the Umbles court-martial, however, Sergeant Thomas H. Allsup testified that on August 1, only thirteen men rode or walked in to the Bull Creek campsite with Umbles; the number, if no trooper had deserted, should have been fourteen (fifteen counting Umbles). See Nolan to Taylor, August 20, 1877, LR, Dept. of Texas, AGO, GR 94, NA; Testimony of Thomas H. Allsup, October 17, 1877, Proceedings of a General Court Martial, Fort McKavett, Texas; Special Orders No. 169, Headquarters, Department of Texas, San Antonio, September 26, 1877, trial of Sergeant William L. Umbles, convened on October 15, 1877, photocopy in Museum Research Library and Archives, Fort Concho National Historic Landmark, San Angelo, Texas (hereafter Umbles Court-martial); Leckie, *The Buffalo Soldiers,* 162. But see also Cook, *The Border and the Buffalo,* 289.
13. Testimony of Private Isaac Thompson, October 16, 1877, in Umbles Court-martial.
14. Ibid.; Testimony of Private Steven Floyd, October 16, 1877, and testimony of Corporal Charles H. Gilmore, October 18, 1877, both in Umbles Court-martial. One wonders how the soldiers could have prevented their very thirsty horses from going for a drink.

15. Testimony of Private Isaac Thompson, October 16, 1877; testimony of Private Smith Johnson, October 17, 1877; and statement of Sergeant William L. Umbles, October 22, 1877, all in Umbles Court-martial.
16. Testimony of Sergeant Thomas H. Allsup, October 17, 1877, testimony of Lieutenant Robert G. Smither, October 18, 1877, statement of Sergeant William L. Umbles, October 22, 1877, all in Umbles Court-martial; Nolan to Taylor, August 20, 1877, LR, Dept. of Texas, AGO, RG 94, NA; Leckie, *The Buffalo Soldiers,* 162.
17. Miles, "Fort Concho in 1877," 36; Haley, *Fort Concho and the Texas Frontier,* 244–45.
18. Miles, "Fort Concho in 1877," 36–38, 40; Testimony of Lieutenant Robert G. Smither, Adjutant, Tenth Cavalry, October 18, 1977, in Umbles Court-martial.
19. Testimony of Lieutenant Robert G. Smither, Adjutant, Tenth Cavalry, October 18, 1877, in Umbles Court-martial; Nolan to Taylor, August 20, 1877, LR, Dept. of Texas, AGO, NA; Leckie, *The Buffalo Soldiers,* 162.
20. Nolan to Taylor, August 20, 1877, LR, Dept. of Texas, AGO, RG 94, NA; Cook, *The Border and the Buffalo,* 289.
21. Nolan to Taylor, August 20, 1877, LR., Dept. of Texas, AGO, RG 94, NA.
22. Ibid.; Lehmann, *Nine Years with the Indians,* 186–87.
23. Nolan to Taylor, August 20, 1877, LR, Dept. of Texas, AGO, RG 94, NA; Testimony of Sergeant Thomas H. Allsup, Tenth Cavalry, October 17, 1877, in Umbles Court-martial.
24. Nolan to Taylor, August 20, 1877, LR, Dept. of Texas, AGO, RG 94, NA; King Medical Report, 6; a copy of King's report can be found in Nunn, "Eighty-six Hours Without Water on the Texas Plains," 356–64.
25. Cook, *The Border and the Buffalo,* 282–83; Statement of Sergeant William L. Umbles, October 22, 1877, in Umbles Court-martial.
26. Cook, *The Border and the Buffalo,* 283, 287; Haley, *Fort Concho and the Texas Frontier,* 251.
27. Haley, *Fort Concho and the Texas Frontier,* 251–52; *Roswell Record,* June 10, 1892; Cook, *The Border and the Buffalo,* 283, 287; Sandoz, *The Buffalo Hunters,* 308–309.
28. First and last quotes from Cook, *The Border and the Buffalo,* 287; Williams quote from Williams, "From Dallas to the Site of Lubbock in 1877," 13.
29. Williams, "From Dallas to the Site of Lubbock in 1877," 14; Cook, *The Border and the Buffalo,* 287. See also Myers, ed., *Pioneer Surveyor—Frontier Lawyer,* 41–46.
30. Cook, *The Border and the Buffalo,* 288–90.
31. Ibid., 287–90. See also Rex W. Strickland, ed., "The Recollections of W. S. Glenn, Buffalo Hunter," *Panhandle-Plains Historical Review* 22 (1949): 62–64.

CHAPTER 8. BACK FROM THE DEAD

1. Miles, "Fort Concho in 1877," 40.
2. Testimony of Lieutenant Robert G. Smither, Company A, Tenth Cavalry, October 18, 1877, Proceedings of a General Court Martial, Fort McKavett, Texas; Special Orders No. 169, 1877, trial of Sergeant William L. Umbles, convened on October 15, 1877, photocopy in Museum Research Library and Archives, Fort Concho National Historic Landmark, San Angelo, Texas (hereafter Umbles Court-martial).
3. Testimony of George Smith and Henry Williams, citizens of Tom Green

County, October 18, 1877, and statement of Sergeant William L. Umbles, October 22, 1877, in Umbles Court-martial.

4. Miles, "Fort Concho in 1877," 40.
5. Cited in Ibid., 41.
6. Ibid. Testimony of Lieutenant John J. Morrison, Tenth Cavalry, October 19, 1877, in Umbles Court-martial.
7. Nicholas Nolan to J. H. Taylor, Asst. Adj. Gen., Department of Texas, August 20, 1877, Letters Received (LR), Department of Texas, 1877, Adjutant General's Office (AGO), Record Group (RG) 94, National Archives (NA) (copy in H. Bailey Carroll, "Nolan's 'Lost Nigger' Expedition of 1877," *Southwestern Historical Quarterly* 44 (July 1940): 55–75); Miles, "Fort Concho in 1877," 43.
8. Miles, "Fort Concho in 1877," 43.
9. Lieutenant Robert G. Smither, Tenth Cavalry, to Colonel Benjamin Grierson, August 28, 1877, in Miles, "Fort Concho in 1877," 46; See also Grierson to his wife, August 21, 1877, in Benjamin H. Grierson Papers, 1827–1941, Southwest Collection, Texas Tech University; Frank M. Temple, "Colonel Grierson in the Southwest," *Panhandle-Plains Historical Review* 30 (1957): 47–48.
10. Miles, "Fort Concho in 1877," 46.
11. Naomi H. Kincaid, "Rath City," *West Texas Historical Association Year Book* 24 (1948): 46; Cook, *The Border and the Buffalo,* 290.
12. Rathjen, *The Texas Panhandle Frontier,* 137, 182; Sandoz, *The Buffalo Hunters,* 314–17; Cook, *The Border and the Buffalo,* 291; Frank Collinson, *Life in the Saddle,* 69.
13. Joe S. McCombs, "On the Cattle Trail and Buffalo Range," *West Texas Historical Association Year Book* 11 (1935): 99–101; Cook, *The Border and the Buffalo,* 291.
14. Eckhart, "Rath City," 42, 44; Rathjen, *The Texas Panhandle Frontier,* 136–37; Sandoz, *The Buffalo Hunters,* 317.
15. Eckhart, "Rath City," 45; E. Douglas Branch, *The Hunting of the Buffalo,* 198–99; Cook, *The Border and the Buffalo,* 294, 299; Tom McHugh, *The Time of the Buffalo,* 276–77; Rathjen, *The Texas Panhandle Frontier,* 136–37; McCombs, "On the Cattle Trail and Buffalo Range," 100–101; Collinson, *Life in the Saddle,* 172–80.
16. Eckhart, "Rath City: Texas Hide Town," 45; Kincaid, "Rath City," 46; Donald F. Schofield, *Indians, Cattle, Ships & Oil: The Story of W. M. D. Lee,* 34, 50–51. The former site of Rath City rests in the middle of a wheat field. It is a place that, after harvest time, archeologists on occasion work and tourists view. A little museum dedicated to the place, and to the bison hunters who traded there, is located in the town of Hamlin, a few miles south.
17. Thomas T. Smith, *The Old Army in Texas: Research Guide to the U.S. Army in Nineteenth-Century Texas,* 72, 116.
18. U.S. Dept of War, Returns from United States Military Posts, 1800–1916, Fort McKavett, October 1877, Roll 690, Microcopy No. 617, Record Group 94, National Archives (hereafter Post Returns, MC617, RG 94, NA). Apparently, because it was a general court-martial, the court examined separate and unrelated cases of soldiers from other regiments as well, for a Private John Hartley of the Tenth Infantry was also tried. See Special Order No. 187, Headquarters Department of Texas, October 26, 1877, in Umbles Court-martial. Joseph T. Glatthaar, *Forged in Battle: The Civil War Alliance of Black Soldiers and White Officers,* 172.

19. Registers of Enlistments in the United States Army, 1798–1914, Volumes 76–77, 1871–1877 (Registers of Enlistments), Roll 40, Microcopy No. 233 (MC233), Records of United States Army Commands (RUSAC), Record Group (RG) 98, National Archives (NA).
20. Ibid., Roll 38; Miles, "Fort Concho in 1877," 33.
21. Registers of Enlistments, Roll 39, MC233, RUSAC, RG 98, NA.
22. U.S. Department of War, *Cases Tried by a General Court Martial,* Fort McKavett, Texas, General Court Martial Orders No. 45, November 21, 1877, Headquarters, Department of Texas, San Antonio (hereafter *Cases Tried by a General Court Martial*), 1–7 (photocopy in Southwest Collection, Texas Tech University).
23. Ibid. See also appendices and attachments (particularly Special Order No. 187, Headquarters Department of Texas, October 26, 1877), in Umbles Court martial.
24. Special Order No. 187, Headquarters Department of Texas, October 26, 1877, in Umbles Court-martial.
25. *Cases Tried by a General Court Martial,* 6–7.
26. Post Returns, Fort Concho, November 1877, Roll 241, MC617, RG 94, NA.
27. Ibid.; Miles, "Fort Concho in 1877," 48–49.
28. Post Returns, Fort Concho, December 1877, Roll 241, MC617, RG 94, NA; Alice Grierson to Benjamin Grierson, December 11, 1877, in Miles, "Fort Concho in 1877," 49.
29. See, for example, Sandoz, *The Buffalo Hunters,* 298–303; Haley, *Fort Concho and the Texas Frontier,* 248–51; Cook, *The Border and the Buffalo,* 268–69, 285; and Carroll, "Nolan's 'Lost Nigger' Expedition of 1877," 61.
30. Haley, *Fort Concho and the Texas Frontier,* 248.
31. Ibid., 249; Alice Grierson to Benjamin Grierson, August 14, 1877, in Miles, "Fort Concho in 1877," 43. Nolan and Mrs. Grierson had their information on Keyes wrong. Keyes was accused of cowardice but was not court-martialed. See Leckie, *The Buffalo Soldiers,* 138–39, 139–40 n45.
32. Cook, *The Border and the Buffalo,* 268–69.
33. Haley, *Fort Concho and the Texas Frontier,* 250–51. See also Sandoz, *The Buffalo Hunters,* 303.
34. King Medical Report, 5–6. King's report can also be found in Nunn, "Eighty-six Hours without Water on the Texas Plains," 356–60.
35. Nolan to Taylor, August 20, 1877, LR, Dept. of Texas, 1877, AGO, RG 94, NA.
36. Ibid.; Cooper to his father, August 30, 1877, as cited in *Lynn County News,* Tahoka, Texas, October 19, 1933. Copies of the letter also appeared in the *New York Tribune,* September 8, 1877, and in Nunn, "Eighty-six Hours without Water on the Texas Plains," 360–64; Cook, *The Border and the Buffalo,* 268; Testimony of Private Smith Johnson, Tenth Cavalry, October 19, 1877, in Umbles Court-martial.
37. Cook, *The Border and the Buffalo,* 284–85; Nolan to Taylor, August 20, 1877, LR, Dept. of Texas, AGO, RG 94, NA. See also Leckie, *The Buffalo Soldiers,* 160–61; and Sandoz, *The Buffalo Hunters,* 311–12.
38. Testimony of Lieutenant Robert G. Smither, Tenth Cavalry, October 18, 1877, and Private Smith Johnson, Tenth Cavalry, October 19, 1877, in Umbles Court-martial; Cooper to his father, August 30, 1877; Nolan to Taylor, August 20, 1877, LR, Dept of Texas, 1877, AGO, GR 94, NA.

39. Cook, *The Border and the Buffalo,* 284–85; Registers of Enlistment, Roll 39, MC233, RUSAC, RG 98, NA. See also Sandoz, *The Buffalo Hunters,* 311–12; and Leckie, *The Buffalo Soldiers,* 160–61.
40. Clipping of a War Department file, n.d., in Box 1, folder marked "Hard Copy," Nicholas M. Nolan Papers, in possession of author (hereafter Nolan Papers); Statement of Military Service of Nicholas Nolan, Headquarters Department of the Amry, Washington, D.C., December 6, 1927, copy in Box 2, Folder No. 1, Nolan Papers; Francis B. Heitman, *Historical Register and Dictionary of the United States Army,* I: 750; William A. Dobak and Thomas D. Phillips, *The Black Regulars, 1866–1898,* 170, 317 n29.
41. Heitman, *Historical Register and Dictionary of the United States Army,* I: 325.
42. Registers of Enlistments, Rolls 38, 39, 40, MC233, RUSAC, RG 98, NA.
43. William T. Hagan, *United States-Comanche Relations: The Reservation Years,* 141; John A. Wilcox, Fourth Cavalry, to Asst. Adt. General, Department of Missouri, Jan. 17, 1879, in Box one, Fort Elliott folder, Nicholas M. Nolan Papers, in possession of author; Haley, *Fort Concho and the Texas Frontier,* 327–28; Nye, *Carbine & Lance,* 238; John Warren Hunter, "Corporal Douglas' Battle with Chief 'Black Horse,'" *Frontier Times* 7 (June 1930): 405–409. See also Loyd M. Uglow, *Standing at the Gap: Army Outposts, Picket Stations, and the Pacification of the Texas Frontier, 1866–1886,* 19, 36.
44. William T. Hagan, *Quanah Parker, Comanche Chief,* xv.
45. See, for example, *The New York Times,* August 9, 1877; *Saint Louis Globe-Democrat,* August 9, 1877; *San Antonio Herald,* August 7, 1877; New York *Daily Tribune,* September 8, 1877; and the *Atlanta Daily Constitution,* August 7, 1877.
46. See *Testimony taken by Committee on Military Affairs in Relation to Texas Border Troubles,* 45th Cong., 2d sess., 1879, H. Misc. Doc. 64, 157–82.
47. *Lubbock Avalanche-Journal,* July 23, 1978.

Bibliography

MANUSCRIPT SOURCES

Boggs, Hershel J. "A History of Fort Concho." Master's thesis, University of Texas, Austin, 1940.

Buffalo Soldiers. Reference File. Southwest Collection, Texas Tech University.

Chamberlain, Cynthia Ann. "Colonel Ranald Slidell Mackenzie's Administration of the Western Section of Indian Territory, 1875–1877." Master's thesis, Texas Tech University, 1971.

Fenton, James Irving. "An Unwitting Autobiography: Staked Plains Etiological Prehistory and History." Ph.D. dissertation, Texas Tech University, 1991.

Grierson, Benjamin H. Papers, 1827–1941. Southwest Collection, Texas Tech University.

Lost Troop (Lost "Nigger") Expedition. Reference File. Southwest Collection, Texas Tech University.

Mooar, John Wesley. Papers. Southwest Collection, Texas Tech University.

Mooar, Margaret McCollum (Mrs. John W.). Papers. Southwest Collection, Texas Tech University.

Mooar, Miss Lydia Louise. Collection. Mooar Family Papers. Southwest Collection, Texas Tech University.

Nash, Robert. Papers. Southwest Collection, Texas Tech University.

Nash, Robert. Reference File. Southwest Collection, Texas Tech University.

Nolan, Nicholas M. Papers. In possession of author.

Nolan, Nicholas M. Reference File. Southwest Collection, Texas Tech University.

"An Overview of a Cavalry Reenactment: The Lost Nigger Expedition of 1877 Scheduled July 26–27–28 and 29 of 1978 on the Arid Plains of West Texas near the Present Day City of Lubbock," typewritten manuscript, n.d., n.p. Copy in Southwest Collection, Texas Tech University.

Rath City. Records. Back to Rath's Trail Museum. Hamlin, Texas.

Rister, Carl Coke. Papers. Southwest Collection, Texas Tech University.

Shafter, William R. Papers. Stanford University Library, Stanford, California. Photocopy, 1861–1898, Southwest Collection, Texas Tech University.

Shafter, William R. Reference File. Southwest Collection, Texas Tech University.

Silver Falls. Reference File. Southwest Collection, Texas Tech University.

U.S. Department of War. Adjutant General's Office. "Map of the Country Scouted by Colonels Mackenzie and Shafter, Capt. R.P. Wilson and Others in the Years 1874 and 1875." Drawn by Alex L. Lucas. Record Group 94. National Archives (photocopy in Southwest Collection, Texas Tech University).

———. Post Medical Reports, Fort Concho, Texas, December, 1867–June, 1891, Books No. 401-403-404-407. Old Records Division. National Archives (microfilm copy in Southwest Collection, Texas Tech University).

———. Post Medical Reports, Fort Davis, Texas, June–July, 1871, Books No. 7-9-12. Old Records Division. National Archives (microfilm copy in Southwest Collection, Texas Tech University).
———. Regimental Returns, Tenth Cavalry, 1866–86, roll 96. Microcopy No. 774. Record Group 94. National Archives.
———. Returns from United States Military Posts, 1800–1916. Fort Concho, Texas, July–August 1877, roll 241. Microcopy No. 617. Record Group 94. National Archives.
———. Returns from United States Military Posts, 1800–1916. Fort Davis, Texas, Sept. 1854–Dec. 1878, roll 297. Microcopy No. 617. Record Group 94. National Archives.
———. Returns from United States Military Posts, 1800–1916. For McKavett, Texas, Sept.–Nov. 1877, roll 690, Microcopy No. 617. Record Group 94. National Archives.
———. Selected Letters Received Relating to Texas, 1875–76. Record Group 94. National Archives.
———. Proceedings of a General Court Martial, Fort McKavett, Texas; Special Orders No. 169, Headquarters, Department of Texas, San Antonio, September 26, 1877; trial of Sergeant William L. Umbles, convened on October 15, 1877 (photocopy in Museum Research Library and Archives, Fort Concho National Historic Landmark, San Angelo, Texas).
———. Records of U.S. Army Commands. Registers of Enlistments in the United States Army, 1798–1914, Tenth Cavalry, Rolls 38, 39, 40. Microcopy No. 233. Record Group 98. National Archives.

NEWSPAPERS

Amarillo Sunday News-Globe. Golden Anniversary Edition, August 14, 1938.
Atlanta Daily Constitution, August 7, 1877.
Army and Navy Journal, 1877.
Bailey County Journal. Golden Anniversary Edition, June 30, 1963.
Dodge City Times, 1877.
Galveston Daily News, 1877.
Lubbock Avalanche-Journal, July 23, 1978; April 20, 2002.
Lynn County News (Tahoka, Texas), October, 19, 1933.
Morton (Texas) *Tribune,* January 28, 1971.
New York *Daily Tribune,* September 8, 1877.
The New York Times, August 9, 1877.
The Portales (New Mexico) *Tribune,* November 19, 1937; Historical and Progress Edition, April 1, 1938.
Roswell Record (New Mexico), June 10, 1892.
San Angelo Standard-Times, May 16, 1948.
San Antonio Daily Express, August, 5, 7, 17, 1877.
San Antonio Herald, 1877.
Saint Louis Globe-Democrat, August 9, 1877.

ARTICLES, BOOKS, AND GOVERNMENT DOCUMENTS

Anderson, Charles G. *In Search of the Buffalo: The Story of J. Wright Mooar.* Seagraves, Texas: Pioneer Press, 1974.
Anderson, John Q. "Fort Elliott, Texas: Last Guard of the Plains Indians." *Texas Military History* 2 (November 1962): 243–54.

Armes, George Augustus. *Ups and Downs of an Army Officer.* Washington, D.C.: n.p., 1900.
Baker, T. Lindsay, and Billy R. Harrison. *Adobe Walls: The History and Archeology of the 1874 Trading Post.* College Station: Texas A&M University Press, 1986.
Baldwin, Alice B. *Memories of the Late Frank D. Baldwin.* Los Angeles: Wetzel, 1929.
Barrett, Arrie. "Western Frontier Forts of Texas, 1845–1861." *West Texas Historical Association Year Book* 7 (1931): 87–99.
Biggers, Don Hampton. *Buffalo Guns & Barbed Wire.* Lubbock: Texas Tech University Press, 1991.
Biggers, Don L. "On the Buffalo Range of Texas." *Frontier Times* 18 (May 1941): 369–76.
Branch, E. Douglas. *The Hunting of the Buffalo.* Lincoln: University of Nebraska Press, 1962.
Capps, Benjamin. *The Warren Wagon Train Raid.* New York: Dial Press, 1974.
Carlson, Paul H., ed. "100 Years Ago on the Llano Estacado." *Southwest Heritage* 5 (Summer 1975): 18–21.
Carlson, Paul H. *"Pecos Bill": A Military Biography of William R. Shafter.* College Station: Texas A&M University Press, 1989.
Carroll, H. Bailey. "Nolan's 'Lost Nigger' Expedition of 1877." *Southwestern Historical Quarterly* 44 (July 1940): 55–75.
Carroll, John M., ed. *The Black Military Experience in the American West.* New York: Liveright, 1971.
Carter, Robert G. *On the Border with Mackenzie, or, Winning West Texas from the Comanches.* Washington, D.C.: Eynon Printing Co., 1935.
Cashin, Hershel V., et al. *Under Fire with the Tenth Cavalry.* Chicago: American Publishing House, 1899.
Cashion, Ty. *A Texas Frontier: The Clear Fork Country and Fort Griffin, 1849–1887.* Norman: University of Oklahoma Press, 1996.
Clendenen, Clarence C. *Blood on the Border: The United States Army and the Mexican Irregulars.* New York: Macmillan, 1969.
Collinson, Frank. *Life in the Saddle.* Edited by Mary Whatley Clark. Norman: University of Oklahoma Press, 1963.
Connellee, C. U. "Some Experiences of a Pioneer Surveyor." *West Texas Historical Association Year Book* 6 (1930): 80–94.
Cook, John R. *The Border and the Buffalo.* Topeka, Kansas: Crane & Co., 1907.
Copeland, Fayette. *Kendall of the Picayune.* Norman: University of Oklahoma Press, 1943.
Counselman, Frank B. "The Permian Basin: From Desert to Energy Empire." *West Texas Historical Association Year Book* 50 (1974): 21–30.
Crane, R. C. "Stage-coaching in the Concho Country." *West Texas Historical Association Year Book* 10 (1934): 58–67.
Crimmins, Col. M. L. "Captain Nolan's Lost Troop on the Staked Plains." *West Texas Historical Association Year Book* 10 (1934): 16–31.
Crimmins, Col. M. L., ed. "Shafter's Explorations in Western Texas, 1875." *West Texas Historical Association Year Book* 9 (1933): 82–96.
Curry, W. Hubert. *Sun Rising on the West: The Saga of Henry Clay and Elizabeth Smith.* Crosbyton, Texas: Crosby County Pioneer Memorial, 1979.
Dary, David A. *The Buffalo Book: The Full Saga of an American Animal.* Chicago: Sage Books, 1974.
———. *Entrepreneurs of the Old West.* New York: Knopf, 1986.

Dixon, Olive K. *Life of "Billy" Dixon: Plainsman, Scout and Pioneer.* Austin: State House Press, 1987.

Dobak, William A., and Thomas D. Phillips. *The Black Regulars, 1866–1898.* Norman: University of Oklahoma Press, 2001.

Eckhart, Jerry. "Rath City: Texas Hide Town." *True West* 39 (September 1992): 42–45.

Fehrenbach, T. R. *Comanches: The Destruction of a People.* New York: Knopf, 1974.

———. *A History of Texas and the Texans.* New York: Macmillan, 1968.

Fleming, Elvis E. "'Buffalo Soldiers' and Buffalo Hunters: The Story of 'Nigger Hill.'" *Southwest Heritage* 3 (1973): 13–18, 24–26.

———. "Captain Nicholas Nolan: Lost on the Staked Plains." *Texana* 4 (Spring 1966): 1–13.

Flipper, Henry O. *Black Frontiersman: The Memoirs of Henry O. Flipper, First Black Graduate of West Point.* Compiled and edited by Theodore D. Harris. Fort Worth: Texas Christian University Press, 1997.

Flores, Dan. *Caprock Canyonlands: Journeys into the Heart of the Southern Plains.* Austin: University of Texas Press, 1990.

———. *Horizontal Yellow: Nature and History in the Near Southwest.* Albuquerque: University of New Mexico Press, 1999.

Fowler, Arlen L. *The Black Infantry in the West, 1869–1891.* Westport, Conn.: Greenwood Publishing Corporation, 1971.

Franks, Lan (Don L. Biggers). *History That Will Never be Repeated.* Ennis, Texas: n.p., 1902.

Gard, Wayne. *The Great Buffalo Hunt.* New York: Knopf, 1959.

Gibson, Arrell Morgan. "The St. Augustine Prisoners." *Red River Valley Historical Review* 3 (Spring 1978):259–70.

Gibson, T. B. "Texas Rangers Scout after Apache Indians." *Frontier Times* 11 (February 1934): 220–231.

Gilbert, Miles. *Getting a Stand.* Tempe, Arizona: Hal Green, 1986.

Glass, E. L. N., ed. *The History of the Tenth Cavalry, 1866–1921.* Tucson: Acme Printing Co., 1921.

Glatthar, Joseph T. *Forged in Battle: The Civil War Alliance of Black Soldiers and White Officers.* Baton Rouge: Louisiana State University Press, 1990.

Graves, Lawrence L. ed. *A History of Lubbock.* 3 vols. Lubbock: West Texas Museum Association, 1959–1962.

Griggs, William C. "The Battle of Yellowhouse Canyon in 1877." *West Texas Historical Association Year Book* 51 (1975): 37–50.

Hagan, William T. *Quanah Parker, Comanche Chief.* Norman: University of Oklahoma Press, 1993.

———. *United States-Comanche Relations: The Reservation Years.* New Haven: Yale University Press, 1976.

Haley, James L. *The Buffalo War: The History of the Red River Indian Uprising of 1874.* Garden City, N.Y.: Doubleday, 1976.

Haley, J. Evetts. *Charles Goodnight: Cowman and Plainsman.* Boston: Houghton Mifflin, 1936.

———. *Fort Concho and the Texas Frontier.* San Angelo, Texas: San Angelo Standard-Times, 1952.

Haywood, C. Robert. *Trails South: The Wagon-Road Economy in the Dodge City-Panhandle Region.* Norman: University of Oklahoma Press, 1986.

Heitman, Francis B. *Historical Register and Dictionary of the United States Army.* 2 vols. Washington, D.C.: Government Printing Office, 1903.

Hill, Frank P. "Indian Raids on the South Plains." *Panhandle-Plains Historical Review* 7 (1934): 53–69.
———. "Plains Names." *Panhandle-Plains Historical Review* 10 (1937): 36–47.
———. "The South Plains and Our Indian History." *West Texas Historical Association Year Book* 12 (1936): 34–44.
Holden, William Curry. *Alkali Trails or Social and Economic Movements of the Texas Frontier, 1846–1900.* Dallas: The Southwest Press, 1930.
———. "Buffalo of the Plains Area." *West Texas Historical Association Year Book* 2 (1926): 8–17.
Holliday, Vance. *Paleoindian Geoarchaeology of the Southern High Plains.* Austin: University of Texas Press, 1997.
Hunter, J. Marvin. "Captain Arrington's Expedition." *Frontier Times* 6 (December 1928): 97–102.
———. "Rangers and Reservation Indians Battle." *Frontier Times* 15 (March 1938): 269–72.
Hunter, John Warren. "Corporal Douglas' Battle with Chief 'Black Horse.'" *Frontier Times* 7 (June 1930): 405–409.
Isenberg, Andrew C. *The Destruction of the Bison: An Environmental History, 1750–1920.* New York: Cambridge University Press, 2000.
Katz, William Loren, ed. *The Black West: A Documentary and Pictorial History.* Rev. ed. Garden City, N.Y.: Doubleday, 1973.
Kavanagh, Thomas W. *Comanche Political History: An Ethnohistorical Perspective, 1706–1875.* Lincoln: University of Nebraska Press, 1996.
Kelton, Elmer. *The Wolf and the Buffalo.* Garden City, N.Y.: Doubleday, 1980.
Kenner, Charles L. *The Comanchero Frontier: A History of New Mexican-Plains Indians Relations.* Norman: University of Oklahoma Press, 1994.
Kincaid, Naomi H. "Rath City." *West Texas Historical Association Year Book* 24 (1948): 40–46.
Kinevan, Marcos E. *Frontier Cavalryman: Lieutenant John Bigelow with the Buffalo Soldiers in Texas.* El Paso: Texas Western Press, 1998.
King, Edward, and J. Wells Champney. *Texas: 1874, An eyewitness account of conditions in post reconstruction Texas.* Edited by Robert S. Gray. Houston: Cordovan Press, 1974.
King, Joseph Henry Thomas. *A Brief Account of the Sufferings of a Detachment of United States Cavalry from Deprivation of Water During a Period of Eighty Six Hours while Scouting on the Staked Plains of Texas.* Fort Davis, Texas: Charles Krull, post printer, 1877.
———. *Experience of Troop A, 10th Cavalry on the "Staked Plains," Texas, July 1877.* Fort Davis, Texas: Charles Krull, post printer, 1877.
La Vere, David. *Life Among the Texas Indians: The WPA Narratives.* College Station: Texas A&M University Press, 1998.
Leckie, Shirley Anne. *The Colonel's Lady on the Western Frontier: The Correspondence of Alice Kirk Grierson.* Lincoln: University of Nebraska Press, 1989.
Leckie, William H. *The Buffalo Soldiers: A Narrative of the Negro Cavalry in the West.* Norman: University of Oklahoma Press, 1963.
Leckie, William H., and Shirley A. Leckie. *Unlikely Warriors: General Benjamin H. Grierson and His Family.* Norman: University of Oklahoma Press, 1984.
Lehmann, Herman. *Nine Years with the Indians, 1870–1879: The Story of the Captivity and Life of a Texan Among the Indians.* Edited by J. Marvin Hunter. Austin: Von Boeckman-Jones, 1927.

Lewis, Preston. "Bluster's Last Stand: The Battle of Yellowhouse Canyon." *True West* 39, Part I (April 1992): 14–18; Part II (May 1992): 20–25.

Marcy, Randolph B. *Exploration of the Red River of Louisiana in 1852.* 32d Cong., 2d sess., 1854. S. Exec. Doc. 54.

Marshall, J. T. *The Miles Expedition of 1874–1875: An Eyewitness Account of the Red River War.* Edited by Lonnie J. White. Austin: The Encino Press, 1971.

McClung, Donald R. "Second Lieutenant Henry O. Flipper: A Negro Officer on the West Texas Frontier." *West Texas Historical Association Year Book* 47 (1971): 20–31.

McCombs, Joe S. "On the Cattle Trail and Buffalo Range." Contributed by Ben O. Grant and J. R. Webb. *West Texas Historical Association Year Book* 11 (1935): 93–101.

McConnell, H. H. *Five Years a Cavalryman; or, Sketches of Regular Life on the Texas Frontier, Twenty Odd Years Ago.* Jacksboro, Texas: J. N. Rogers & Co., 1889.

McHugh, Tom. *The Time of the Buffalo.* New York: Knopf, 1972.

McIntire, Jim. *Early Days in Texas: A Trip to Hell and Heaven.* Kansas City: McIntire Publishing Co., 1902.

Meadows, William C. *Kiowa, Apache, and Comanche Military Societies.* Austin: University of Texas Press, 1999.

Miles, Susan. "Fort Concho in 1877." *West Texas Historical Association Year Book* 35 (1959): 29–49.

Miller, Edna Clark. "Mushaway (Mucha-Que) Peak." *The Permian Historical Annual* 15 (December 1975): 7–14.

Mooar, J. Wright. "The First Buffalo Hunting in the Panhandle." *West Texas Historical Association Year Book* 6 (1930): 109–11.

———. "The Frontier Experiences of J. Wright Mooar." *West Texas Historical Association Year Book* 4 (1928): 89–92.

Morris, John Miller. *El Llano Estacado: Exploration and Imagination on the High Plains of Texas and New Mexico, 1536–1860.* Austin: Texas State Historical Association, 1997.

Murrah, David J. *C. C. Slaughter: Rancher, Banker, Baptist.* Austin: University of Texas Press, 1981.

———. "Mushaway or Muchaque? A Hill by Any Other Name . . ." *The Cyclone,* newsletter of the West Texas Historical Association, 7 (August 15, 2000): 1–2.

Myers, S. D., ed. *Pioneer Surveyor–Frontier Lawyer: The Personal Narrative of O. W. Williams, 1877–1902.* El Paso: Texas Western College Press, 1966.

Neeley, Bill. *Quanah Parker and His People.* Slaton, Texas: Brazos Press, 1986.

Noyes, Stanley. *Los Comanches: The Horse People, 1751–1845.* Albuquerque: University of New Mexico Press, 1993.

Nunn, W. Curtis. "Eighty-six Hours Without Water on the Texas Plains." *Southwestern Historical Quarterly* 43 (January 1940): 356–64.

Nye, Wilber S. *Carbine and Lance: The Story of Old Fort Sill.* Norman: University of Oklahoma Press, 1938.

Owen, Keith R. "Doans: The Birth and Death of a Frontier Town." *West Texas Historical Association Year Book* 71 (1995): 85–94.

Parkes, Henry Bamford. *A History of Mexico.* Sentry Edition. Boston: Houghton Mifflin, 1969.

Pierce, Michael D. *The Most Promising Young Officer: A Life of Ranald Slidell Mackenzie.* Norman: University of Oklahoma Press, 1993.

Pike, Albert. *Prose Sketches and Poems Written in the Western Country.* Edited by David J. Weber. College Station: Texas A&M University Press, 1987.

Potter, Col. Jack. "Killing the Lobo Wolf." *Panhandle-Plains Historical Review* 11 (1938): 52–54.
Rath, Ida Ellen. *The Rath Trail.* Wichita, Kansas: McCormick-Armstrong Co., 1961.
Rathjen, Frederick W. *The Texas Panhandle Frontier.* Rev. ed. Lubbock: Texas Tech University Press, 1998.
Richardson, Rupert Norval. *The Comanche Barrier to South Plains Settlement.* Glendale, Calif.: Arthur H. Clark Co., 1933.
Rickey, Jr., Don. *Forty Miles a Day on Beans and Hay: The Enlisted Soldier Fighting the Indian Wars.* Norman: University of Oklahoma Press, 1963.
Rister, Carl Coke. *Fort Griffin on the Texas Frontier.* Norman: University of Oklahoma Press, 1956.
———. *The Southwestern Frontier, 1865–1881.* Cleveland, Ohio: Arthur H. Clark Co., 1928.
Robinson, Charles M. III. *The Buffalo Hunters.* Austin: State House Press, 1995.
Roth, Jeffrey M. "Civil War Frontier Defense Challenger in Northwest Texas." *Military History of the West* 30 (Spring 2000): 21–44.
Sandoz, Mari. *The Buffalo Hunters: The Story of the Hide Men.* New York: Hastings House, 1954.
Schofield, Donald F. *Indians, Cattle, Ships & Oil: The Story of W. M. D. Lee.* Austin: University of Texas Press, 1985.
Smith, David Paul. *Frontier Defense in the Civil War: Texas' Rangers and Rebels.* College Station: Texas A&M University Press, 1992.
Smith, Thomas T. *The Old Army in Texas: A Research Guide to the U.S. Army in Nineteenth-Century Texas.* Austin: Texas State Historical Association, 2000.
———. *The U.S. Army and the Texas Frontier Economy, 1845–1900.* College Station: Texas A&M University Press, 1999.
Strickland, Rex W., ed. "The Recollections of W. S. Glenn, Buffalo Hunter." *Panhandle-Plains Historical Review* 22 (1949):21–64.
Tate, Michael L. *The Indians of Texas: An Annotated Research Bibliography.* Metuchen, N.J.: The Scarecrow Press, 1986.
Temple, Frank M. "Colonel Grierson in the Southwest." *Panhandle-Plains Historical Review* 30 (1957): 27–54.
Uglow, Loyd M. *Standing in the Gap: Army Outposts, Picket Stations, and the Pacifiction of the Texas Frontier, 1866–1886.* Fort Worth: Texas Christian University Press, 2001.
United States. Army. Cavalry, Tenth. *Roster of Non-commissioned Officers of the Tenth U.S. Cavalry; with Some Regimental Reminiscences, Appendixes, Etc., Connected with the Early History of the Regiment.* Washington, D.C.: Government Printing Office, 1897 (reprinted Bryan, Texas: J. M. Carroll & Company, n.d.).
———. Congress. *Report of the Secretary of War.* House Exec. Doc. 1, 44th Cong., 1st sess., 1875, vol. 1, part 2.
———. *Report of the Secretary of War.* House Exec. Doc. 1, 44th Cong., 2d sess., 1876, vol. 1, part 2.
———. *Report of the Secretary of War.* House Exec. Doc. 1, 45th Cong., 2d sess., 1877, vol. 1, part 2.
———. *Report of the Secretary of War.* House Exec. Doc. 1, 45th Cong., 3d sess., 1878, vol. 1, part 2.
———. *Report of the Secretary of War.* House Exec. Doc. 1, 46th Cong., 2d sess., 1879, vol. 1, part 2.

———. *Special Committee of the House of Representatives to Investigate Texas Frontier Troubles.* 44th Cong., 1st sess., 1876, H. Report. 343.

———. *Testimony Taken by Committee on Military Affairs in Relation to Texas Border Troubles.* 45th Cong., 2d sess., 1879. H. Misc. Doc. 64.

———. Department of War. *Cases Tried by a General Court Martial,* Fort McKavett, Texas, General Court Martial Orders No. 45, November 21, 1877, Headquarters, Department of Texas, San Antonio (photocopy in Southwest Collection, Texas Tech University).

Utley, Robert M. *Frontier Regulars: The United States Army and the Indian, 1866–1890.* New York: Macmillan, 1973.

———. "'Pecos Bill' on the Texas Frontier." *The American West* 6 (January, 1969): 4–13.

Wallace, Ernest, and E. Adamson Hoebel. *The Comanches: Lords of the South Plains.* Norman: University of Oklahoma Press, 1952.

Wallace, Ernest, ed. "The Journal of Ranald S. Mackenzie's Messenger to the Kwahadi Comanches." *Red River Valley Historical Review* 3 (Spring 1978): 227–46.

———. *Ranald S. Mackenzie's Official Correspondence Relating to Texas, 1871–1873.* Lubbock: West Texas Museum Association, 1967.

———. *Ranald S. Mackenzie's Official Correspondence Relating to Texas, 1873–1879.* Lubbock: West Texas Museum Association, 1968.

Wallace, Ernest. *Ranald S. Mackenzie on the Texas Frontier.* Lubbock: West Texas Museum Association, 1964.

———. *Texas in Turmoil.* Austin: Steck-Vaughn Company, 1965.

Wellman, Paul I. *Death on the Prairie.* New York: Macmillan, 1934.

Weniger, Del. *The Explorers' Texas: The Lands and Waters.* Austin, Texas: Eakin Press, 1985.

Wentworth, Edward N. *America's Sheep Trails: History, Personalities.* Ames: The Iowa State College Press, 1948.

White, Lonnie J., ed. "Texas Panhandle News Items 1877–1885, from the *Dodge City Times.*" *Panhandle-Plains Historical Review* 40 (1967): 1–162.

Williams, O. W. "From Dallas to the Site of Lubbock in 1877." *West Texas Historical Association Year Book* 15 (1939): 3–21.

Wooster, Robert. *Soldiers, Sutlers, and Settlers: Garrison Life on the Texas Frontier.* College Station: Texas A&M University Press, 1987.

Index

ISBN 1-58544-253-4
90000
9 781585 442539